PLANET VC

Every owner of a physical copy of this edition of

PLANET VC

can download the eBook for free direct from us at Harriman House, in a DRM-free format that can be read on any eReader, tablet or smartphone.

Simply head to:

ebooks.harriman-house.com/planetvc

to get your copy now.

PLANET VC

How the globalization of venture capital is driving the next wave of innovation

BY TERRANCE PHILIPS
AND JAME DIBIASIO

HARRIMAN HOUSE LTD
3 Viceroy Court
Bedford Road
Petersfield
Hampshire
GU32 3LJ
GREAT BRITAIN
Tel: +44 (0)1730 233870

Email: enquiries@harriman-house.com
Website: harriman.house

First published in 2023.

Paperback ISBN: 978-0-85719-997-3
eBook ISBN: 978-0-85719-998-0

British Library Cataloguing in Publication Data
A CIP catalogue record for this book can be obtained from the British Library.

CONTENTS

FOREWORD BY BILL TAI

BEFORE co-founding Apple Computer, Steve Wozniak had a company with Steve Jobs selling phone-freaking devices called "the blue box."

The US phone system had a set of switches whereby if you played a 2600-hertz frequency into a payphone, you could unlock the computer switching system and make free phone calls.

There was a hacker network that published something called "2600." It was a bible for people who liked to mess around with electronics. When I was in junior high school, I took apart my Radio Shack 101 kit and made a blue box. I'd ride my bicycle around Moraine Valley Community College, Illinois, making free phone calls.

That led me into electronics.

Fast-forward to 2012, when Eric Yuan, an ex-Cisco software engineer, asked me to invest in his startup. It was a video-conferencing idea, like Skype but without the user needing to have an account—you could just log in. I became the first investor in Zoom. I invited everyone I knew to my annual kite-surfing get-together on Necker Island and made them all try it.

Zoom became the ultimate tool for venture capitalists. We could operate anywhere, any time. The global companies that I invested in, like TreasureData, Bitfury, and Canva, could not have been built without Zoom: Bitfury had 700 employees in 16 countries but never had an office. Canva was founded in Perth, Australia, which would have meant a lot more flying.

Most of all, Eric's company was cloud-native, unlike the competition, so it could scale. By 2019, shortly after Zoom listed on Nasdaq—valued at $15.9 billion—the infrastructure for Zoom was designed to support 30 million meetings a day. Then Covid hit. By February 2020, when the world was scrambling to work from home, Zoom could handle 200 million meetings a day. It was doing 300 million by March.

The book you're reading wouldn't have been possible without Zoom. *Planet VC* is a pandemic baby. Terrance Philips and Jame DiBiasio conducted all their interviews on Zoom. Even without Covid, it would have been too expensive and time-consuming for them to track down in person all the venture capitalists interviewed in this book.

I first met Terrance in the early 2000s when he was with Silicon Valley Bank (SVB), for a long time the world's leading financial service provider to venture capital and innovation companies. Terrance was the banker of choice for VC firms being established in places like India, China, Israel and the UK. He had inherited a small book of VC relationships from SVB's Pacific Rim team and, under the leadership of SVB Global head Ash Lilani, helped the bank expand innovation beyond the traditional networks of Silicon Valley.

I later reconnected with Terrance in Hong Kong, where he now leads Citi Private Bank's private equity client coverage, serving Asia's biggest private equity firms investing locally and globally.

He's still building and maintaining relationships with private capital worldwide, and one of the introductions he made to me is Jame. During our conversations, Jame asked perceptive questions and told me about his work as a journalist and author. The two of them seem to make a good team; this book is testament enough.

It's an important book because the innovation economy and the role of venture capital is not well understood. But I'm especially supportive of this work because its focus is not on Silicon Valley, but on the rest of the world.

It's personal for me. I feel that in many ways, the story Terrance and Jame have told is a version of my own life and career, writ large.

I was accepted to Princeton University but blew it off as they did not have a good electronic engineering department. I went to the University of Illinois, home to one of the three inventors of the transistor. I studied digital logic computing design and semiconductor physics. I paid for college by doing contract work for Caterpillar and Texas Instruments.

By the time I got out of college, I joined the CEO of Fairchild in a startup called LSI Logic. This company was a hit, and I got exposure to its three main investors: Don Valentine of Sequoia, Tom Perkins of Kleiner Perkins, and Reid Dennis of Institutional Venture Partners—the godfathers of venture capital.

I completed my MBA at Harvard and went to Alex. Brown & Sons, one of the investment banks specializing in tech companies, while still working at LSI Logic. I happened to pick up an industry magazine and read an article about Taiwan wanting to start a semiconductor industry. I wrote the editor and got the fax number for his sources in Taipei. I sent them my resume and they immediately hired me.

So I deferred my job at Alex. Brown to go help the government of Taiwan. I landed there before I even graduated from Harvard to help create a capacity plan for what would become the island's first fab. The company was not incorporated until November that year. Today Taiwan Semiconductor Manufacturing Corporation (TSMC) is the tenth most valuable company in the world. There is not a single device that you use today that does not have TSMC silicon inside.

In that era, there was a heavy concentration of technology companies within 100 square miles of Silicon Valley. Don Valentine said you should never fund something that is more than an hour away from your office. All of the value creation was happening nearby. I could see, though, hints of things to come on the international scene. After returning to Alex. Brown, I decided to shift to venture capital. I wanted to be closer to the companies. I wanted to be involved in the early-stage companies in Asia, where there was differentiation, and therefore advantages.

It was the dawn of the globalization of VC and a series of waves of innovation. The first wave is silicon, which rippled from the invention of the transistor—silicon was the rock thrown into the pond.

Then came computer and communication systems that couldn't exist without that silicon, in terms of performance, footprint, and power consumption. Those chips became the key components to digitize the phone companies to create the internet—the third wave.

The fourth wave was the applications layer that's on top of the internet: cloud, mobile apps, software-as-a-service. Now we're in the wave of data science, artificial intelligence, machine learning—the knowledge base that helps drive all of the information coming off the cloud.

The waves caused by the original silicon continue to get bigger and occupy a larger percentage of world gross domestic product. Incremental productivity now comes from software, and in future will come from better asset utilization and other things related to the deployment of software.

You will learn about these waves of innovation in this book. More importantly, you will learn how the ripples of change flowed out of the United States and into the rest of the world—but not always easily or successfully. You will learn the special role that venture capital played in that transition, and how it has helped create new clusters of innovation in some unexpected places. You'll learn what that means for the future.

Terrance and Jame have spoken with many of the pioneers—people with stories like mine—to shape a lens through which to view the world. I love the title of this book. It's a prophecy foretold.

Bill Tai
San Francisco, August 2023

INTRODUCTION

SILICON Valley is a byword for innovation. It has been so since the commercialization of the transistor, which is to say, since the onset of the Information Revolution.

The advent of the transistor, followed by microprocessors, bifurcated technology businesses into those built on "bits" or "atoms." Bits refers to the zeroes and ones of digitizing information, and related intellectual property (IP). It is about the virtual universe of software. Atoms have mass and physical properties that require energy to move and manipulate: think moon landings and nuclear reactors.

In 2012, the venture capitalist Peter Thiel criticized his industry for over-investing in companies focused on bits. Software is easy to scale so its most successful companies can blossom quickly, delivering investors a huge payoff.

"Scale" is a term frequently used in business, especially among tech startups, usually in tones of reverence, referring to making something or patterning something based on a rate or a standard.

Think of a McDonald's hamburger, which is a repeatable, mechanized output of a formula, versus the hand-made burger made on a backyard grill. The latter might taste better, but the griller couldn't sell their burger on the market anywhere as cheaply as McDonald's can sell a Big Mac. The ingredients, the griller's per-hour salary and the cost of the grill and its fuel, to say nothing of the costs of advertising the availability and deliciousness of their backyard burger to passersby, must all be factored in.

They'd have to charge $100 a burger just to break even; in most of the United States, a Big Mac costs around $4.50. At the end of the day, the griller might net a couple hundred bucks, assuming they could find nine or ten people willing to pay $100 for lunch (beer or soda not included); while in 2022, McDonald's reported $23 billion in revenues, of which $13 billion was a profit. That's the power of scale.

Software scales at an incredible rate. A software business needs only a small number of coders. Its product is the same everywhere, with no quirks of minute physical differences (a little too much mustard, a few too many fries). It can ship its products electronically. It has almost no overhead. And because its users are people with smartphones or businesses with laptops, things that almost everyone already owns, the addressable market of customers is global. The unit costs of producing software are therefore far below those of producing a Big Mac.

Scale is not unique to the Information Revolution. It is intrinsic to innovation. But the potential for scale within computer and communication businesses became so big, at such a fast pace, that it drove the creation of companies that have defined life in the early twenty-first century.

Think of a company such as Meta, the corporate organization behind Facebook. Thiel made his reputation as a venture capitalist as the first outside investor in Facebook, acquiring a 10.2 percent stake for $500,000 in 2004. That half a million became a $1 billion-plus payout when Thiel sold down most of his shares in 2012.

He was enormously enriched by this deal because Facebook scaled like wildfire. Along the way, though, it also transformed the attitudes, habits, and opportunities for people worldwide. For some people, it enabled an enduring connectivity with others. As an advertising platform, Facebook and Google have given businesses, even small ones, a new way to reach customers around the world. In some developing countries such as the Philippines and Indonesia, Facebook serves as many people's portal to the internet.

But Facebook and other social media have also caused problems. Its algorithms are written to maximize user engagement, which it turns out means catering to base desires and hatreds. Social media have been accused of debasing democratic norms and behaviors in the US, Europe, and beyond.

These companies did not materialize out of thin air. Someone had to finance them. Even in software, which may only need a few devoted programmers wearing hoodies in their parents' basements, money is essential to commercialize whatever the nerds are cooking up. Facebook wouldn't exist without its co-founder, Mark Zuckerberg, but nor would it have become a sustainable business without backers such as Thiel.

The allure of easy and exponential scaling has made software businesses the focus for two generations of entrepreneurs and investors. But can venture capital do better—and solve meaningful problems—by investing more in companies focused on atoms?

"We wanted flying cars, instead we got 140 characters," Thiel quipped. Since then, the big-scale challenges the world faces, including pandemics, demographic upheaval, and climate change, are not just bigger. They are existential. We need innovation if we are to meet them.

Global challenges require diverse solutions. Although Silicon Valley remains the most important center of technology and innovation, it is no longer unique. That is true within the United States, and it is especially true worldwide.

Silicon Valley's own model enabled the rise of other tech clusters; some as complements and others as rivals. The most important innovation to come out of the Valley is not the iPhone or the PC or Amazon's platform. It is venture capital, the key to unlocking innovation.

This book is the story of how Silicon Valley exported VC to the rest of the world—and what the future of innovation and competitive advantage looks like now that everyone has their own key, of one fit or another.

Innovation isn't the same thing as invention. Invention is as old as civilization: agriculture, fire, the wheel, paper, gunpowder, boats, compasses, money itself—these are all inventions and the list of them is as endless as history. Innovation is turning ingenuity into commercial ideas, and it only began to drive economies with the advent of the Industrial Revolution and the creation of scale through technology. The invention of the transistor set the stage for the Information Revolution, but it took innovation to put silicon-based semiconductor chips inside our devices. Commercial risk requires funding, and VC was invented to channel big pools of money into risky startup companies.

VC is primarily about aligning incentives. Roughly nine out of ten startups fail because they are small companies with no profile, untested technology, and unknown founders who come from modest backgrounds. They need money to get started, to grow, to market themselves, build sales channels, and deal with whatever hurdles come their way. If you give just one startup your money, you are very likely to lose it all. If you give ten startups some money, and one of them is the next Google, you will become rich regardless of how the others perform.

This sounds simple, but to achieve this kind of alignment is not easy. It took VC several iterations in the US to land on the right formula. Exporting it was even harder. Incentives include options, tax breaks, and other aspects of a business environment that companies and investors cannot control. In most cases, governments had to take steps to nurture a VC industry, either by removing obstacles or, in the case of China, by coopting VC for its own purposes.

Even then, there is no guarantee that VC will be effective. Culture matters too, which explains VC's weakness in Europe and Japan, despite those places having sophisticated industrial bases and technically excellent people. Other markets such as India are embracing VC and the innovation economy with relish, but are doing so as relatively poor countries (in per-capita gross domestic product (GDP) terms) with weak infrastructure. Are these markets the future of innovation or merely stomping grounds for big US and Chinese tech companies?

The good news is that much of the world has learned how to foster VC, or is feeling its way there. This means innovation is to be found almost everywhere, and this is grounds for optimism. The scale of problems like climate change suggests our future will depend on these many clusters of innovation being able to collaborate.

The bad news is that US–China geopolitical tensions are throwing up barriers—to trade, to capital, to flows of data and information—and the VC industry is in the crosshairs. Politics within the US, notably an anti-immigrant nativism, also threatens to weaken Silicon Valley's attractiveness or accessibility for the brightest entrepreneurs from other countries.

Planet VC tells the story of how VC went global, how governments as different as Israel and Indonesia played roles in developing VC industries, and what this means for the next wave of innovation. The true answer to Thiel's "bits versus atoms" question is that we will need innovation in both, and increasingly it will come from outside of the US.

This book is the result of a partnership between Terrance Philips, a banker, and Jame DiBiasio, a journalist—a partnership that extends across the worlds of finance, tech, public policy, and academia. *Planet VC* is written for professionals with similar interests.

From the heights of geopolitics to the nitty-gritty of planning the next investment, technological disruption continues to shape every decision. Knowing the financial history behind innovation in the key centers of the world provides a framework to make sense of today's headlines and appreciate the big picture of where opportunities will lie.

Planet VC is organized to tell a single story that unfolds across various countries at different times. Chapter One narrates the importance of innovation and VC's role, with illustrations of early successes in China. Chapter Two explains VC's American origins. Chapter Three explains why VC failed to take root in Europe as well as its belated successes.

The next set of chapters, Four to Six, relate VC's carving out of beachheads beyond Silicon Valley, in Israel, Taiwan, and Singapore. They look at the interplay between governments, VCs, and tech companies, and put VC's rise in the context of the geopolitical environment.

Chapters Seven and Eight return to the US, the shift of investment from hardware to software, and the rise of the PC. This occurred amid an important part of tech history: Japan Inc.'s efforts to displace the US as the world's leading tech player. VC played an important role in maintaining Silicon Valley's dominance, and its subsequent leap into the internet.

The internet enabled the rise of China as the only true challenger to Silicon Valley. China's story—including its rise, its impact on global VC, and most recently its self-inflicted setbacks—is recounted in Chapters Nine through Twelve.

Chapter Thirteen looks at India and Southeast Asia, the up-and-coming markets where VC is going to have an outsized influence over the next decade. India has the potential to join China and the US as a full-fledged tech power, with its VC industry now leading the way.

Chapter Fourteen concludes by looking ahead. The rise of VC since the ashes of the dotcom crash in 2001 has benefited from a benign macro environment of ever-falling interest rates and relative stability. In 2022 that environment changed irrevocably. Global equity and fixed-income markets crashed, and no sector was hurt more than technology. The business models of most VCs, predicated on cheap or free money, were made irrelevant almost overnight.

There are reasons for optimism, and the opportunities for VC are bigger than ever, but only if the industry is considered in its proper global context rather than as just a US story.

Terrance Philips and Jame DiBiasio
Hong Kong, July 2023

Note: Dollar amounts in this book are US dollars, unless otherwise stated.

1

VENTURE CAPITAL: THE GREATEST EXPORT

WHEN we think of innovative companies changing the world, we probably think about the likes of Apple, Google, Amazon, Facebook, and Netflix: the giants of Silicon Valley.

These companies are important not just because they are huge—although they *are* huge, with Apple's market capitalization surpassing $3 trillion in January 2022.

They are important because they have transformed our lives. We rely on them even if we also fear their access to our personal data, or don't trust some of the things they're developing, like artificial intelligence (AI).

Think of what the Covid-19 pandemic would have been like without Amazon or online delivery services to sustain our economy, or without Zoom or social media to keep us connected and let a substantial part of the workforce operate remotely.

Nor is innovation just about computers and the internet. It's also about biotech. Where would we have been these past years without the incredible vaccines developed by companies like Moderna?

So far, we are talking about innovation as an American phenomenon, with a list of the most famous Silicon Valley companies.

However, in *Planet VC* we show that more of the next generation of tech companies, and the innovation they produce, will be found outside of the United States. And we also show that the secret ingredient that has unlocked this innovation wave, both in the US and abroad, has been the means of financing risky startups with institutional money: venture capital.

Venture capital is Silicon Valley's greatest export. Not the iPhone or the personal computer, not e-commerce or genetically engineered drugs.

Why?

Because venture capital is the toolkit to unlock creativity that all humans can possess and turn it into fast-growing businesses. Countries that have figured out venture capital, or VC as it's known, are now creating their own Silicon Valleys.

Some of these new centers of innovation are complementary to America's. They grow the pie through trade and allowing consumers around the world to benefit from what they create.

And some are becoming competitors. The story of VC's globalization is also a way to tell the story of America's place in the world and the rise of direct competitors such as China, as well as emerging centers of power such as India that seek to carve out their own geopolitical path.

As we'll see, VC is not a given. It doesn't just happen. It has to be created. The toolbox must be opened and the tools applied in the correct manner, sometimes by VCs themselves, other times by governments.

EARLY WIN: BAIDU

To get a sense of what's possible for VC outside of the US, let's look at the Chinese company Baidu Inc. Its story shows how venture financing made a critical difference in the early days of China's internet industry—and delivered incredible returns for its investors, including its private VCs as well as ordinary American retail investors.

Baidu has done as much as any American Big Tech company to shape life in the twenty-first century. It operates the world's second-most popular search engine, after Google, and is a leader in AI and autonomous vehicles. Its co-founder Robin Li is an internet pioneer with a net worth as of April 2021 of $14.7 billion, according to *Forbes*.

Non-Chinese media still refer to Baidu as "China's Google," but the search technology that Li developed, using hyperlinks to rank a site's relevance, predates Google. He built the prototype of his search engine in 1996 while working at Dow Jones, helping the company develop the *Wall Street Journal's* online business.

Robin Li Yanhong was born to factory workers in Yangquan, an ancient but small (by Chinese standards) city in Shanxi Province, far from the wealth and bustle of coastal cities like Beijing, Shanghai or Guangzhou. He had enough brains and grit to get into the prestigious information management department of Peking University.

From there he won admittance to the doctorate program for computer science at Buffalo University—landing in another small factory town. Li was part of a small but growing wave of young, talented Chinese getting a first-class education in the United States.

He settled for a master's degree in 1994, skipping the doctorate in favor of getting a job, and began working for a unit of Dow Jones in New Jersey, where he developed his search-scoring algorithm, which he called Rankdex. Li got a US patent for it in 1996, and Google co-founder Larry Page even cited it when, two years later, his company filed their own patent for search.

Li then worked as an engineer at Infoseek, a nascent internet search company that was the default engine on Netscape's browser, Navigator. In 1999 he returned to China and teamed up with Eric Xu Yong to launch Baidu.

Eric Xu had also studied at Beida (as Beijing University is known) as a biologist. He parlayed that into a PhD degree from Texas A&M University and a post-doctoral research fellowship at University of California, Berkeley. While in California he also worked at two biotech startups.

Li and Xu incorporated Baidu in 2000 in Beijing. They are among the first wave of Chinese who studied and worked in the US, especially in its technology sector, and returned to China to create their own businesses.

CHINA'S EARLY INTERNET

In the wake of the 2008 global financial crisis that embroiled the US and Europe, China's economy powered ahead, and Beijing began rolling out programs to attract more returnees. The government recognized the value of wooing home its most entrepreneurial citizens who were immersed in Silicon Valley's culture of innovation.

But in 1999, when Li and Xu went back to China, they were early in this trend and what government support existed wasn't suited to private startups. They were building their network from scratch, and it wasn't easy.

China had caught dotcom fever in the late 1990s, just like the US. Its most prominent players were portals—companies that provided web browsers to surf the internet. Sina, Sohu and NetEase were all founded in the mid-1990s and were duking it out for Chinese-language eyeballs, not just in the mainland but in the US and Hong Kong.

These browsers were modeled after Netscape Navigator and served as a "yellow pages," with directories for all kinds of websites, from games to news. The Chinese aesthetic was "more is more," giving these portals a madcap vibe as they stuffed as much as possible onto their sites, hoping to cater to every type of click.

Li knew his search algorithm could transform Chinese-language search. He had the US patent to prove his chops. But this required a dedicated team of engineers and salespeople.

Most of all, Baidu had to prove it could beat the portals. These companies depended on revenue from advertising. Online ad spend in China amounted to about $30 million by 2000,[1] a pittance compared to that in the US, and the big three portals were all struggling. But Sina got the ball rolling with a spectacular first, getting approval to list on Nasdaq in April 2000, raising $68 million. Sohu and NetEase quickly followed.

This was the very top of the dotcom bubble on Wall Street, and Sina and the others put China on the map. They were China's Goliaths, and Robin Li wanted to be the underdog with the deadly slingshot.

But for that slingshot to hit its mark, Baidu was going to need money. Real money: ten million American dollars.

And there was no money for a startup in China.

THE SEARCH FOR FUNDING

China had plenty of entrepreneurs, but not in the iconic sense: not as Silicon Valley, Steve Jobs-type visionaries.

In 1979, Chinese paramount leader Deng Xiaoping launched his "reform and opening-up," gradually creating space for private enterprise to support the government's investment-led growth strategy. The economy took off, and soon small enterprises accounted for more growth and employment than the state-owned enterprises (SOEs). But the state never relinquished control over the economy's commanding heights. Credit remained the purview of state-owned banks, which were ordered to lend to SOEs.

Small-business owners had to rely on friends and family to get started. This was fine for small-scale factories or other cottage industries that people understood. No one, however, was prepared to lend to untested startups in risky businesses—certainly not companies that were surely going to rack up years of losses before they could turn the corner.

Sohu got its start because its founder had studied at Massachusetts Institute of Technology (MIT) and had American contacts willing to back the company. Sina's various founders also had overseas educations, and they assembled the company out of a series of mergers and acquisitions (M&As). NetEase emerged from its humble roots in Guangzhou in 1997, at a time when there was hardly any competition, and won backing from Baring Private Equity in Hong Kong. By 2000 the nascent Chinese internet was hotly contested, but no one was making a profit.

Robin Li and Eric Xu cobbled together $1.5 million from "friends and family" investors. This was an impressive sum, but only 15 percent of what they thought they needed to make Baidu a success. They had no choice but to turn to the one place in the world with an industry full of people crazy enough to give an unknown, risky startup the other $8.5 million: the US.

They traveled to Silicon Valley and pitched dozens of venture capital firms. This was in the wake of the Sina initial public offering (IPO), so some people in the VC industry had a hazy awareness of China: lots of people, lots of eyeballs, "the Wild East." That was about it. Amid the dotcom craze, there were a lot more reliable home runs in the US of A.

What Li and Xu didn't appreciate was that the VC community in Silicon Valley was parochial. The industry gathered around the nexus of Sand Hill Road, a nondescript highway connecting Palo Alto, Menlo Park, and Woodside, home to many tech companies and Stanford University. It had become a truism that investors would only back startups within a stone's throw of Sand Hill Road.

The Baidu team found no takers.

Now they were getting desperate, mailing letters to any VC firm cold. They sent one to John Fisher, co-founder of Draper Fisher Jurvetson (DFJ). Fisher and his partners received hundreds if not thousands of such letters a year, but Fisher knew one of Baidu's angel investors. He passed the letter to an associate, who agreed to meet Li and Xu. She was impressed by their pitch, but so had been others, and the matter might well have ended there. DFJ, however, had something unique: an office in Asia.

DFJ'S GLOBAL VENTURE CAPITAL FUND

In the year 2000 there were hardly any venture capital firms operating outside of the United States. A handful had begun to see that the rest of the world offered a growth story for tech companies.

Silicon Valley was filled with immigrants, from Europe, Israel, Taiwan, mainland China, India, and beyond.† Some of these people saw the potential to take the Silicon Valley model back home. Many were engineers and entrepreneurs. But none of them could succeed without venture capital—the secret ingredient to Silicon Valley's success.

† For simplicity, references in this book to China refer to mainland China, while references to ethnic Chinese people include people from mainland China, Taiwan, Hong Kong, and Southeast Asia.

DFJ was an exception to the parochial norm. Its partners, though Americans, had a feeling that the rest of the world was going to follow America's example, so it would be better to get in early, find the best entrepreneurs, and make a killing.

They set up ePlanet, the first global VC fund. It was special in two ways. First, it was aimed at late-stage companies in the US—that is, private companies that had matured beyond the "startup in the garage" phase and now needed much bigger funding to achieve scale. The second was to allocate money to early-stage companies in Europe and Asia. ePlanet raised $650 million, of which about 10 percent would be allocated to Asia.

"They weren't bullish on Asia, but they wanted to ride the wave early," says Finian Tan—the man DFJ ePlanet recruited to invest that 10 percent. "I had about $60 million to work with."[2]

FINDING DFJ'S ASIA PARTNER

Tan grew up in Singapore. After a promising education in the UK—at Cambridge, then an engineering degree at University of Glasgow—he returned home to work, first at Shell Eastern Petroleum, then at commodities trading firm J. Aron (which was later acquired by Goldman Sachs).

His real break came in 1997 when he was recruited into government. Since its founding, Singapore—a city-state of just four million people situated among big, sometimes dangerous neighbors—has prided itself on effective and clean governance. The government and bureaucracy attracted the best and the brightest, a reputation it maintains today.

Although elite, the culture was prone to groupthink. Singapore's mandarins had guided the country to prosperity, but they saw it needed to make the jump to tech and high-end services. They acknowledged they needed some outside expertise, and recruited Tan to serve as deputy secretary at the Ministry of Trade and Industry—the highest position ever given to a non-bureaucrat.

Tan's mission was to help make Singapore into an entrepreneurial country, a story that we will tell later. While in government, Tan brought under his wing a young associate, Jixun Foo. When Tan decided to return to the private sector, he took Foo with him.

While in government, Tan had visited Silicon Valley, so he was a known quantity to any VC with an interest in Asia. When DFJ launched ePlanet, they recruited Tan to serve as their founding partner for Asia.

TAN'S VISION FOR THE CHINESE INTERNET

Tan didn't operate like a typical VC fund.

Usually, venture funds take equity stakes in startups knowing that these are risky companies that may not ever turn a profit. The classic model is to seed ten companies and expect seven to go bust, two to muddle through, and one to take off like a rocket. It's a business of strikeouts and grand slams, not base hits and walks.

But Tan didn't want to operate that way. Perhaps it's his Singaporean side, or his time in government, or just the lack of deals in Asia at the time. He was cautious.

"I was confused about the internet," he says. He looked at companies like Amazon and Yahoo!—then still in their infancy—and wondered how their business models would survive if transported to Asia. "How do eyeballs become money?"

He knew only two things.

First, the internet would grow like wildfire.

Second, China's economy would grow like wildfire.

How could he make money when both things became true?

Tan looked at the previous computer revolution: the personal computer. Microsoft was the clear winner of the PC. Its rivals had been software companies writing applications like Lotus123 and WordPerfect, but it was Microsoft's operating system that captured all the money. From within this fortress, Microsoft could then produce copycat apps and services: Excel, Word, or its own browser, Explorer. Its services didn't have to be as good as Lotus123 or WordPerfect, but the convenience factor meant that packaging these with Microsoft's operating system gave the company an insurmountable advantage.

Tan could see therefore that the leaders in China's internet business, the browser companies, were giants lumbering on feet made of clay. But he wasn't sure yet what was the equivalent of Microsoft's PC operating system for the internet; what was the new killer edge?

He had one idea: search. He noticed the first thing his friends in China did when they opened Sina or Sohu browsers was conduct a search on their directories.

Search was more than just a function: it influenced user behavior. Robin Li's idea was to get rid of the clutter of Chinese portals and present them with a clean screen that asked them to query for what they really wanted to see.

Finian Tan found out that US browsers such as AltaVista and Yahoo! relied on third-party search engines such as Inktomi to power their directories; some used a Taiwan startup called Openfind for the Chinese-language market in Asia, but it wasn't available in mainland China.

When DFJ in Silicon Valley sent the Baidu team to Finian Tan, he knew he had found what he had been looking for.

INVESTING IN BAIDU

He and Jixun Foo organized a call from Singapore with Robin Li and Eric Xu while the two founders were still in the US. They followed this up with dinner in Beijing at the Kerry Hotel. Located near to the Beida campus, the Kerry had become the unofficial ePlanet headquarters in China, at a time when capital was scarce and investors could require founders to visit them where they pleased.

Tan had one essential question: Sina had just completed its IPO, making it the first China listing on Nasdaq, and it was what everyone in Asia's tech circle was talking about. Could Baidu beat them?

This was a sensitive question, because Baidu's business model was to serve as the search engine for Sina, Sohu or NetEase. The Baidu team was careful to include Sina and Sohu executives in their negotiations with Tan, to the point that Robin Li prevented Tan from meeting them on his own. Tan and Jixun Foo did their own asking around to make sure they were confident that Baidu had the goods. And it did: its search was both faster and more relevant than what the browsers were using.

Baidu needed $10 million to absorb several years of expected losses, given the high costs of the engineering talent required. It also needed a cushion in case Sina and Sohu didn't grow quickly enough, which would mean they had too few consumers conducting online searches. Baidu intended to charge Sina Rmb000.1 ($0.000015) per click. Over time, that would become a ton of money—if everything worked. Even optimistic scenarios, however, meant Baidu would burn money. It needed deeper pockets than the $1.5 million of angel backing it had already won.

Tan, because of his particular view of China and the internet, was convinced. "Baidu was one of a hundred deals for other VCs," he says. "But for me, it was one of one. This was the only company I wanted."

By now Tan had been running ePlanet's Asia business for 18 months without a single deal. The internet had confused him until he had met Baidu. He decided to put all his chips on the table and offered to back the entire $8.5 million ask.

In the end, another VC, IDG Capital, persuaded him to give it a $1 million allocation; we'll meet IDG later but suffice to say it was about as venerable a name as you could find in Asian VC, and it already had the on-the-ground presence that ePlanet lacked. Finian Tan agreed to share some of the action with this more established rival.

IDG's version of this story is a little different: it says it was the first institution to commit to Baidu's raise, under the leadership of its partner Fei Yang.[3] But it confirms the business case: Baidu's search prowess was far superior and knew how to please Chinese internet surfers, who were growing in number by nearly 60 percent year-on-year. Also, importantly, IDG saw that Baidu's team, with Western experience and a focus on the Chinese user, would be best positioned to take on Yahoo! and Google.

BAIDU TAKES ON THE PORTALS

ePlanet ended up taking a 25 percent stake in Baidu and two of seven seats on the board, both of which Tan assumed, although informally he included Jixun Foo. He now had equal weighting on the board to Li and Xu.

Tan portrays the operations of the board as essentially decisions between him and the two co-founders. "All we did was say yes, because Robin and Eric had good ideas," he says.

The biggest challenge was being tethered to Sina and Sohu, which provided most of Baidu's revenue. As their traffic skyrocketed, the browsers forced Baidu to renegotiate, demanding they pay only a tenth the rate agreed per click. At this rate, Baidu would never turn a profit, no matter how quickly China internet usage grew. Staying small was not an option for an investor like ePlanet: to survive and thrive, venture capitalists needed grand slams.

Worse for Tan and Foo, the Baidu executive team began worrying they might have to sell the company. That wouldn't be a home run, to stay with the baseball analogy: it would be three strikes and you're out.

The only other option was to combat the browsers head-on. Baidu didn't have the customers, but it had the algorithm. The company launched its own website called Sherpa, "powered by Baidu." The hedged marketing didn't fool Sina and Sohu, which severed ties to Baidu, thinking they'd crush it. But Baidu's search engine proved to be far more useful than a browser's portal.

Eventually Eric Xu left the business due to an internal dispute, but he exited as a billionaire. In 2005, Baidu went public on Nasdaq.

BAIDU'S NASDAQ IPO

The listings of Sina, Sohu and NetEase had been a big deal in Asia, but these were small deals in the US. When the dotcom bubble collapsed in early 2001, their combined market caps were below $200 million, recalls Jixun Foo. But from 2000 to 2005, China's internet user base exploded from zero to almost 400 million people.

"Baidu became the de facto gateway for everyone," Jixun Foo says. And the ad revenues followed.

The old browser companies still exist but by 2005 they had all diversified into other businesses, because the browser model was dead. Sina launched Weibo, known as China's answer to Twitter. Sohu went into video hosting, NetEase into gaming. Baidu's pure search model elevated it into the BAT, as the new Chinese triumvirate of Baidu, Alibaba and Tencent became known. Baidu was one of the winners of the Chinese consumer internet business that would power the country for the next two decades.

Baidu's IPO on Nasdaq was a watershed. It put China tech on Wall Street's map and to this day remains the most lucrative ADR in Nasdaq history (ADRs being American Depository Receipts, the term for listing US-based shares of a foreign company).

Goldman Sachs, Piper Jaffrey and Credit Suisse First Boston underwrote the IPO, with the ADRs offered at $27. Trading opened at $66. By the end of the first day, the price had reached $122: the best performance by an overseas company in Nasdaq history. (That was despite Goldman and Piper analysts spending the first year talking down the stock, claiming its true valuation was only $27 a share, an abuse that Baidu's executives preferred to play down.)

The company's IPO valued it at around $1 billion but by the end of 2006, it had reached a market cap of around $4 billion; and by end 2007, it was trading around a $10 billion valuation. In early 2015, at the stock's peak, Baidu was worth $114 billion.

VC'S SUCCESS BEYOND AMERICA

The deal did more than put China tech on everyone's radar screen: it also proved that venture capital could work in Asia, in a language that everyone on Wall Street understood.

IDG held on to its Baidu shares until 2007, when it exited and realized a return of nearly a hundred times on its investment.

Baidu made the careers of Finian Tan and Jixun Foo, who soon left DFJ ePlanet having banked a 40x valuation on their $7.5 million bet. They went on to pursue their own careers in venture, with Tan founding Vickers Venture and Foo becoming a founding partner of GGV Capital.

The Baidu story shows that the world outside of the US is chock full of entrepreneurs, ideas, innovation, and eager customers. But it took an arm of an adventurous Silicon Valley VC to provide the money that Baidu needed to launch, pivot against bigger competitors, and get listed.

Capital has always been the necessary partner, the secret sauce, to innovation. For most of the twentieth century, venture capital was an American phenomenon. The story of how other innovation centers, from Beijing to Bangalore, have emerged depends on when and how venture capital emerged in those markets. In the case of Baidu, the VC firm was American. But once the template is found, local capital also begins to form.

When and how local venture capital emerges also colors the nature of innovation in those places. Tech scenes from Tel Aviv to Taipei may complement America's, or not—but they are all different.

But as the next chapter will show, exporting VC wasn't easy. In fact, in the earliest days, these efforts failed. Let's find out why.

2

USA: THE FUNDING OF CHANGE

VENTURE capital was invented in Boston in the 1940s. It was a deliberate act. There was nothing natural about creating a fund to invest the money of other institutions into risky, unknown startups. Venture capital was itself a risky innovation and its first iterations were flawed, and almost failed.

In this chapter we will look at the birth of venture capital in the United States, the conditions that created it, why it mattered, and the first home run in VC, scored by an East Coast firm called American Research and Development Corporation (ARD). This will help us to appreciate the first attempts at exporting the US VC model.

THE MYSTERY OF TAKEOFF

Although people have always invented, economies and living standards grew very slowly through most of history. This changed radically in the middle of the nineteenth century, first in Great Britain, then in France, Germany, and the United States.

Historians have calculated that Britain's real GDP per person (adjusted for prices) grew by 0.2 percent from 1270 to 1700. At that rate, no one would have experienced a sense of change in their lifetime. It accelerated slightly in the eighteenth century. Then Britain experienced takeoff, with GDP per person rising 1.25 percent by the mid-1800s.[1]

By the 1870s, the industrialized Atlantic world spun out one life-changing invention after another, while the rise of corporations commercialized these for another new phenomenon: the mass market.

The classic economists could not explain this. Adam Smith, writing a century earlier, said labor created wealth. Karl Marx, writing in 1867 as takeoff was being imprinted on society, ascribed wealth creation to labor and capital, with capitalists exploiting workers through their ownership of the means of production. But no one could explain why things were changing so quickly.

Joseph Schumpeter is the intellectual author of the innovation economy. Born in the Austro-Hungarian Empire in 1883, he moved to the US in 1932 to teach at Harvard. He framed economics in terms of business cycles, entrepreneurial "creative destruction", and the role of money in funding change.

Schumpeter benefited from experiencing the rise of corporations, capital markets, and the fruits of scientific advancement that were rudimentary in Smith's time. His heirs have also benefited from seeing how Schumpeterian change unfolded in cumulative waves. The most prominent of these is Carlota Perez, a Venezuelan-British scholar who, writing in the early 2000s, recast Schumpeter's business cycles in terms of technological diffusion.

Perez argued new technology systems did more than just impact business and growth patterns. They changed the way businesses operated, requiring new regulations, new training, and new ways of doing things. In other words, transformative innovations do not stand alone but arrive in mutually supportive waves, until eventually their impact wanes and they are displaced by a new set of breakthrough technologies.

She phrased these waves as "great surges": the Industrial Revolution; the Age of Steam and Railways; the Age of Steel, Electricity and Heavy Engineering; and the Age of Oil, Automobiles and Mass Production. Her fifth wave is the Age of Information and Telecommunications—an age that has defined our lives, and is now giving way to something else.

Finance has been critical to all of these waves, but the manner of that funding the information and telecommunications revolution has a story of its own: venture capital.

FINANCING CHANGE

VC firms invest in privately owned startups in the hope that one of these companies will hit it big—and knowing that most will deliver mediocre returns or fail outright. It is a style of investing that is deliberately risky. But that's what makes VC work.

The venture capitalist is an intermediary. VCs manage money on behalf of large institutional investors like pension funds, insurance companies, sovereign wealth funds, university endowments, and wealthy families. These are the asset owners, often managing funds on behalf of others (such as pensioners). They lack the expertise to select which entrepreneurs to support, so they invest in VC funds to do the work for them.

Such asset owners are referred to as limited partners (LPs) because they put their money into a VC fund as partners with no active say in how the business is run—that is up to the VC's people, its general partners (GPs). These GPs operate the fund and get compensated for their performance.

VCs serve as a buffer, taking on the risks of venture investing on behalf of asset owners, while getting paid handsomely when they strike gold. Their structure is designed to fill the need of risky new companies: in the US, typically 50 percent of startups will fail within five years[2] and so traditional banks won't lend to them.

VC funds therefore provide the capital to help the best of these startups survive those initial years. The leading VCs have played a critical role in the development of American business and life. From 1972 to 2019, companies backed by Sequoia Capital—just one VC—had an aggregate value of over $3 trillion.[3]

But VC only flourished in the US since the 1960s, and remained niche and obscure for its first two decades.

EARLY MEANS OF FUNDING ENTREPRENEURS

Throughout most of history, innovation was financed by wealthy partners using family money.

The early Industrial Revolution in Britain was financed this way: Richard Arkwright wasn't alone when he invented the spinning frame; he had financial partners who invested in him because they saw the potential for the invention to transform British textiles. Ditto for James Watt, an engineer who relied on financial partners to turn his steam engine into something that could be marketed and sold.

Over time, new financial arrangements emerged to support entrepreneurs.

The emergence of giant corporations in the late nineteenth century in the US, Germany and Japan created a model for massive, well-funded, in-house research labs. Big companies can be very innovative, but they do not create entrepreneurs. Their brilliant employees are encouraged to remain with the company, which is good for the company but not for the diffusion of knowledge—which means their learnings remain bottled up, and their impact on society is limited. This overweening corporate culture is a big reason why the technological stars of Japan and Germany didn't strike out on their own, denying their communities a pool of entrepreneurs.

These people chose to remain in their big companies because they could see how difficult it would be to go independent. The most fundamental problem would be surrendering their salaries and bonuses and having to secure funding from somewhere else.

They could try asking a bank for a loan. In theory, financial institutions can help fund entrepreneurs. The reality is, however, that banks are never going to lend to risky startups that often have no revenues and may not even have a product. Banks prefer to lend to companies that don't need the money.

Similarly, startups could try tapping the stock market. There are periods of time when stock market investors are willing to take a flutter, such as in the 1920s, when dozens of radio startups were able to list on the New York Stock Exchange's secondary bourse, the Curb market. The mania only lasted a few years, though, and then these stocks collapsed—leaving the future of radio in the hands of a combination of giant conglomerates.

Bank loans and corporate labs are not suited to financing entrepreneurs. Innovation is risky and the startups that bring new ideas are untested. Entrepreneurs, where they exist, have traditionally relied on the patronage of rich families.

FROM FAMILIES TO FUNDS

The first generation of professional VC firms in the US stemmed from earlier funds and personal networks set up by very wealthy industrial families, such as the Rockefellers, the Phipps, and the Carnegies: the titans of oil, steel, and railways. These wealthy pools of capital backed startups in the next generation of industries, such as aviation, automobiles, and photography. McDonnel Douglas, Henry Ford's Detroit Motor Company, and George Eastman's Kodak were all backed by family funds.[4]

These family funds would later morph into the first generation of professional VC funds, including Venrock (Rockefellers) and Bessemer Venture Partners (Phipps). However, in their early years, they remained small and relied on an interested family member to drive their investments almost like a hobby.

Passion was required because returns were not very attractive. Laurence Rockefeller, who launched the family's venture fund in 1938, made 3.2 times his money over the next three decades—but the S&P 500 Stock Composite Index returned 8.6x in the same period (calculated to compensate for the index's formal creation in 1957). Some 44 percent of Laurence Rockefeller's investments lost money.

"Venture capital endeavors are not for the impatient, the faint of heart, [or] the poor loser," he said.[5]

There simply were not enough rich families with a taste for adventure to fuel America's growing need for financing new companies. Banks and new pools of institutional capital, such as insurance companies and pension funds, were very conservative and would never lend to a company without profits and a solid reputation. A few insurers did try venture investing, but their lack of expertise quickly disabused them of the notion.

Investments in risky assets were made even more unattractive by taxes on capital gains, levied as part of Franklin D. Roosevelt's New Deal programs. Capital gains were taxed at 39 percent, top-bracket incomes at 79 percent, and startups were taxed like big companies once they began to expand. The US emerged victorious from the Second World War in 1945, but for all its manufacturing prowess, industry in the 1940s and 1950s had a worryingly poor record of new company formation.

ARD: THE FIRST VC COMPANY

Old-money wealth, banking and insurance was centered in Boston, New York, and Philadelphia. Philly had old money, New York had Wall Street, and Boston boasted Harvard, MIT, and the labs conducting most of the military's wartime research and development (R&D). It was from this East Coast milieu that a new idea of venture funding sprang to life.

Ralph Flanders, a Vermont engineer and industrialist, was serving as governor of the Boston seat of the Federal Reserve System. He, along with Karl Compton, the President of MIT, established ARD in 1946, in Boston.

Although some of ARD's backers included old-money families such as the Whitneys and the Rockefellers, ARD was the first company designed to channel the money of institutions—endowments, pension funds and insurance companies—to entrepreneurs commercializing new technologies.

ARD was created as a listed company on the Boston bourse that would take equity stakes in promising startups, as well as their convertible debt or convertible preferred stock. It would nurture its companies with managerial help and, via its MIT connection, technical advice.

THE GENERAL TAKES COMMAND: GEORGES DORIOT

Flanders was meant to head ARD but that same year he was elected to the US Senate, so the job went to Georges Doriot, a French immigrant who had served as the US military's quartermaster general during the war—and thus was often known simply as "the General."

Doriot was a natural leader. Born in Paris in 1899, his father was an engineer who helped Peugeot build some of the first cars. Doriot *père* sent Georges to the US to study, but by 1921 Doriot *fils* had become the teacher, at Harvard Business School. There he would nurture many pioneers of the venture world, including the founders of Greylock Partners and Fidelity Ventures, two of the most eminent East Coast VCs.[6]

The challenge for Doriot was to prove the ARD model, which is to say, to prove the idea that a professional fund could deliver its institutional investors a good return while supporting the development of innovative companies.

It didn't work—at first. ARD's portfolio companies lost money during its early years, therefore ARD lost money too. It depleted its initial capitalization of $3.4 million and struggled to raise more.

Doriot inherited four big problems when he took over ARD. First was its capital structure: as a listed company, it had to provide dividends, which often meant selling out of its best-performing companies to oblige its shareholders. Also, ARD was set up as a closed-end fund, which meant it could not create new shares to meet any increased demand; only the existing shares could trade.

His second problem was tax. ARD was not considered a pass-through entity for tax purposes, which meant ARD had to pay capital gains taxes (which meant its partners were paying tax twice, once on their income, and again on their capital gains). And although ARD charged a management fee, it levied this on its portfolio companies, instead of its investors. This only hobbled its companies' performance.

Third—fatally—ARD couldn't retain its best people because it couldn't offer its directors stock options in the portfolio companies. Doriot recognized the need to offer his team outsized returns to compensate for the fact that most of ARD's investments made losses. But as a publicly listed company, Doriot's attempts to do so ran afoul of the Securities Exchange Commission, which considered this a conflict of interest.

ARD's fourth problem was the sole one that Doriot could address: it struggled to find good investments. In 1957 he finally struck gold.

DAWN OF THE INFORMATION REVOLUTION

By this point, the underpinnings of the Information Revolution were being erected. Early telecommunications, radio, television, sound recordings and radar all relied on vacuum tubes: airtight tubes in which electric currents could zip back and forth, amplifying things like radio signals. General Electric and AT&T were among the key developers of various types of vacuum tubes, and they pooled their patents into a new conglomerate, RCA.

Vacuum tubes were problematic, though: they used up a lot of electricity, consumers had to periodically replace them, and they were big and clunky.

The vacuum tube's fate was sealed in 1947 when John Bardeen, Walter Brattain and William Shockley, researchers at AT&T's Bell Labs in New Jersey, invented the first workable transistor (for which they'd share a Nobel Prize in physics in 1956).

Like tubes, the transistor amplifies or switches electronic signals and electrical power, but via a solid-state material. This is usually in the form of a sliver of conductive material like germanium or silicon, rather than a fussy, power-hungry glass ensemble. The transistor made electronics increasingly cheaper, faster, and more precise in their use.

It is a bedrock invention that formed the basis for consumer electronics, computers, and smartphones: the moment when Carlota Perez's next wave of innovation changed the world.

But in the 1940s and 1950s, few people had any inkling of a transistor's potential, let alone the know-how to turn chips into a business.

One of the first companies to commercialize transistors was Texas Instruments (TI), which was established in 1951 by veterans of the oil exploration industry. It licensed AT&T's transistor technology for $25,000.

TI had evolved out of petroleum-tech companies, so it wasn't a startup built from scratch. But its research did require capital, so it went public in 1953 by merging with a sleepy rubber manufacturer listed on NYSE. That infusion of money from this backdoor listing financed TI's production of the first transistor radio, in 1954.[7]

Four years later, one of its researchers, Jack Kilby, invented the integrated circuit (IC): putting multiple transistors on one piece of semiconductor material (in this case germanium), creating a device exponentially faster, smaller, and cheaper than a series of single electronic components.

Kilby wasn't alone. In California, Robert Noyce of Fairchild Semiconductors independently developed the IC, so both men are considered the inventor. Noyce's design was the more sophisticated, while Kilby's was intended for cheap, mass-produced things like pocket calculators. One of Noyce's most important innovations was the selection of better semiconductor material: silicon.

THE FIRST COMPUTERS

The IC (or microchip) would launch the Information Revolution. But what would ICs power? Computers!

Charles Babbage in 1830s England first worked out the idea of a machine that could carry out a sequence of mathematical or logical operations, but his government funding ran out before he could complete his hand-built device.

By the 1930s, Britain, the US, and Germany were building early computers powered by vacuum tubes, with German engineer Konrad

Zuse replacing Babbage's decimal calculations with a simpler, binary one—just ones and zeros were needed to trigger electronic switches. The term for a signal or datum that is expressed in zeros and ones is *digital.*

In 1936, the British mathematician Alan Turing proposed the idea of a universal computer that could calculate anything that is computable by being fed instructions (a stored program, i.e., software, which at the time meant punch cards or a tape).

These prototypes ran on hundreds of bulky, expensive, and unreliable vacuum tubes. During the war, Turing led the British effort to decrypt German naval codes with the aid of electromechanical machines. After the war, British government funding supported the creation of the first stored-program computers, at the University of Manchester. These still operated on cathode ray tubes rather than transistors and were designed purely to solve math experiments, but the designs were contracted to a local engineering firm, Ferranti, which produced the first commercial, general-purpose computer. (Manchester remains a center of cutting-edge computer science today.)

The commercialization of the computer achieved scale, however, with IBM. Founded in 1911 as the Computing-Tabulating-Recording Company in Endicott, New York, the company restructured under the zealous leadership of Thomas J. Watson, Sr., who ditched the firm's clunky name for International Business Machines.

IBM built computers for the US military and then released its first commercial product in 1952, which was based on vacuum tubes. The company switched to transistors in 1958 and became the dominant commercial vendor for mainframe computers—that is, physically large computers that conducted bulk data processing. It would not be until 1964, however, with the launch of the IBM System/360, that its mainframes became a must-have for large enterprises.

Although IBM would go on to dominate mainframe sales into the 1980s, one entrepreneur believed he could outwit "Big Blue" and build business computers that were smaller, cheaper, and faster.

ARD'S BIGGEST BET: DEC

Ken Olsen was an engineer at MIT who researched projects for the military, including early work on building computers run by transistors. He and a partner, Harlan Anderson, wanted to bring a superior product to the market. In 1957 they pitched their idea to Georges Doriot.

Doriot recognized Olsen's talent and liked his humble, modest lifestyle. Doriot even groomed the men's wives. Doriot, progressive in many ways, was backward when it came to gender. He would allow spouses to attend his classes at Harvard so he could train them to become supportive housewives of absentee husbands.

Doriot was satisfied by the response of Mrs. Olsen and Mrs. Anderson to his terms for investing in their husbands' company. Doriot must have been eager to make this deal, as by now ARD was in its 11th year with little to show. Nonetheless, he drove a hard bargain: he'd invest $70,000 in the startup, for 70 percent of the equity—take it or leave it.[8]

Olsen and Anderson took it and founded Digital Equipment Corporation (DEC). DEC would go on to produce the minicomputer. It thrived because initially it wasn't trying to compete with IBM or other mainframe vendors. Like any good disrupter, it was designing computers for the mass business market, not a few elite mega-corporations.

By the time IBM introduced smaller, cheaper products, DEC's minicomputer business was well established and able to compete against its giant rival.

DEC VALIDATES THE VC MODEL

It was Doriot who took the lead in helping DEC go public, in 1966. Olsen and Anderson had no experience with Wall Street, so ARD could add value by supporting this process. This involved more than coaching the company: ARD helped educate their underwriter,

Lehman Brothers, whose bankers didn't know what a minicomputer was.

Doriot and Olsen conducted a series of pitch meetings with investors arranged by Lehman. DEC went public at $22 a share, making Olsen's 13 percent stake worth $7 million—and ARD's stake (by then reduced to 65 percent) worth $38.5 million, a return on investment of nearly 55,000 times.

In one stroke, Doriot and Olsen validated the venture capital fund. ARD's other mediocre or loss-making investments didn't matter: its one bona-fide success compensated for the losers many, many times. And it put Boston's Route 128, the beltway around the city, on the map for the tech industry.

The VC model worked for the entrepreneur, too. Olsen made the kind of money that no manager of even the biggest corporations would even have dreamt about.

Most importantly, ARD showed how a professionally managed fund could take institutional capital and deploy it to companies and entrepreneurs whose ideas introduced innovative technologies that delivered widespread social benefits.

DEC would go on to become very profitable, with a market valuation that rivaled IBM's. By the 1980s Olsen was on the cover of *Fortune* magazine, having become the emblem of American tech entrepreneurship. It wouldn't last. Olsen didn't take personal computers seriously: in 1977, he said, "There is no reason for any individual to have a computer in his home."[9] By 1992, the company he built was gone, acquired by Compaq, a PC maker.

At least DEC enjoyed a good run for several decades. ARD, on the other hand, died shortly after its crowning success. Doriot's inability to give his directors options in DEC led to resentments once the company went public, and his best people left. Doriot was also his own worst enemy: he refused to groom a successor, nor would he take ARD private. In 1972 he sold the business.

ARD was a one-hit wonder. Its legal structure was unwieldy and unsuited to venture capital. It would take a new set of investors operating on the West Coast to create the durable model for VC funds. But Doriot, through sheer hard work and insight, helped show that institutional money could be put profitably to the task of supporting startups.

Moreover, he also played a role in the first attempts to export venture capital to other parts of the world. As we'll see in the next chapter, though, finding the next DEC outside of the US would prove frustrating.

3

EUROPE: THE SETBACK

IF creating a venture capital industry was as simple as correlating to a certain level of national wealth, per-capita income, industrialization, or some vague idea of being "Western," then it should have spread from the United States to other rich countries with ease.

That's not what happened.

In fact, venture investing barely survived on the US East Coast.

Two men, rivals, tried to export the VC model beyond American shores: Georges Doriot and Peter Brooke.

We'll begin with Doriot. A transplanted Frenchman who helped America win the Second World War, he naturally had an international outlook. He was an educator, having used his position at Harvard Business School to mentor the first generation of American corporate leaders. He was an evangelist for venture funding for startups to jumpstart economic growth.

And Europe certainly needed a shot in the arm.

POST-WAR EUROPE

Europe lay prostrate in the aftermath of the war. The United States helped trigger European recovery with the 1948 Marshall Plan. For the next four years, the US transferred over $13 billion in economic aid to Western European nations. (The Soviet Union and its vassal states in Eastern Europe refused the funds.) In return, recipients removed trade barriers and enacted laws to help modernize their industry.

Europeans quickly took charge of their own recovery with transnational institutions that were designed to embed West Germany among its former enemies and thereby prevent another war.

France, West Germany, Italy and the Benelux nations established the European Coal and Steel Community in 1951, pooling the coke, iron and steel industries—the raw materials of a war machine—into a single market overseen by a European regulator. This was the kernel of what would become the European Economic Community, which emerged in 1973 when the UK, Ireland and Denmark joined the group.

The three decades following the war became known in Europe as *Les Trentes Glorieuses*, a period of rapid growth underpinned by European institutions, freer trade, and American military security. Throughout most of the period, socialist parties ran European governments. They succeeded in overseeing growth, democracy, and the rise of a middle class. But they were also bureaucratic and statist. They viewed innovation as the purview of large corporations tied to government-directed banks and bureaucracies.

DORIOT MOVES FIRST

Doriot's first initiative abroad was to found INSEAD in 1959, in Fontainebleau, France. INSEAD, short for L'Institut Européen d'Administration des Affaires, was intended to be Europe's answer to Harvard Business School. The school was designed from the start as a European institution: business courses were taught in German and English as well as French, which was unique at the time.

INSEAD was a success and remains a leading business school today. Like Harvard Business School in the US, INSEAD became the training ground for Europe's top business talent.

Nurturing talent takes time, however, and it didn't happen soon enough to support Doriot's next gambit: the creation of a pan-

European venture fund. Modeled after ARD, he set up European Enterprise Development Company (EED) in 1963 (he also established a similar business in Canada).

EED was designed to invest in startups, but Europe wasn't ready. Doriot recruited directors to EED but these people lacked the skills or experience to hunt for good entrepreneurs and nurture their businesses. An even bigger problem: there were no entrepreneurs!

Even if there were such people, they faced an uphill battle if they tried to scale their operations. At this stage, the European Common Market was still more idea than reality. European socialist governments were focused on economic nationalism led by state-guided corporations.

In post-war Europe, there was no appetite or even understanding of what a startup could do, let alone how it could be financed through private capital.

EUROPEAN FAILURES

There were, however, some early attempts in the UK to create a local VC industry. The UK government had set up a development company meant to stimulate private investment into industry in the 1930s, called Charterhouse. Immediately after the war, the government also founded a bank to lend to new companies, called Industrial and Commercial Financial Corporation. It didn't prosper because its focus on debt, rather than equity, was unsuited to the needs of young companies.

There were also private efforts at equity investment in the 1960s, including New Court & Partners, established by the Rothschild family, and Spey Investments. These efforts lost money and the funds closed, but out of the wreckage emerged some of Britain's future investors, such as the banker John Incledon, who co-founded a financial advisory firm, IDJ, that would support equity investments into technology companies.[1]

Continental Europe was barren. At best, there were some government efforts to organize funds to invest in US technology companies. There was only one similar effort in the private sphere in the form of a company called Wagnisfinanzierung Gesellschaft, organized by Deutsche Bank.

It didn't get anywhere. Socialist governments were interested in full employment, which led to massive subsidies to companies for hiring people. This might have been useful in the 1950s when Europe was still licking its wounds. By the 1970s, European economies had closed the wealth gap with the US but become rigid in their ways. Companies were incentivized to win government subsidies, not to take risks or be creative. Innovation, to the extent it was encouraged, was reserved for the labs of corporations, such as the pharmaceutical and chemical giants of Germany and Switzerland.

To be fair to the Europeans, VC was a fringe industry even in the United States. VC was still getting established in Silicon Valley, and American institutions generally avoided the sector throughout most of the 1970s.

EED folded in 1974. But Doriot's failure was a noble one. During EED's lifetime, he taught people how to structure venture deals and showed the potential for startup-led innovation. INSEAD and EED championed pan-European solutions to business needs.[2]

Bigger changes were needed, however, before Europe was going to support entrepreneurship. Some of these involved high-level questions about taxation and how governments managed their economies. But it would also require people with vision and patience to bring VC to Europe.

In the United States, meanwhile, VC was undergoing a transformation. It was headed West.

USA: EAST COAST TO WEST COAST

Although ARD proved the VC model, it did so despite a terrible structure. Doriot's successors weren't going to make the same mistake. They founded the modern VC as a limited partnership.

This structure was private instead of listed on a public stock market, so there were no conflicts about owning shares in portfolio companies, which meant firms could provide incentives to their partners. It was tax efficient, so the company could avoid paying capital gains tax; instead, the profits, or "carry," was passed on to the owners in the form of income. This meant if the founders of a startup deferred getting paid, they could keep earnings within the business and not pay tax on them, which could be critical for building a startup.

Limited partnerships brought additional benefits. These firms launched funds of specific duration, usually ten years, which made it easier to measure performance. And the limited partnership could launch consecutive funds, creating "permanent capital" that could be deployed repeatedly into the same companies but at different stages.[3]

The first VC limited partnership to make money was Greylock Partners, co-founded by Bill Elfers, a Doriot mentee from ARD. Despite this success, Greylock suffered from a different kind of problem: it was part of the East Coast establishment. It would soon have to pivot to California, because by the 1970s, that's where the action was.

San Francisco boasted the first VC limited partnership, DGA, set up in 1959 by a team including William H. Draper, Jr., a prominent US banker and diplomat, and with a mix of family and bank money. However, the fund is probably best known for another VC trend: paying itself better than its backers.

The company introduced the 2-and-20 fee structure, with an annual 2 percent management fee on the assets and a 20 percent performance fee. By the end of the fund's eight-year life, its investors would have been better off putting their money into the S&P 500 and reinvesting the dividends.[4] But DGA's GPs flourished, and the firm created the template that other VCs would follow.

The Silicon Valley venture model had been born, and it facilitated the shift of innovation to California. Even Greylock, despite being more financially successful than DGA, felt compelled to shift its operations west. But why, when America's technology and financial expertise was entrenched on the East Coast? And what lessons would this hold for future VCs worldwide?

STANFORD'S CATALYTIC ROLE

One of the pivotal figures in California's early innovation culture was Frederick Terman, a radio engineer and a professor at Stanford University. Terman recognized the importance of marrying academic research with ways to commercialize it.

From 1925, he taught courses on vacuum tubes and circuits. But he was annoyed that his students kept heading east to make their careers, so in 1939, Terman dangled fellowships to two of his former students, promising to put them in touch with local California engineers and potential customers. The two students, Dave Packard and William Hewlett, agreed. They set up their company in Packard's garage with $539 of working capital. With Terman's help, Hewlett-Packard (HP) began to sell audio products to the likes of Disney and International Telephone & Telegraph, as well as to the military.

California was still a mere outpost compared to the East Coast, but it offered a freer environment, without the snobby hierarchies of traditional firms. Defense companies were flocking there, providing a natural market for tech companies. And the weather was great. But those conditions alone wouldn't suffice. Visionaries had to build what today we'd call its ecosystem.

Terman played an important role in encouraging big companies to set up and hire local talent. As Dean of Stanford's engineering school, in 1951 he launched what became Stanford Research Park. This industrial park encouraged researchers to start their own companies, and leased its landholdings to the likes of HP, Eastman Kodak, and General Electric.

This forged a connection between academia and business, but before this emerging hub could become important, it needed one more ingredient: financing.

SHOCKLEY'S MOVE

ARD and the East Coast family funds such as Venrock were creatures of a traditional, conservative culture. The West Coast would prove fertile for a more swashbuckling style of investing. This new breed of risktakers would cut its teeth on semiconductors.

William Shockley, co-inventor of the transistor at Bell Labs, had more self-regard than his colleagues. He initially accepted a consulting job at Raytheon in Boston, because Boston was America's tech hub. But the Raytheon brass objected to paying him $1 million over three years, so Shockley decamped for Mountain View, California, instead, where he could be close to his mother, or so he claimed.[5] In 1956 he opened Shockley Semiconductor Laboratory and attracted the best engineering talent.

Shockley had always suffered from a big ego and managed to alienate his co-inventors. After winning the Nobel Prize, he became insufferable. Nor did Shockley grasp the West Coast culture, which didn't abide his domineering style, and which encouraged talented people to move among companies, which Shockley tried to stop at his company. The progenitor of Silicon Valley was very much a fish out of water.

Shockley's best engineers, disillusioned with him, wanted to set up on their own. Semiconductors required a lot of capital. There was no precedent for engineers to create their own company with that kind of financial barrier. One engineer, Eugene Kleiner, wrote to his father's brokerage asking for advice, and the letter landed on the desk of Arthur Rock.

ARTHUR ROCK AND THE TRAITOROUS EIGHT

Rock was a New York investment banker at a firm called Hayden Stone specializing in helping small high-tech companies raise money. In 1957 he flew to California to meet seven unhappy engineers at Shockley Semiconductor; an eighth, Robert Noyce, signed on after Rock said he'd help them form a company and find someone to lend them the money.

Easier said than done! Rock tried 35 companies but no one liked the idea of lending money to a startup. It simply wasn't the way things were done. Then Rock met Sherman Fairchild—whose father had helped set up IBM as Tom Watson Sr.'s partner. Fairchild was now the largest single owner of IBM stock. He was also an inventor in his own right: he developed cameras for use on airplanes. Fairchild's camera company would front $1.5 million with an option to buy all of the stock, which was divided 10 percent to each of the eight engineers, and 20 percent to Hayden Stone.[6]

Thus the "Traitorous Eight," as Shockley would dub them, set up Fairchild Semiconductor Engineering, with Arthur Rock greasing the wheels.

If one single company deserves credit for making Silicon Valley, it's Fairchild Semiconductor. Fairchild's engineers, led by Robert Noyce, invented the IC, the first to use silicon as its solid-state material. Noyce's colleague, Gordon Moore, would predict to a reporter that ongoing miniaturization would allow chips to double their power every two years, an observation—and a challenge to engineers—that became known as "Moore's Law." From here on out, every electronics business sought to fulfil Moore's prediction, making miniaturization and cheapness the industry's driving ethos. This drive transformed a cluster of sleepy California towns into a center of global power that became known as Silicon Valley. Fairchild even laid claim to the moniker, which was coined in 1971 by a journalist who had been a company publicist.

CHANGING COMPLEXIONS

Shockley, meanwhile, would quit business to teach at Stanford, where he would spew ugly, racist theories about eugenics. White supremacists were delighted to have a Nobel Prize winner in their ranks, while engineers and entrepreneurs were dismayed by Shockley's making speeches about sterilizing minority women instead of talking semiconductors. Although his reputation declined, Stanford continued to let Shockley lecture there into the 1980s.

For America's VC industry today, as it seeks to attract talent across gender, race, and nationality, Shockley's legacy is one that needs a reckoning. Even the engineers who abhorred his racist views were of a type: there is a famous photograph of the Traitorous Eight that portrays eight middle-aged white men in the 1960s uniform of suit and tie.

But even at that early moment, the tech industry was not solely a white man's realm. Back at Bell Labs in New Jersey, the two men who had refined the original transistor into the model that ultimately went into chips were Mohamed Atalla and Dawon Kahng, an Egyptian-American and a Korean-American respectively.

Congress passed the Immigration and Nationality Act in 1965, abolishing race and nation-based quotas in favor of preferences based on skills and professions, as well as factors such as family ties or refugees. Also known as Hart-Celler, for its Senate sponsors, the legislation transformed American society at large but had an outsized impact on Silicon Valley.

This represented a sea change in America's attitudes toward immigration, particularly from Asia. Washington first established quotas based on race in 1882 with the Chinese Exclusion Act. From 1920, the US enacted racial quotas on all immigrants, with virtual bans on people from East and South Asia. White American views of Asians hit a nadir during the Second World War when the US forcibly moved about 120,000 people of Japanese ancestry into concentration camps along the West Coast.

This arrangement became an embarrassment amid the Civil Rights Movement of the 1960s. But Silicon Valley interests also lobbied to ensure Hart-Celler was crafted to attract engineers and scientists.

From 1965, the US threw open its doors to migrants from Asia, as well as Africa and Latin America. But it was China, Taiwan, Korea, and India that had castes of well-trained engineers from elite schools who could meet the sudden demand in the US for their skills.

"Entire classes from National Taiwan University or Indian Institute of Technology migrated to the US," writes AnnaLee Saxenian, a scholar of migrant networks in Silicon Valley.[7]

Although the Valley attracted people from Israel and Europe, those people had a home market they could go back to. Japanese, Korean, and French students were more likely to return to their native corporations—but there were no such companies in Greater China or India. These people stayed in the US.

"Silicon Valley is powered by ICs," jokes Thomas Tsao, a Brooklyn-born, ethnic Taiwan Chinese who co-founded Gobi Partners, a venture firm focused on East Asia. "Not integrated circuits, but Indians and Chinese."[8]

The data bears this out. From 1975 to 1990, Silicon Valley created 150,000 jobs. Of these, one-third of the scientists and engineers were born overseas, mostly in Greater China and India.[9] These workers would also encounter glass ceilings in Silicon Valley (few were promoted to senior management), which encouraged them over time to use their knowledge and network to take a slice of Silicon Valley back to their home country—the story of this book.

FOUNDING INTEL

But to understand the story of VC's globalization, we need to continue with its story in the US and Europe.

Back to Shockley: his personal shortcomings set the stage for the creation of Fairchild, which would become the Valley's benchmark firm, both for its engineering successes and for its financial history.

First, Fairchild Semiconductor wouldn't have been created without Arthur Rock's vision and network.

Second, the company's engineers gradually quit over the lack of stock options, establishing a new business culture of entrepreneurial rewards and fluid movement of talent. The business did incredibly well, especially thanks to military contracts. But Sherman Fairchild died, and his heirs viewed the idea of giving employees stock options as anathema. One by one, the engineers peeled off to other ventures where they could be better rewarded.

The last of the Treacherous Eight to leave were Noyce and Moore, who hung in there until 1968. The reason for their lingering was that they didn't want to join another company: they wanted to create their own. Once more, they turned to Arthur Rock.

By now Rock had quit his New York securities job to move to California and start his own venture fund, Davis & Rock, the first successful West Coast VC managing institutional money. Rock asked the two engineers how much they'd need: $2.5 million, they said. Then he asked how much each man could put up: $250,000, which Rock knew represented most of their net wealth. Rock drew up the business plan, a mere page and a half, but after a few phone calls he already had raised the rest of the money. Investors knew Rock, and they knew Noyce and Moore, who for founders could insist on keeping unusually large equity stakes.[10]

The two men founded Intel that year, which by the early 2000s was supplying 80 percent of the world's semiconductor chips. Rock was on the board from day one. "I was a co-founder," he once told an interviewer. "Not in the sense of leading the science, but I had founder stock, and I signed the corporation papers."[11]

Arthur Rock has come to epitomize a style of venture investing: the networked financier. His Rolodex helped the Traitorous Eight find a corporate backer, and then his contacts with wealthy families let him quickly find the money to create Intel. Soon others would create different types of venture investment strategies, but they all relied on the same limited partnership structure pioneered by DGA.

VC in the 1970s was still a cottage industry, but it had gained purchase in sunny California, eclipsing Boston's Route 128. Could the Silicon Valley model be replicated elsewhere? Intel was founded shortly before the collapse of Doriot's EED. It would be up to another American investor to carry VC's torch to Europe.

SECOND MOVER: ADVENT

Peter Brooke would pick up where Doriot left off. The two men disliked one another. Brooke had been studying at HBS, enrolled in Doriot's class, sat in the front row, and walked out. He didn't like the General's harping on about the need for businessmen (Doriot only admitted men to his classroom) to work endless hours.

To Brooke, it seemed Doriot was just trying to turn people into corporate drones so they could work at IBM—the kind of place where you could wear any color of buttoned-down shirt so long as it was white. Doriot never forgot the slight. The two men would cross paths many times but there was no admiration beneath their professional courtesies.[12]

Brooke was a Boston Brahmin—that class of wealthy, cultured Northeasterner inculcated with old-fashioned manners and a sense of noblesse oblige. He was a natural fit in New England's conservative, blue-blood business circles. But—like Doriot—he also had a vision for VC as a global force for good. Inspired by the Marshall Plan, he thought VC could be applied as a purely private tool to kickstart growth and innovation, by backing startups.

He built a career in Boston banking creating what would become VC investing: one of his early banking clients was An Wang, co-founder of Wang Laboratories, an early tech company in Cambridge, Massachusetts. Wang sold computers to the US government but had no idea how to market his wares commercially. Brooke convinced his bank to provide Wang with finance and with business advice, essentially serving as a venture capitalist.

He came to view VC as most effective when practiced in an environment in which the public sector and the private sector collaborated to promote economic development. And he wanted to take this experience to the rest of the world.

Brooke went on to found TA Associates in 1968. TA was an early private equity (PE) firm. PE is a cousin to VC. VC provides equity to startups and early-stage companies. PE invests in large, established companies, with a view to restructuring them to create shareholder value. In the 1960s, the lines between VC and PE were blurry. TA did both and in the 1970s made some very successful investments into early biotech companies such as Biogen.

FRANCE AND SOFINNOVA

As Brooke's partners steered TA more toward buyouts of mature companies, he began hopping the globe in search of partners and ideas to take VC global. Like Doriot, he wanted to create a pan-European network. Unlike Doriot, he was wary of an actual pan-European VC fund, because he believed VC had to adapt to local market conditions.

To that end, he envisioned TA becoming an enabler of other, local VCs, providing them with financial, managerial, and logistics services, as well as a network. A local team was necessary to manage relationships, scout for deals, support local entrepreneurs, and avoid any political minefields around being a foreign company acquiring local businesses.

His first attempt was in France, where in 1972 he helped establish Sofinnova Partners. It only happened because Brooke met Christian Marbach, a young deputy minister at the Ministry of Industry who was intrigued by VC and decided the state would need to help create it. This proved necessary, because Brooke struggled to find European institutions willing to invest in a venture equity business. Marbach brought in state-owned lender Crédit National, as a third backer behind Sofinnova.

Sofinnova was designed to support European biotech, but opportunities were thin on the ground. It achieved commercial success initially by investing in US tech. France and other markets had plenty of cutting-edge technology—cooped up in the labs of large companies with state connections. These companies took good care of their technologists, who were not going to leave for a risky, no-name startup.

Nonetheless Sofinnova survived thanks to its French political protection, gaining a reputation as France's first "American-style" VC firm. It struggled for a long time, serving more as a vehicle for European investors to access US tech firms. It didn't launch its first European fund until 1989.

BRITAIN AND ADVENT

Brooke found Britain a much easier environment. Throughout the 1970s it suffered from the same sclerosis as the continent. It was a high-tax, low-productivity market, with a legal system that discouraged equity investments.

That changed dramatically with Margaret Thatcher's becoming prime minister in 1979. She rammed through three changes that were friendly to VC. First, she cut the top tax rate on income from 83 percent to 60 percent (and later to 40 percent). She also abolished a separate tax on investment income.

Second, her government wrote legislation to allow for limited partnerships for VC funds, along with tax advantages for supporting startups. Third, she backed the creation of a second board at the London Stock Exchange, the Unlisted Securities Market, to provide a venue to trade shares in small companies.

Together the Thatcher initiatives transformed the landscape in the UK. But there was still no one with experience in VC.

Brooke helped support the creation of Advent Limited as the first venture firm in Europe that followed the US limited partnership model.

The company was founded in 1981 and over the next few years launched several funds. These were rolled into Advent Capital, the successor fund, in 1985. Led by David Cooksey, Advent Capital enjoyed an early success by backing Filtronic, a company that developed compounds that went into antimissile systems sold to the British military. The technology had proved itself in the Falklands War of 1982, and was being commercialized for use in cellular communications tech.

Filtronic reminded Brooke of successful companies from Boston: its founder was an engineer who came out of Leeds University, developed a business that could get off the ground thanks to government contracts, and then could commercialize and scale.

"After establishing a foothold in a country—France—where the conditions were relatively difficult, I had found a much more congenial environment in Britain," Brooke wrote in his memoir.[13]

Filtronic listed on the London Stock Exchange in 1994, providing Advent with a handsome return and Europe with its first DEC-like, VC-backed success story.

Europe, for all its wealth and sophisticated corporations, nevertheless was difficult territory for venture investing. Stories like Filtronic were rarities.

BAD TERROIR

Europe remained better at consuming and regulating technology rather than creating it. It fostered an environment that supported incumbent corporations, didn't commercialize university-led research, and was hostile to startups, which faced the same red tape and tax levels as the incumbents. These barriers to scale and profitability kept venture capitalists away, and prevented the accumulation of talent and experience—in engineering, investing, or business.

The paradox is why the UK, with an institutional and cultural setting comparable to the US, didn't become a VC or startup hub. Germany actually attracted more early-stage investment than the UK into the early 2000s.[14] London was such a lucrative financial hub that it didn't attract technologists, and its mighty pension sector was content to invest quite conservatively.

German universities cranked out engineers. While its bank-dominated financial sector was aimed at supporting its conglomerates, the government did support small businesses with funding programs—which is why most German startups failed to scale, once they had to wrangle with banks to get larger investments.

France, in the meantime, tried to support VCs directly with a number of funding schemes, tax breaks, and—*trés* important—allowing government employees to retain their status as civil servants if they quit to run a fund.

Despite these efforts, though, the large presence of banks as investors in these funds almost guaranteed they would have to operate more conservatively.

SKYPE

Success breeds success, and a blockbuster deal can spark a trend, proving to founders and investors that a VC-backed startup can make it big. Europe got its blockbuster in 2005. That was the year when eBay acquired Skype.

Skype was a truly innovative startup founded by two technologists, Niklas Zennström of Sweden and Janus Friis of Denmark, along with four developers from Estonia. They released their product in 2003: using Voice-Over-Internet-Protocol design, their users could make phone calls over the internet for free, even to other countries.

The service attracted funding from DFJ ePlanet, but most of its VC backing came from Europe, including a Luxembourg-based VC, Mangrove Capital Partners, which had only gotten started a few years earlier. Mangrove invested $1 million for a roughly 25 percent stake in Skype to finance its rapid growth. The bet was a spectacular win: in 2005, eBay acquired Skype for $4.1 billion in cash and stock, giving Mangrove an exit and turning its $1 million into $200 million, says Peter Jackson, partner.[15] Skype would also be the biggest moneymaker for ePlanet.[16]

Skype would subsequently go on a rollercoaster ride. eBay decided it had overpaid and sold it at a loss to US later-stage VCs Silver Lake and Andreessen Horowitz, who eventually sold it to Microsoft in 2011 for $8.5 billion. The company innovated video chat and money-transfer capabilities for its mobile app, which Microsoft integrated into its own platform.

By any measure Skype was a hit: disruptive tech, great consumer product, massive user base, and terrific financials. Yet it speaks to the barrenness of the European startup and VC scene that nothing like it followed for another decade.

EUROPE'S EVENTUAL EMERGENCE

The European scene began to perk up in the 2010s, as more founders with experience in Silicon Valley returned to start companies in their home countries. The rise of scalable software made it cheap to start a technology company, while by the mid-2010s a critical portion of European consumers and businesses were now online.

The year 2015 was a watershed, with Europe and the UK experiencing takeoff in terms of the number of startups hitting unicorn status—valuations of $1 billion or more. Europe had just 22 unicorns in 2010, but by 2021 it had more than 220.

European venture investment rose steadily throughout the decade. The first mega-round of €100 million or more was struck in 2013; in 2019 rounds began to exceed €250 million and total investment hit €20 billion. In line with a global boom, VC in 2021 invested €49 billion.[17]

Europe's industry is mostly home grown, with little presence among Silicon Valley's marquee firms. Instead European VC is led by smaller firms such as Berlin's Global Founders Capital, Hiventures in Budapest, and High-Tech Gründerfonds, a Bonn-based VC with public and private backing.[18]

US VCs FINALLY RETURN

It's only recently that brand-name Silicon Valley firms have set up shop, with Sequoia finally opening in London in 2020. VCs had been investing in Europe from global funds managed from the US, but such deals were rare, with US VC accounting for only 3 percent of European startup funding as late as 2013. That portion rose steadily over the decade, however, with US firms accounting for 19 percent of funding by 2019.[19]

The only major Valley firm with a longstanding presence in Europe has been Accel, which established itself in London in 2001 to run funds dedicated to European Series A and Series B raises, under autonomous leadership. Other attempts didn't work out: IDG came and left, while Benchmark Europe, an outpost of the US firm, spun out on its own as Balderton, in 2007.

The current wave of US interest may not last, either, as a major factor was sky-high valuations in Silicon Valley; European startups were cheaper. But since the market crash of 2022, that may no longer be the case. US firms prefer to invest at home, where they have deep networks, a vast ecosystem, and an IPO market that delivers eye-popping returns.

What will make them stay? Great companies. The likes of music-sharing platform Spotify and AI neural network DeepMind have begun to showcase scalable European innovation.

However, the biggest sector in Europe over the past few years has been fintech, with companies like Sweden's buy now, pay later (BNPL) platform Klarna and Dutch payments company Adyen reaching incredible valuations at their peak in 2021. The tech bust in 2020 has been vicious: in June, Klarna raised a "down round," that is, the company sold more shares at a price lower than in its previous financings, which forced all of its backers to revise their estimates of its worth. In Klarna's case, it was valued at $6.7 billion, a precipitous drop from its private valuation of $45.6 billion from its previous raise, in June 2021. VCs that had bought shares on the assumption of a higher valuation had to accept their position had lost money.

UNDERPERFORMANCE

Overall the story of VC in Europe is one of constant setbacks, despite the region's wealth and maturity.

There is more to tech than VC-backed companies: countries such as Germany have built world-beating manufacturing companies supported by a backbone of small, sophisticated enterprises, the *Mittelstand*. European consumers still benefit from the innovations pouring out of the US, while its regulators have emerged as a global brake on Big Tech's most egregious behavior.

But European companies failed to set standards, change the world, or produce job-creating dynamism and wealth. The most talented people will flock to where there's action and opportunity, and that's still Silicon Valley.

In recent years, the story has begun to change. Europe finally boasts a vibrant startup scene funded by its own VCs. As it begins to take its place along the US and Asia, though, the 2022 market crash risks a different kind of setback.

Niklas Zennström, the co-founder of Skype and now co-founder of London-based VC Atomico, says Europe's startup scene, having learned to embrace risk, must learn to accept failure. "The real danger is that the failure stigma that used to stop Europeans from starting tech companies, will now hold founders back from ending them."[20]

Better to free experienced founders and skilled engineers to start anew on companies that can solve social problems, than have them run zombie businesses that burn VC cash.

Where might these entrepreneurs turn next? The UK, despite its superficial similarities to US-style capitalism, is still playing catch-up when it comes to startups. London is a center for fintech and some enterprise software, but it is too easy to make money in finance rather than in technology, while UK pension funds still turn up their noses at scrappy startups. Nonetheless, Britain boasts strong research institutions and a global capital market, and its English language makes it an easy setting for entrepreneurs from around the world. By itself, Britain can't rival Silicon Valley, but it should play an outsized role in a broader European startup environment.

The brightest spots in Europe for actual tech entrepreneurs have been smaller countries, such as Estonia and Ireland, which have taken pains to lay out attractive tax and other rules for VC—often copying Israel.

Russia and Ukraine, with their long history of talented engineers, have also grown some VC-backed companies. Russia is now a pariah, though, after its disastrous invasion of Ukraine in February 2022. When Oleg Tinkov, founder of Moscow-based Tink—one of Europe's most successful fintechs and digital banks—criticized the war, the Russian government confiscated the business and sold it to a pro-regime tycoon for pennies on the dollar. That's the end of VC-backed innovation in Russia.

Ukraine's armed forces are fighting against the bigger Russian force by relying on ingenuity and flexibility straight out of the Silicon

Valley playbook. The Russians' inability to adapt and learn on the battlefield is reminiscent of a sclerotic corporation getting outclassed by an agile disruptor. A rebuilt, post-war Ukraine will be a source of engineering talent, and could become a startup hub. Ukraine, with its dynamic, open but militarized society, looks like the next Israel in the making.

We've referred to the Israeli model before. What's special about Israel? Everything: it was here, when Israel was an economic backwater in the war-torn Middle East, that VC first took root beyond America's shores.

4

ISRAEL: THE BREAKTHROUGH

THE first attempts to export US VC focused on other wealthy, industrialized economies like France, Germany, and the UK, where they largely failed. These other places lacked a culture of entrepreneurialism, an appetite for risk, and the very idea that such things were important. They were complacent.

What the innovation economy needed was hunger. With hindsight it seems obvious that the first place VC took root was a small, peripheral, and troubled economy: Israel. How did this economic backwater, surrounded by enemies, bereft of natural resources, become an innovation powerhouse?

As we'll see, Israel combined technical expertise, entrepreneurial grit, and smart government initiatives to activate its startup economy. What made Israel's tech scene endure and thrive were the personal connections between its people—its investors and entrepreneurs—and the United States.

Today Israel's high-tech industry is undeniably successful. As of 2022, although the industry employs only 10 percent of the workforce, it is responsible for 15 percent of GDP and 43 percent of Israeli exports, and its workers contribute 25 percent of income taxes.[1]

THE ISRAELI STARTUP MYSTIQUE

In 2021, Israeli companies raised a record funding amount of $25 billion, led by cybersecurity and fintech. The biggest driver behind these sums were 77 "mega-rounds" for deals valued at $100 million or more going to unicorns—private companies valued at $1 billion and above.[2] That same year, the aggregate value of 85 Israeli companies trading on Nasdaq and the New York Stock Exchange exceeded $300 billion.[3]

Israel has become a model that other countries seek to emulate. In 2009 two journalists, Dan Senor of the *Wall Street Journal* and Saul Singer of the *Jerusalem Post*, dubbed it the "Startup Nation" in a book of that name, a label that Israelis happily embrace. This narrative explained much of the mystique that has grown around Israel's success, notably the blunt, self-reliant, and inventive culture forged from participation in the Israel Defense Forces (IDF).

While these factors are real, the enduring power of Israeli tech stems from its connectivity with Silicon Valley and the US market. Put another way, Israel's small size meant its talented people had to focus on building companies that ignored the home market—a lesson that would color VC in other regions.

BASKET CASE: ISRAEL'S ECONOMY AND EARLY VC

Today Israel has a population of over 9 million, but in 1980 it was only about 3.9 million, not including the people in the West Bank and other Palestinian lands. The economy was dominated by seven local banks locked in incestuous trading relationships.

The country was better known for conflict than business: in 1982 it invaded Lebanon in an attempt to wipe out the Palestinian Liberation Organization (PLO). The PLO fled Beirut but the IDF found itself bogged down in Lebanon's civil wars and had to stage a messy withdrawal—only for Israel to face the first *intifada*, violent protests by Palestinians in Israeli-occupied territories.

The upheavals weren't just political and military. They were economic too, with Israel suffering from runaway inflation. The economy went from 13 percent inflation in 1971 to nearly 400 percent in the early 1980s. The turmoil led to a financial crisis that threatened to bring down the banking system and the Tel Aviv Stock Market. The government shut the stock market down for 18 days in 1983 and converted bank equity into government bonds, effectively nationalizing the sector.[4]

Who in their right mind would consider this economic basket case to be the place to launch a tech startup?

MILITARY KNOW-HOW, US CONNECTIONS

What Israel did have was talented people. First they were trained: the IDF taught its best people electronics, optics and communications. Second, they were international: from 1978 to 2000, more than 14,000 professional and technical Israelis moved to America, and many would be employed by Silicon Valley or Route 128 companies.[5]

These people would take their know-how back to Israel, sometimes while leaving their families in the US. There was no comparable circulation of tech talent from Western Europe.

Leading companies such as IBM, Microsoft, and Cisco were prepared to allow their best-performing engineers to return to Tel Aviv and continue to work from Israel. This was unusual for American companies, but they valued these people too much to let them go. Intel, for example, let its staff set up an integrated chip factory in Israel. In other cases, Israelis working in the US campaigned for their bosses to set up an operation in Israel to take advantage of its mass of skilled engineers.

The next step was for these Israeli returnees to set up new businesses. But that required more than tech expertise: it needed people who understood commercialization, sales, and marketing. Israel lacked such people.

FIRST FUND: FRED ADLER AND ATHENA

This began to change with the creation of Israel's first VC, Athena Fund.

Athena was co-founded by Fred Adler, a lawyer-turned-VC investor in New York. Adler was one of the VC industry's early success stories. An avuncular workaholic, he told the *New York Times* in 1981 that he had built his wealth as an investor from $500,000 in 1967 to over $100 million.[6]

Starting in the late 1970s he began accepting European and Middle Eastern money into his venture funds, a prelude to his becoming one of the founders of the Israeli VC industry. In 1985 he launched the Athena Fund with two Israeli partners, a former Israeli Air Force general named Dan Tolkowsky and his son, Gideon Tolkowsky. The idea was to invest half of Athena's assets in US companies and the other half into Israeli ones.

Dan Tolkowsky was already involved in supporting local tech, as vice chairman of the Discount Bank Investment Corporation, which was spun out of a bank. But it was Adler's insight to seek exits in the US, not on the Tel Aviv Stock Exchange. Adler had some experience with this, having already backed the first Israeli company to list on Nasdaq: Elscint, a medical imaging company.

Athena was groundbreaking, but its activities were minuscule in the scheme of things, even for a small country like Israel. Its example showed the importance of US connections, maybe to a fault: for years, it was the only VC operating in Israel, eventually closing in 1997. Other than Adler, no American investor would touch Israeli companies, as they regarded the country as just another dead end in the Middle East. Neither was there a conduit to sell startups to corporate acquirers in Europe or the US.

Israel needed a VC industry, and fast.

GOVERNMENT FUNDING

Israeli government officials had been trying to foster the nation's tech scene for years. In 1974 the Ministry of Industry and Trade established the Office of the Chief Scientist, an agency designed to fund Israeli startups and tech incubators. It still exists, now branded as the Israel Innovation Authority. But handing out grants then was like throwing seeds on barren soil. Nothing grew.

Fred Adler saw the value of a VC firm wasn't just the money. It was the ability to connect startups to the people they needed to commercialize their technology: people who knew marketing, sales, distribution, finance and accounting, legal and compliance, and licensing.

They needed people who knew how to find and build reliable business partnerships, how to test a market's demand, and how to engage with customers and users. This was all the stuff that Israel lacked, no matter how many shekels a government agency spread around.

The second alternative for Israeli entrepreneurs was to apply for a grant from Binational Industrial Research and Development (BIRD), a fund backed by the US and Israeli governments to promote joint ventures. BIRD was run by Ed Mlavsky, a US citizen born in the UK who moved to Tel Aviv to operate the fund.[7] BIRD was successful, helping match Israeli companies with American partners that could commercialize the tech, but it remained small.

The more fundamental drawback to Athena and BIRD was that Israelis remained dependent on US-backed institutions for funding and connections.

The government was acutely aware of this weakness. In the 1980s it tried to develop an indigenous fighter jet, the Lavi. Israel wanted an air force that could defeat enemies including Egypt and Saudi Arabia, which were armed with US weaponry. The US helped Israel develop the Lavi, but the Pentagon was hostile to the project, which it feared would create a competitor in global arms sales. The engineering that went into the Lavi made it a showcase of Israeli technical sophistication, but the mounting costs forced the government to cancel the project in 1987—a humiliating reversal.

The Lavi had employed 5,000 scientists and engineers, making it the focal point for channeling IDF skills into big high-tech projects. Their numbers were expanding with the import of Russian Jews: under Soviet Union leader Mikhael Gorbachev, some 900,000 Russians would migrate to Israel in the 1980s and 1990s. That was a vast number considering Israel's population was only about 4 million at the time.

These migrants didn't speak Hebrew (let alone English) and had no experience with business or capitalism. But about one-third of them were technical.

"It was tough for the economy," recalls Yossi Sela, who would co-found Gemini, a local VC, in partnership with BIRD's Ed Mlavsky. "But they brought a lot of music, engineers, and scientists. Physics, chemistry. Researchers that brought skills we lacked."[8]

But with Lavi canceled, indigenous talent was out of a job, and there were few places to put the growing ranks of Russians. The Lavi episode made clear Israel's dependence on American capital. Israel couldn't be independent until it resolved this weakness.

YOZMA

The country needed to develop a homegrown capacity for venture investing, in both the public and private spheres. It would create this by getting these two worlds to work together.

The impetus came from Yigal Erlich, who since 1984 had been running the Office of the Chief Scientist. He noticed a coterie of promising startups was emerging from Israel's technology sector and realized they needed help with commercialization.

First, in 1991 he launched a government-backed insurance company called Inbal to limit the downside of VCs backing startups that listed on the local stock market. It didn't work because it was built on short-term assumptions and lacked the incentives to attract

VC professionals, notably by excluding them from being able to contribute to the operating of a company once it went public.

What Erlich learned was the importance of giving VCs and management a free hand when it came to compensation, including options, and the advantages of early exits to quickly raise capital for new funds.

Erlich launched a second initiative in 1992 that incorporated these lessons. The Yozma program (from the Hebrew for "initiative") would back ten VC funds. Each fund had to have at least one financial institution from Israel and one from abroad, so that VC know-how would be transferred to young Israelis. They had to be new funds that operated independently of incumbents.

The funds had to raise a minimum of $10 million, with Yozma's own government-sponsored fund (managed by Erlich) contributing 40 percent to 80 percent, for a total of $100 million in government money. This matching program of $100 million catalyzed a greater pool from private sources.

The challenge was how to attract foreign LPs to back these new funds. Erlich's critical innovation was to grant LPs a call option on the government's share after five years. A call option is the right (but not the obligation) to buy a security at a future time and price. By writing these contracts, Erlich was giving LPs an incentive to partner with Yozma. They would both reap the rewards of investing in startups, plus be able to leverage the government's upside at a discount (assuming the IPO was a success).[9]

Yozma jumpstarted Israel's VC industry. Ten funds were launched with foreign partners, including one involving Advent Venture Partners out of Boston, whom we met in Chapter Three. Other foreign LPs came from Germany, the Netherlands, Japan, and Singapore. They raised $263 million in total capital and invested in 217 companies, of which eventually 122 (or 56 percent) went IPO—a very high success rate for risky startups.

Israel had come a long way in a short time from the Lavi disaster. "The project failed but the country succeeded," says Michael Eisenberg, partner at Tel Aviv-based Aleph VC.[10]

Yozma sowed the seeds for a homegrown venture industry that would eventually support world-class companies. Eisenberg, for example, would go on to be one of the first investors in companies such as Lemonade (digital insurance) and Wix (website builder).

But Yozma was a one-off. It would take a lot more building for Israel to create VCs like Aleph.

THE HARVEST

Erlich sun-setted the Yozma program. After the initial ten funds were created, it stopped investing and the government later sold its stakes to partner LPs. It's unusual for a government program to be shuttered, especially when it's successful. But the government had the right idea. It knew the industry needed a kickstart, but having germinated the ecosystem, the Office of the Chief Scientist got out of the way.

The fruits of Yozma included the first generation of local VCs, some of which continue to operate, such as Gemini (partnering with Advent), Pitango, Jerusalem Venture Partners, and a local subsidiary of US firm Walden International.

None of the foreign LPs came from top-tier US venture firms. There was no Sequoia, no Kleiner Perkins (KP), no Accel or Benchmark. Not yet. But the smaller players were enough to give Israel's startup and venture scene critical mass. Most of these ten funds would go on to raise follow-up funds. In 1995 they managed $163 million; by 2000, they were managing $3.2 billion, representing more than half of the capital raised by the Israeli VC industry.

The point to having a VC industry, however, is not to raise assets but to support startups. And the Yozma program did that. In the early 1990s, VC-backed startups represented only 10 percent of startup creation, but by 1996, they accounted for 55 percent.[11]

These companies also took a page from Fred Adler's playbook and exited by listing on Nasdaq. Yozma funds accounted for more than half of Israeli IPOs on Nasdaq in 1998–2001. Strategic M&A became an important exit too.

What counted more than numbers, though, was the learning that Yozma enabled. By creating an industry and leaving it to its devices, the government replicated the benefits of Sand Hill Road, with VCs and entrepreneurs sharing knowledge about deals, due diligence, supporting portfolio companies, and structuring IPOs or sales.

"We were the first to write a term sheet [in Israel]," Yossi Sela says. The culture was fearless and maybe a little naïve. "My partner Ed Mlavsky used to say, 'Babies and drunks, when they fall they don't get hurt.'"[12]

After Yozma, there might still be plenty of falling over—most startups still end in failure—but Israel could boast a sustainable high-tech cluster. Gemini, for example, has closed its fifth fund and now manages $700 million.

ANGEL INVESTORS: MICHAEL EISENBERG AND PICTUREVISION

Initially, deals were backed by angel investors (individuals) rather than by venture funds. "There wasn't any difference, though, because there was almost no VC," says Michael Eisenberg—who was one of Israel's first angels before starting up a professional fund.[13]

In 1993 Eisenberg, an American Jew, migrated to Israel fired by the idea of investing in the brand-new world of the internet. Two years later he was introduced to a struggling entrepreneur named Yaacov Ben-Yaacov who had developed a way to transfer images over the internet. In 1995 this was a radical notion, because most people accessed the internet through slow dial-up modems connected by telephone landlines, and which could barely handle email. It took about one hour for Ben-Yaacov to demo his technology. The man was broke and no one would fund his crazy idea.

Eisenberg teamed up with Shlomo Kalish—the founder of Jerusalem Venture Partners—to co-invest $50,000 to invest in the company and help it raise more money by asking investors if they would like to send photos to faraway friends and family over something called "the internet." The business was called PictureVision. In 1998, Kodak acquired 51 percent of the company for $50 million cash, valuing the business at $100 million. AOL acquired another 20 percent a few months later, and then Kodak acquired full control for $90 million.

Sadly, in 2001, Kodak shuttered the business. Ben-Yaacov went into VC, founding a firm called Yazam. Eisenberg and Jerusalem Venture Partners each made a return of just over 10×, an encouraging start. And Israel had its first VC-backed internet exit.

Eisenberg would co-found Aleph in 2013, a VC dedicated to supporting Israeli startups whose seed investments included digital insurer Lemonade, AI-driven marine risk manager Windward, and WeWork, the controversial SoftBank-backed co-working space company.

ANGEL INVESTORS: YOSSI VARDI AND MIRABILIS

The company with the biggest impact in the early days of the internet was Mirabilis, a startup that invented peer-to-peer messaging. It too was enabled by an angel investor, Yossi Vardi. Or rather, the creation of Mirabilis by four friends in 1996 transformed Vardi into an angel investor: one the founders was his son, Arik.

Vardi was already a technologist and entrepreneur with a career in the government-linked energy sector. He agreed to help fund his son's company without asking too many questions, but was astounded by what they came up with: a service called ICQ, a play on "I Seek You," that could connect any two people on computers using any network, anywhere in the world, in real time.

Now the internet was not just a way to plug into the "information superhighway" but a means of communicating with everyone else. People could now chat in real time with distant friends and family, for free. The service was immediately popular in Israel, and the team relocated to Los Angeles to refine the software and grow a US base; within a year, the service had over 1 million users.

The founders had no business plan, as ICQ was released for free, but they knew creating a huge audience would lead to opportunities to monetize. US tech companies knew this too. Vardi helped raise additional seed money from his personal network. He represented

Mirabilis in negotiations, ultimately selling the company to AOL in 1998 for $407 million. Mirabilis is Latin for "wonderous" and the sale lived up to the company's name, netting Vardi a return of 130× and earning $70 million for the co-founders—each.[14]

"The turning point for investing in Israeli tech was the ICQ deal," says Robby Hilkowitz, an independent investor.[15]

Vardi went on to a career of angel investing in Israeli companies, while AOL drove ICQ's audience to 100 million users. Eventually the shift from PC to mobile would threaten ICQ's dominance. AOL sold ICQ, bought it back again, and then finally sold it once more; it's now owned by DST Global, a late-stage VC founded by Yuri Milner, and Mail.ru, the Russian internet portal Milner also helped create. ICQ is used mainly in the Russian-speaking world, but the company continues to operate out of Tel Aviv.

BMR AND CHECKPOINT

Professionally organized venture firms were going to be able to provide the support founders needed to expand to global markets, particularly the US. Indeed, no Israeli startup could afford to focus on the domestic market. It was too small.

"We all had to be global from day one," says Avi Zeevi, who founded Israeli VC firm Viola Ventures in 2000, and would go on to back financial technology startups such as payments business Payoneer. "The addressable market needs to be worldwide. We spend a lot of time living and traveling abroad. The B2Bs [businesses selling to businesses] keep the tech and the R&D in Israel, but the CEO and the business development team are abroad, mostly in the US, usually with their families."[16]

The iconic example of this was Checkpoint, a cybersecurity startup whose founders came out of Unit 8200, a highly regarded communications team in the IDF. The company was founded in 1993 but had no access to US VC money.

A new local venture group called BRM lent Checkpoint $250,000 in return for 50 percent of the company. This wasn't classic VC (it was a loan, for starters), and BRM was inexperienced. It was the product of an earlier company whose founders had developed antivirus software while studying at Hebrew University. Two brothers, Eli and Nir Barkat, joined to help commercialize the tech, and they sold the company. They decided to use the money to provide seed money to other startups.

This was chutzpah—a Hebrew term for audacity—but the underlying tech was solid and the Barkats helped Checkpoint set up a headquarters in Redwood City, California, from where it struck deals supplying Sun Microsystems and HP. These wins made Checkpoint into the world's leading firewall vendor. In 1996 the company went public on Nasdaq and raised $67 million.

The windfall made BRM and Checkpoint leaders in the Israeli tech scene. The money was astounding. Checkpoint employees would go on to found their own businesses, making the company the epicenter of Israeli commercial cybersecurity akin to how spinoffs from Fairchild Semiconductor populated the US chip industry. It put BRM on the map and helped fuel Nir Barkat's later political career as mayor of Jerusalem. It proved that Israeli capital could enjoy the kind of home runs usually affiliated with American VCs like Venrock or Sequoia.

ISRAEL SEED PARTNERS AND COMPUGEN

But were there enough stories like Checkpoint to sustain a domestic VC industry?

A teenage Jon Medved showed up in Tel Aviv from his hometown Berkeley to be a tour guide, which meant fooling around and having fun. His father had once started and sold a startup to XeroxPARK, a famous high-tech lab in Silicon Valley. His father paid a visit to Israel in 1982, and Medved found him in the basement with six men fiddling with transmitters and receivers.

Medved preferred to smoke nargile and flirt with women. But his dad dragged him to a meeting with the other men at a guarded compound. When Medved told a scientist there about his time in

Tel Aviv, the man replied, "What a total waste. There are thousands of guys like you. But the guys we need are doing startups, building factories, like your dad."[17]

He later learned the compound belonged to Rafael, the government's military technology agency. It would be spun off as a private company in the 1990s and later co-develop Israel's Iron Dome missile defense.

Chastened, Medved joined the family business and discovered his entrepreneurial side. He moved to New York, started his own business, and sold it. He returned to Israel in 1991.

"The place had changed," he says. "The bureaucrats saw the prowess in Israeli defense and electronics, but needed venture capital." He tried to start a fund to join the Yozma program but was too late.

But he also identified a need: there were plenty more startups that needed seed money. One of these was a biotech founded in 1993 called Compugen. Its founders noticed that the recent decoding of the human genome was producing more data than big pharmaceutical companies could process. Compugen was founded to provide the software and computing power to allow the pharmas to analyze and predict bioinformation.

Medved and a business partner, Neil Cohen, then the business editor of the *Jerusalem Post*, saw the potential, but Compugen needed more funding than a Yozma VC could handle.

Medved launched an investments business, Israel Seed Partners, in his garage, with Cohen and Michael Eisenberg, whom we met earlier. They cobbled together $2.5 million to invest in Compugen, but the company needed $4 million, so they raised a second fund.

Compugen went on to IPO on Nasdaq in 2000, raising $50 million.

Israel Seed Partners is still in operation, having made 108 early-stage investments over four funds managing $300 million. Medved left in 2006 but continued to invest in startups.

"Israel is the place for reinvention," he says. "There's a Zionist pioneer song that goes, 'I'd come to Israel to build, and to be built.'"

BIG AMBITIONS

By the time Dan Senor and Saul Singer published their book, *Startup Nation*, Israel had produced many stories in addition to Checkpoint and Compugen. By 2000, there were more than 100 VC firms investing a collective $1 billion a year into Israeli startups, including by premier US firms such as Benchmark, Lightspeed, Sequoia, and Intel Capital. This made Israel's cluster the third-largest recipient of venture capital, after Silicon Valley and Route 128, and more than all of Europe.[18] Foreign governments from Singapore to Scandinavia flocked to Tel Aviv to learn Israel's secret.

But the VC industry was in for a rude awakening. In the early 2000s, the global internet boom turned to bust, wiping out most local VCs. Only a handful of the original players from Yozma, such as Pitango, Jerusalem Venture Partners, and Gemini, survived. Israel's financial sector remained small and backward, its local stock exchange home mainly to minor family businesses. The Startup Nation was still tethered to a weak domestic economy.

This only brought home the truth that Israeli founders needed global VC and a global business strategy. With Yozma closed down, and no big pot of oil money to dominate the local scene, private VC became the industry's jet fuel.

Until 2004, all funding was domestic, says Avi Zeevi, with a new crop of VCs founded to support new internet companies. A mini-bubble developed, with the industry raising $6.5 billion in 2004—and promptly burst, forcing many of these new firms to shut.

"We didn't know how to grow companies," says Yossi Sela of Gemini.[19] The 2000s were years of uncertainty, with most tech companies getting acquired before they could become sizeable.

Progress was steady but it was only in the mid-2010s that deal sizes became big—matching the growing ambitions of Israeli founders, who began to look past a big sale to an AOL-type of buyer, and aimed to IPO instead. It had taken time for the surviving Israeli VCs to produce a track record, and their attractive numbers caught the attention of US VCs.

"Since 2000, Israeli VC investment per capita has been the highest in the world," says Zeevi.

FROM PRODUCTS TO COMPANIES

This success and new infusion of capital—tracking trends in the US—led to a mindset shift among founders and investors.

The aim of the early founders was different then: they were technologists who had a product they wanted to sell.

"We didn't trust ourselves to build category-leading companies that would be independent for life," says David Cohen, a partner at Gemini who left to help establish the local office for Silicon Valley Bank (SVB), a specialist lender to venture companies. "In the early days, a $5 million syndicate was considered a big investment, and the dream exit was a $100 million sale to Cisco."

Cohen says things began to change around 2013, when a new crop of VCs were created to focus on growth investing, coming in later, bigger rounds designed to build up the company to a size where it could contemplate a US IPO. More of these funds were run by Wall Street jocks instead of techies.

Now VCs began to look for founders focused on the business rather than the technology.

"We began building large companies," Cohen says. This meant a willingness to give founders and key executives bigger salaries, so they could relax about their finances and focus on the business. It also meant VCs could be more aggressive about replacing those founders or executives if they weren't up to scaling the business.

But eventually specializations emerged that could sustain bigger ventures, many launched by internet-savvy Israelis who had worked in the US and wanted to be entrepreneurs back home.

"We now have over 500 companies here in cybersecurity," Sela says.

The beginning of the 2020s saw frenetic activity and a rise in unicorns. Israeli companies making hundreds of millions of dollars in annual revenues included Wix (software for websites), Fivr (gig economy platform), Cyberark (cybersecurity), and Monday (financial services).

This was a change from the traditional background in fundamental tech that Israel was known for. In the 2000s, startups were focused on semiconductors and communications for enterprise customers. Now they were building consumer apps in fintech, e-commerce, gaming, and healthcare.

"I see a lot of tech, but I also see a lot of social-this and social-that," Sela says.

STAYING CLOSE TO HOME

Foreign, especially US, venture funding became key to this growth. Israeli VCs reinvented themselves as local trustworthy partners, perhaps ready with some blunt advice when trouble loomed. "Israeli VCs proved they can support founders when life is tough, when foreign VCs might lose interest," Cohen says. "It's sad because Israeli companies still pick top-tier US VC over locals," with 90 percent of funding coming from overseas.

Growth equity is valued because it requires a lot of capital to catapult a company into fast, massive rates of growth, which may include acquiring competitors, poaching talent, or expensive digital marketing campaigns.

It's difficult for Israeli growth funds to compete with the heavyweights in the US—not just early-stage VCs but the late-stage hedge funds such as Tiger Global Management, Coatue Management, and Japan's SoftBank. As a result, the local scene is fragmented, with a large number of angel investors.

Local pension funds and other investors into Israeli venture funds are increasing their allocations to support the domestic VC industry, but they remain tiny compared to the vast demand for capital.

Israeli investors, meanwhile, stick primarily to investing in Israeli companies. They might have a small allocation to startups in the US but these are invariably founded by Israelis and part of a personal network.

By 2021, Israel enjoyed a higher per-capita income than the UK, and its startup ecosystem boasted 70 unicorns, 10 percent of the global total. The VC culture permeates the highest office in the land: even a prime minster, Naftali Bennet, got his start as a tech entrepreneur, funded by John Medved's Israel Seed Partners.

The country has even innovated a new form of VC.

OURCROWD

The oddity about the VC industry is that, while it is in the business of financing change, it doesn't itself change. The essential model was set in California by DGA in 1959: a limited liability partnership, management and performance fees, options in the portfolio companies, and other mechanisms to ensure the partners prospered first.

Even today VCs mostly operate in the same way. They're basically old-fashioned partnerships, with decisions on portfolio companies made by mostly white males sitting around a boardroom table. Maybe they don't wear ties and suspenders and drink martinis and smoke cigars, but if they did, no one would notice.

It was, and remains, a clubby world. There are only a few hundred LPs in the world—"limited partners" that invest in VC funds, such as pension funds, university endowments, and a handful of family offices investing on behalf of super-wealthy people. VCs chase the LPs for funding. The LPs rely on the VCs to give them early access to exciting private companies. VCs have no interest in opening up to other investors, because LPs can write big checks and they're in the same professional circuit, speaking the same language. Besides, it's a paperwork headache to manage smaller investors.

Two US companies broke the mold. AngelList and FundersClub both launched in 2010. AngelList was like a dating site, sharing term sheets with a group of investors, and later adding recruitment. It became the back office for angel investors. FundersClub opened investments into founders to non-VCs, letting individuals seed companies and share in the spoils of any eventual exit.

Their launches raised concerns they'd break the law, as they didn't have broker-dealer licenses and they were handling securities transactions in the form of company equity. But in 2013, the US Securities and Exchange Commission blessed the models.

In Israel, Jon Medved thought the retail peer-to-peer approach could be improved upon. He launched OurCrowd in 2013. It finds companies for individuals, conducts due diligence, and pools customer capital into large VC funds it manages.

"We're principal investors, with skin in the game," Medved says. As of 2022 the company managed about $2 billion of assets, had investments in 320 startups located around the world, and had seen 56 exits. The customers aren't VCs but they tend to be experienced professionals in various industries, including many entrepreneurs, who can often lend advice or support to the OurCrowd portfolio companies.

DIVERSIFYING ISRAELI VC

Medved says the early days were tough. "Entrepreneurs were wary of revealing their secrets on a platform with no guarantee of raising money. Today people want our LPs to be part of their funding syndicate."

By opening the doors of VC to a broader spectrum of investors, he says, OurCrowd has been able to attract more women and minorities as individual LPs. This is opening up VC to people who remain marginalized.

According to All Raise, an advocacy group co-founded by Aileen Lee (the venture investor who coined the term "unicorn"), 65 percent of Silicon Valley VCs still have zero female partners.[20]

Worse, of the $330 billion in venture funding spent in the US in 2021, only 2 percent went to all-female founded businesses. Women founders are actually getting less funding in the Valley: in 2019 they accounted for 3.4 percent.[21]

The other big innovation in financing change was the creation of the startup accelerator. The iconic example is Y Combinator (YC), founded in San Francisco in 2005. It runs a boot camp for wanna-be entrepreneurs, including mentoring, networking, case studies, generally whipping their business models into shape—and some seed money. YC has been a huge success, launching mega-startups like Airbnb, Coinbase, DoorDash, Instacart, and Stripe.

There are imitators around the world, some successful, but the business is much costlier than just being an angel or early-stage investor, and most rivals have failed. The Israeli government has sponsored its own accelerator program since 1990, but it wasn't until 2011 that private accelerators began to crop up—but within four years, there were more than 200 of them.

LOOKING EAST: NEW RELATIONSHIPS

Israel is unique for its VC's size relative to the economy. It has nine domestic VC firms with more than $1 billion in assets under management, and in 2020 the industry raised a record $4.5 billion—an amount it repeated in 2022. Among the most prolific dealmakers are OurCrowd and Pitango Capital, along with foreign VCs such as Bessemer Venture Partners from the US and Vertex Ventures from Singapore.

The presence of Vertex shows a growing interest between Israel and East Asia. When China's internet giants were riding high, from 2005 to 2015, companies like Alibaba and Tencent began making investments into Israeli tech startups—usually in companies that had grown a Chinese customer base, such as payments fintech Payoneer.

The election of Donald Trump in the US in 2016 put paid to that: he viewed Chinese tech companies as a threat to national security. As Trump turned the screws on Chinese access to US technology, initially some Chinese firms saw the chance to get what they needed in Israel.

"There are a few Chinese companies here, like Alibaba and Huawei," Yossi Sela says. "They don't have strong relationships but they visit a lot, scouting for technology."

But it's unlikely now that China will find what it wants in Israel, at least not directly.

Although Trump was very friendly to the Israeli establishment,

Israeli VCs and founders understood they now had to choose between the certainty of accessing the US market, or trying to tackle the allure of China. Most chose the US, where many Israelis have families and are happy to call home.

"We won't see Chinese acquirers for our companies," says Avi Zeevi. "It's a shame, but it's the fact."

Trump helped broker the Abraham Accords, a peace treaty between Israel, the United Arab Emirates (UAE), and Bahrain signed in 2020. That has opened new opportunities for Israeli entrepreneurs and the oil-rich UAE. Dubai, the leading commercial emirate within the UAE, has long sought to center itself as a tech hub. Like Singapore, it has tried to copy the Silicon Valley and Israeli models, building industrial parks for internet and biotech startups.

But Dubai has no R&D or innovation-based companies: it's more a center for marketing. Also, like Singapore, the government maintains a strict hold on society and the kind of open, rebellious cultures of the Valley and Israel don't work. But also like Singapore, Dubai has a lot of big state-affiliated funds that have billions to invest. They could emerge as a new wave of LP money for Israeli VCs as well as buyers of Israeli tech.

"We've always had good relations with the Gulf states, only now it's open," says angel investor Robby Hilkowitz.

Its VCs are also looking further east. Will East Asia and India become either sources of capital or markets for portfolio companies to sell into? Will Asia compete with the US for the attention of Israeli VCs and founders? Some realignment seems likely.

In one sign that the global scales are shifting, in 2022 Israel lost its mantle as the country with the highest level of VC investment per capita. Israel's $4.5 billion investment equated to $506 per person. But Singapore's VC industry, with a smaller population, invested the equivalent of $695 per person.[22]

Israel was the first country outside of the US to transform itself by making a home for VC as the primary source of funding innovation. But it wasn't the only one. Indeed, the heart of the VC globalization story is in Asia.

But it wasn't Singapore or mighty China that first emerged as a VC hotspot and tech cluster. It was a place rather like Israel in the 1970s and 1980s: marginal, resource-poor, but talent-rich. And it would take a very different path in relying on its own stock market to list its tech startups rather than go to the US. We now turn to the story of Taiwan.

5

TAIWAN: THE FOUNDRIES

ON the westernmost shore of Asia, Israel was developing a global technology cluster of startups and venture capitalists, focused on commercializing at a global level, piggybacking off an influx of engineering talent and thousands of connections in the United States.

Something interesting was happening on Asia's eastern rim, in another impoverished place that lacked natural resources and was locked in a dangerous relationship with its neighbors.

Like other parts of East Asia, by the 1970s Taiwan had become a low-cost assembly center for multinational companies. It was unable to match the even lower labor costs of Malaysia or Singapore, and it lacked the deep corporate power of Japan or Korea.

Yet by the end of the 1990s, Taiwan was the world's third-biggest producer of information technology (IT) hardware, after the US and Japan; its exports catapulted Taiwan's per-capita income from $6,333 in 1988 to $12,235 in 1999.[1]

Unlike Israel, whose companies aimed to list on Nasdaq, Taiwanese startups tended to go public at home. By 2004 its stock market had become the biggest among emerging markets, with a market cap of $350 billion supporting an industry landscape of thousands of tech companies.[2]

At that point in time, it might have also looked as though Taiwan's tech industry would grow even more. First-generation Taiwanese companies like Acer were replicating American stories such as HP and Fairchild, and spinning off and funding companies, ensuring a future.

That future would not arrive—at least, not on the island of Taiwan. But Taiwan achieved something great. This chapter examines how that happened, and VC's role. First, we need to paint Taiwan itself upon a larger canvas.

TAIWAN'S PLACE IN ASIA

Taiwan's emergence as a VC-fueled tech hub occurred in the context of important political changes. The end of the Second World War darkened into the Cold War. In China, the head of the Kuomintang Party (KMT), Chiang Kai-shek, lost the battle for supremacy to Mao Zedong's Communists.

Chiang and the KMT ensconced themselves in Taiwan, and in 1949 Chiang declared martial law. He oversaw a White Terror in which the core of Taiwan's literati were murdered (a horror for which a future KMT President of Taiwan, Ma Ying-jou, would apologize, in 2008). The US and its allies recognized the KMT as "China," and under Chiang's rule, the island began an economic recovery led by manufacturing, becoming one of Asia's "Four Tigers," along with Japan, South Korea, and Hong Kong.

US semiconductor companies triggered this economic development in Asia through their search for offshore production. Wages in America were high and producing millions of chips was laborious. The US government was eager to anchor its Asian allies in its capitalist embrace as Communist insurgencies rocked the region. Likewise, many Asian political leaders were just as keen to provide jobs for their people to head off unrest, but equally hostile to unions, to the delight of American companies.

Fairchild was the first US company to set up assembly in Asia, opening a factory in Hong Kong, along Kowloon Bay behind the airport, in 1963. Hong Kong was then a British colony, which provided American businesses a degree of comfort.

Assembly-line workers in Hong Kong earned 25 cents an hour, one-tenth the cost of an American worker. Costs were even lower elsewhere: Taiwan, Malaysia, Singapore and South Korea were half as cheap.[3] By the 1970s, most US semiconductor companies shipped their wafers to factories in Asia for final packaging and testing.

By the 1970s, Taiwan's shift to tech began amid bigger changes. US President Richard Nixon made his surprise visit to Beijing in 1971, shocking politicians from Tokyo to Taipei. The US was eager to drive a wedge between China and its erstwhile Communist ally, the Soviet Union.

In 1972, the US and China announced the Shanghai Communique, in which the US recognized Beijing's claim that there was only one China, and that Taiwan was part of it—although the US didn't say who it regarded as the legitimate government of One China, the Communists or the KMT. This ambiguity would leave plenty of room for conflict, but it served to take Taiwan off the table as a flashpoint.

In 1979, the US officially switched diplomatic recognition from Taipei to Beijing, and China accepted the US would continue to maintain business and cultural ties to Taiwan. The Chinese insisted on their claim on Taiwan, including the intention to take the island by force, while the US pledged to defend Taiwan if it were attacked. The peace was uneasy but it allowed all parties to focus on economic development and business ties.

All of these changes were alarming to Taiwan's rulers. China had successfully tested nuclear bombs in 1964, so defending the island against invasion was now impossible without an American security guarantee. Seeing Washington then woo Mao added to the threat.

Meanwhile, although Taiwan hosted semiconductor factories for US companies, there was nothing special about Taiwanese production. Singapore, Malaysia, and Korea promised even cheaper workforces. The brightest Taiwanese engineers went to the US to seek their fortunes. Tech manufacturing was a small part of the economy, which was largely agricultural. In 1962, Taiwan's per-capita GDP was $170—on a par with Zaire (now Congo).[4]

VISIONARY MINISTERS

Taiwan was fortunate at this time to have visionary ministers in key government roles able to put Taiwan on a different path. They saw that Taiwan possessed one advantage: its people. Taiwan's universities were cranking out engineers. Too many were leaving. Taiwan's biggest need wasn't capital to build another factory: it was to develop its own talent.

Sun Yun-suan, or YS Sun, became one of Asia's leading technocrats. In charge of Taiwan's economic affairs, he launched a number of big-ticket infrastructure projects, including in 1973 the creation of the Industrial Technology Research Institute (ITRI) to support entrepreneurs. Sun served as its CEO until he was made Premier of the government in 1978.

Nonetheless, Sun remained frustrated by the bureaucracy's resistance to change and its blinkered insistence on developing national champions that could take the Koreans and Japanese head-on. He assembled a group of advisors, including Chinese Americans, who urged him to focus instead on training and attracting talent. One of these advisors was Hsu Ta-lin, a venture capitalist we'll soon meet.

Another influential politician was Li Kwoh-ting, or KT Li, as he's commonly called. Like Sun, he was born on the Chinese mainland but escaped to Taiwan after the Communists took power. There he became a leading industrialist and, later, the senior official responsible for economic planning for the KMT-run government.

By the 1970s, after several big ministerial roles, KT Li focused his attention on transitioning Taiwan from labor-intensive work to high tech. As a "minister without portfolio" in the government, he promoted science and technology, and established Hsinchu Science Park, modeled after Stanford's industrial park, combining research with commercialization. KT Li also launched policies supporting the infrastructure and incentives to attract entrepreneurs.

Li's pragmatic approach was firmly rooted in private enterprise and private property, but given Taiwan was a poor place with little in the way of natural resources, it would need government support to create conditions for a market economy.

Some of that support was financial. Li could pull levers at China Development Industrial Bank, a state-owned lender. (The bank was privatized in 2001.)

His greatest insight was that while other countries such as Singapore and Malaysia were competing to attract US capital, Taiwan should try to attract talent. There was always going to be a Malaysia that offered cheaper labor and funding for capex-hungry factories, but no innovation ever emerged from the component makers in Penang.

KT Li intuited that supporting entrepreneurs and competition would be one way to lure some of these people back. Taiwan wasn't going to have a national champion like a Fujitsu or a Samsung, but it could nurture thousands of startups that could supply the things needed by US, Japanese, and Korean companies.

To make it happen, KT Li needed not just the entrepreneurs, but the kind of financiers who could take a risk backing them.

VC COMES TO TAIWAN: TA-LIN HSU

Ta-Lin Hsu had an idea: he wanted to run his own company. He had already clocked 12 years doing business development at IBM in the US. Although steeped in ICs, he wasn't interested in starting a technology company. "He wanted to be an investor," recalls his son, Mark Hsu.[5]

The year was 1985. VC was now entrenched in Silicon Valley but rare anywhere else—this was seven years before Israel would launch its Yozma program. In Taiwan, where Hsu had grown up, it was non-existent.

For the last five years he had been traveling throughout the US, Japan, Korea, and Taiwan, sniffing out ways for IBM to take advantage of cheaper labor overseas. Unlike his American colleagues, Hsu wanted to do more than just outsource. Hsu wanted to bring US know-how across the Pacific Ocean: technology, management skills—and capital.

He knew that Taiwan was laying the building blocks to upgrade from low-skilled manufacturing to high tech. The time looked ripe, for the electronics industry was undergoing a new wave of innovation led by the personal computer.

In 1981, IBM launched its first line of PCs, combining its manufacturing scale with Microsoft's MS-DOS operating system and Intel's latest generation of microprocessors to take a bite out of Apple's Macintosh series. The result put the PC on the road to ubiquity. This created new opportunities for other companies to supply chips, peripherals (monitors, printers, and so on), and components.

"The only thing they were missing was venture capital," Hsu told an interviewer. "So I answered the call."[6]

The "call" was an offer to join Hambrecht & Quist (H&Q), extended by a former colleague of Hsu's from IBM. H&Q was the first investment bank that was dedicated to the tech sector. Founded in 1968 in San Francisco, it initially focused on researching the industry, but as the need for capital outstripped the VC industry's ability to supply it, H&Q began helping tech companies access the public markets.

H&Q became known as one of the "Four Horsemen," a quartet of boutique investment banks focused on tech that included two other San Francisco-based firms, Robertson Stephens & Co. and Montgomery Securities, and Baltimore-based Alex. Brown & Sons. From the 1960s to 1990s these specialists dominated the US tech IPO market, buoyed by the stunning success of Apple's 1980 listing, which raised $100 million and made more than 40 of its employees instant millionaires.

Soon H&Q branched out from underwriting tech IPOs to investing in VCs. The firm was interested in funding a VC that could exploit the opening of a nascent tech industry in Asia. Ta-Lin Hsu knew from his jetting back and forth that the region did have entrepreneurs, not to mention supportive bureaucracies. He joined

H&Q and by 1986 he had launched its H&Q HanTech Fund, the first one to back Taiwan's first generation of tech companies.

One of its early bets included Acer, a maker of PCs and related parts that has become one of the world's biggest providers of computers and notebooks. The company was founded in 1976 as Multitech by Stan Shih, a locally trained engineer, along with his wife and three friends with $25,000.

LIP-BU TAN AND WALDEN INTERNATIONAL

Ta-Lin Hsu wasn't going to have Taiwan to himself. A year later, another venture capitalist, Lip-Bu Tan, opened a local fund as part of a franchise of VC portfolios operated by Walden International in California. (Walden would later establish one of the ten Yozma-backed funds in Israel.)

Tan, an ethnic Chinese born in Malaysia and schooled in Singapore, had moved to the US to be a nuclear physicist. The Three Mile Island disaster of 1979 put a chill on the nuclear industry, however. Tan ended up joining Walden Investments, a US-focused VC based in San Francisco, in 1983, just as the VC industry was experiencing a boom.

His timing was fortunate, but Tan came to realize he had an edge against his American-born colleagues: he understood the opportunity in Asia. In 1987 he launched Walden International, still based in San Francisco, which would structure multiple funds focused on specific foreign markets.

He worked with a colleague, Peter Liu, to set things up in Taipei. While he was getting started, Peter Liu received a visit from KT Li, the visionary politician behind Hsinchu Science Park. This was no ordinary business meeting.

"KT Li was also my great-uncle," Liu says. "He asked me to come back to Taiwan to build a local VC. We spent a year negotiating; Taiwan was greenfield for venture capital, and we'd need some government support."[7]

But setting up a venture fund wasn't straightforward. Li brokered a meeting between Peter Liu and YC Wang, the chairman of Formosa Plastics and then the richest man in Taiwan. Within five minutes it became clear to Liu that Wang's investment came with too many conditions: the tycoon didn't trust the idea of a professional investment firm dedicated to risky startups.

"No one understood VC," Liu says. He and Li worked to get funding from the state-owned China Industrial Development Bank, as well as from private individuals and even from the KMT.

More important than sourcing capital, KT Li also helped tailor programs to lure back Taiwanese studying or working in the US. "They were using VC funds as a form of development funding, mobilizing students to bring back technology from Silicon Valley," Liu says.

CHIP FOUNDRIES: MORRIS CHANG AND ITRI

Taiwan's rise as a tech juggernaut involved a combination of VC-backed companies and a few successful corporate giants that were spun out of government agencies. What they had in common was reliance on ethnic Chinese returning from the US.

One of these was Morris Chang, another mainland-born Chinese who left after the Communists took over, moving to the US to study at Harvard University and then MIT. He failed to get his PhD at MIT, so he ended up working at a second-tier semiconductor company, Sylvania. Chang could tell the company wasn't a winner, but he used his experience to get himself into one that clearly was: Texas Instruments.

He joined in 1958 at a time when semiconductors were still a primitive business. Figuring out the right mix of how to make them involved laborious trial and error involving different materials, temperatures, pressures, and points along the production line. Chang figured out the optimal techniques to mass-produce chips, and by 1967 he was running the entire semiconductor side of the business.

His fortunes then wavered when he was put in charge of the consumer electronics business. TI, like other semiconductor companies, kept trying to expand into new businesses. It wanted to both make chips and the products they went into. This drained the company of focus and Chang couldn't turn around the consumer electronics division. He was passed over for the CEO role and took early retirement.

Ethnic Chinese of his stature in America's tech industry were rare. Chang got noticed by KT Li, who courted him to run the government-backed ITRI. His brief: translate research into commercial results, and therefore support all of Taiwan's budding tech industry.

In 1985 Chang left for Taipei. "In 1985 the big money was supposedly in financial venture capital," Chang told an interviewer. But he was more interested in the challenge. "As it turned out, when you don't chase money, money comes to you."[8] Chang didn't know it yet, but he was on the road to becoming Taiwan's most influential industrialist.

Taiwan had been keen to find a way into semiconductors for a long time. In 1975, ITRI had licensed the tech from RCA: the once-great American electronics company, wheezing on its last legs, was selling what remained of the family silver. (YS Sun, then ITRI's chief executive, sealed the deal.[9])

RCA's chip IP was second-rate compared to what Intel or TI could do. But ITRI engineers determined that it was right for Taiwan, as its chip design was suitable for low-power consumer electronics. ITRI had bought RCA's technology to make some kind of commercial industry out of it, not to leap to the cutting edge of technology. That included studying the industry's lifecycle: design, packaging, and testing, as well as production planning, management rules, and relevant regulation. In the end, Taiwan put its best engineers on R&D and over time they developed yields (the portion of transistors on a chip that worked) that outstripped anything RCA could produce.

THE ECOSYSTEM: UMC AND ROBERT TSAO

Robert Tsao led ITRI's RCA project. Tsao's family had fled Communist China when he was just one year old and he was raised and educated in Taiwan. As an electrical engineer, he was assigned to various government agencies, culminating with ITRI.

He took on responsibility for turning RCA's technology into a business. This involved battling with Taiwan's bureaucrats to change outdated laws, auditing requirements, and foreign-exchange controls to make it easier to establish companies. In 1980, ITRI spun out a company to mass produce chips, United Microelectronics Corporation (UMC), with Tsao as general manager. China Industrial Development Bank, a state-owned institution, provided the necessary capital.

Tsao recognized UMC couldn't afford to do everything, integrating design and manufacturing, because the capital required was simply too great. He suggested the idea of becoming an original equipment manufacturer (OEM), in which UMC focused on manufacturing based on clients' own designs. This was an innovation: US and Japanese chip companies all wanted to control both manufacturing and design.

But the government vetoed this idea: Morris Chang was then overseeing ITRI and he told KT Li that it should focus on vertical dynamic random-access memory (DRAM) production (lower-value memory chips). UMC had to do the design as well, so Tsao responded by incubating and spinning out "fabless" design companies, such as MediaTek, which got its start creating chips specialized for TVs and other home entertainment products. UMC began to populate Taiwan with the kind of companies that would need the services of a chip foundry, and these spinoffs often needed third-party VC money to succeed.

TSMC AND THE PURE-PLAY FOUNDRY

Although UMC would eventually transform itself into a foundry, the spoils of this new industry went to another ITRI spinoff, Taiwan Semiconductor Manufacturing Company (TSMC), created and led by Morris Chang.

The company was funded by a $100 million stake from the government, via China Industrial Development Bank, for a 49 percent share, plus another $58 million from Philips, the Dutch electronics company, which also licensed some of its technology to Chang's venture.[10] After that, it would have to rely on the private sector for additional funding—which opened the door to venture capitalists such as Hsu Ta-Lin at HanTech, who became an early investor.

TSMC, launched in 1987, pursued the OEM strategy,[11] while UMC continued to act as an integrated player. UMC now found itself locked in combat with TSMC for manufacturing contracts. Chang had already outmaneuvered Tsao to create Taiwan's first chip foundry, and he wasn't about to see UMC win the kind of volumes that could turn it into a threat. It would take UMC another decade before it could restructure into being just a pure-play foundry for foreign chip companies. In the meantime, though, it was creating conditions favorable to local VC.

Tsao pioneered financial incentives to attract talent as well. He knew Silicon Valley firms offered stock options. But most startups failed, so hardworking employees wouldn't benefit when stocks fell to zero. Also, Taiwan's law did not allow for stock options.

Tsao lobbied hard for UMC to provide stocks to employees in the form of bonuses (not options), to enable a large state-backed company to reward its engineers. Such incentives helped lure Taiwanese back from the US. For a time, this model became widely adopted by local tech companies such as Acer. But TMSC opposed it and eventually adopted US-style options, which Tsao would blame for harming the incentives to keep talent in Taiwan.[12]

Chang also claims credit for the idea of a pure-play foundry, which he had first considered while at TI. He knew Taiwan couldn't compete against the US and Japanese companies. It lacked cutting-edge R&D, design expertise, sales or marketing experience, or its own IP. "The only possible strength, maybe, was manufacturing semiconductor wafers," he told an interviewer.

Even then, TSMC would have to create the market. Chang knew there were engineers at big chip companies that would like to start their own design shops, and the industry assumption was that companies would manufacture their own ideas. TSMC started off manufacturing "leftovers" for big companies like IBM.[13] The presence of a foundry, however, made it economical for standalone design firms to exist. By the early mid-2000s, Chang counted nearly 1,000 design firms in the US, Taiwan, and increasingly in mainland China.

SEEDING STARTUPS

UMC and TSMC were established by ITRI to help Taiwan break into the high-tech world and win back the talented engineers who had migrated to the US. The government had helped finance them via state-owned China Industrial Development Bank.

As these companies battled for a workable business model, they helped spin off more private companies and created an ecosystem beyond chip manufacturing.

This broke the reigning belief at the time that "periphery" countries—what today we'd call emerging markets or the Global South—were fated to serve as low-cost assembly factories, while the rich "core" nations retained all the most valuable know-how.

But Taiwan, a poor country with no natural resources, was able to transform itself into a self-sustaining innovation machine. Its advantages included insightful government ministers, quality universities, political stability, and, most of all, an army of engineers and businesspeople working in the US who were prepared to come home and put their know-how to work in Taiwan.

The opportunities for such people grew as corporate anchors like UMC and TSMC nurtured a local ecosystem that produced hundreds of startups. This blooming industry could not rely on state-backed funding. These entrepreneurs needed private capital.

But Taiwan's wealthy families and industrial groups were focused on investing in low-risk businesses they could control, not taking minority stakes in unproven startups.

Tan later recalled: "The concept [of VC] is very new for Asian investors. You tell them: give me your money, I will take a 20 percent profit share, you have zero say; when the fund makes money, we don't share the losses. That concept is unknown to Asian investors, who tend to be short-term; ten years lock-out, are you crazy?"[14]

Another barrier were tax regimes that punished risk equity. Tan spent a lot of time in Taiwan and other Asian markets advising governments on how to restructure their taxes.

In Taiwan, Premier Li drafted legislation to enable enterprises to set up their own VC funds and to make investments into venture funds tax deductible. He also set up government matching funds. In 1984, Acer took the plunge and set up the first domestic fund, called Multiventure Investment.[15] But Li didn't stop there: he wooed Chinese Americans to bring their Silicon Valley investing style to Taiwan.

This was the environment into which Ta-Lin Hsu launched H&Q's HanTech Fund, and Lip-Bu Tan founded Walden International. Peter Liu, who worked alongside Tan, would establish his own local VC, WI Harper. These VC pioneers got in on the ground floor just as Taiwan's tech sector was getting red hot.

Only Israel fostered more tech companies, but its progeny tended to list in the US, whereas Taiwan was developing its own capital market. Ruchir Sharma, an investor at Morgan Stanley, notes that only two emerging markets consistently enjoyed 5 percent GDP growth rates over 50 years and leaped from poverty to developed-market status: Taiwan and South Korea, which in their own ways have constantly invested in research and developed the chops to stay a little ahead of the competition.[16]

SILICON VALLEY EAST

Taiwan never developed a consumer giant like Fujitsu, Samsung Electronics, Philips, or IBM. Rather it fostered a collaborative network of interdependent but competitive companies—in other words, Taiwan emerged as a technology cluster, exhibiting many of the traits that had made Silicon Valley a success.[17]

And unlike the manufacturing framework of companies like Intel, which might have factories spread around the US West, all of Taiwan's fabs were crammed together in Hsinchu Science Park: UMC's and TSMC's headquarters sit across the street from each other. This concentration drove down costs and facilitated knowledge diffusion.

As a hub, though, Taiwan did not compete with Silicon Valley. It complemented it as its primary outsourcing center, fueled by Taiwanese engineers and connected by ethnic Chinese financiers, who spent their working lives jetting back and forth over the Pacific Ocean.

The nature of financing was also a little different. In addition to the government, Taiwan boasted plenty of rich families prepared to back the local tech industry. But local investors tended to prefer later-stage investments into proven technologies. Local investors and the emergence of Taiwan VCs focused on startups that were making an existing part of the tech industry more efficient. American VCs were more willing to back founders at seed level and prove the tech—they were ready to assume greater risk and lose on most of their bets if they thought a handful would be runaway successes.

Taiwan's most influential IPO was Acer, which listed on the Taiwan Stock Exchange in 1988, raising the equivalent of $88 million—a blockbuster. The island had just held its first democratic elections, even as its businesspeople were becoming more deeply plugged into mainland China. The prospects looked good. Taiwan was now on Silicon Valley's radar as a tech hub in its own right.

Taiwan's rise also coincided with a major wave of change in technology. Silicon Valley got its start with semiconductors, and its first great companies were hardware firms. Their chips went into consumer electronics and into business computers. Moore's Law was still in force, driving miniaturization and economies of scale, to the point that by the end of the 1970s, personal computers were entering the scene. This was a revolution in itself that created the need for a whole new set of software, equipment, and technologies to enable PCs to communicate.

Taiwan's tech industry rose to the challenge. Its startups made all the devices and machines for US, Japanese, and European clients. The state-backed creation of TSMC ushered in a new wave of fabless chip design companies—essentially software businesses that engineered chips for an expanding set of uses, notably for PCs.

Commercializing technology, however, required risk-taking finance. In 1990, Taiwan had 20 VC firms; by 1999, it had 153, investing $1.3 billion across 1,800 startups.[18] By the early 2000s, Taiwan boasted the largest VC industry after Silicon Valley and Israel, and this propelled the Taiwan Stock Exchange into becoming the world's third biggest in volume, after the New York Stock Exchange and the London Stock Exchange.

Nonetheless, Asia's earliest VCs had to prove themselves. It took Georges Doriot's ARD nearly two decades after its creation to cash in on its one big hit, DEC. Arthur Rock was the first to make real money by investing in Silicon Valley startups.

The irony of the Taiwan VC story is that the first smash hit was not in Taiwan. It was a company from Singapore. "That's where we hit the jackpot," Peter Liu says; and that's where our story goes next.

6

SINGAPORE: THE ECOSYSTEM

THE company that caught the attention of VCs operating in Taiwan came from an unlikely place: Singapore.

This is one of the most conservative, careful places in the world. Its best and brightest people go into government, not business. Within the business world, the talent goes to a clique of government-friendly corporations and banks. The education system trains people to follow the rules.

Not great working material for taking risks.

Singapore became a modern nation in 1965. It is an equatorial island nestled at the bottom of the Malay peninsula, strategically dominating the Straits—a chokepoint of maritime trade between China, Southeast Asia, and the Indian Ocean. For 1,000 years it served as an entrepot, a role the British reinvented when they showed up in 1819 and made it their primary free-trade port in their fast-growing colonial empire.

Although there had always been small Chinese communities in this Malay landscape, under British rule the region filled with Chinese and Indian workers, to the resentment of the indigenous people. The cities of the Straits, including Penang, Malacca, and Singapore, became majority Chinese—although within the Chinese community there was a variety of people hailing from different parts of China, speaking their own dialects.

After the Second World War and Japanese occupation, all of Malaysia won independence from Britain in 1963, including Singapore. The leading political force in Singapore was the Political Action Party led by Lee Kuan Yew, who argued for a multicultural, cosmopolitan Malaysia. The Malay political leadership's legitimacy, on the other hand, had been won on an agenda of Malay-first.

These principles clashed immediately, and Singapore was expelled from the federation just two years later. It had no natural resources or hinterland—indeed, it faced hostility from its ethnic Malay neighbors, including Indonesia. To Lee, the direction was clear: to survive, Singapore must transcend its immediate neighborhood, embed itself in global trade, and attract foreign investment to develop export manufacturing. And it had to do so in a disciplined way, with a high degree of state planning. The environment was too risky to tolerate loose cannons.

LOW-END MANUFACTURING

Singapore wasn't the only place looking to develop manufacturing. Malaysia and Hong Kong, then still a British colony on the southern Chinese coast, were also becoming low-cost centers.

Malaysian companies moved into the lowest end of the technology ecosystem. They produced things like passive devices such as capacitors: circuits that don't produce energy or amplify signals. Such items are used to tune radios to particular frequencies or stabilize voltage in power transmission—the simplest parts of a transistor.

"Passive devices have very little IP and are labor-intensive," says Peter Mok. "No wonder many were copied."[1] But the factories to produce them nonetheless required plenty of long-term capital.

Today, Mok is the president and CEO of KLM Capital Group, a consortium affiliated with the airline of technology entrepreneurs who invest in semiconductors and communications. Before setting that up in 1996, however, Mok was a banker in California and then an early VC investor in both the US and Asia in the late 1980s and early 1990s.

Mok recalls that Hong Kong—although another budding hub for low-cost manufacturing, trade, and finance—was not fated to become a tech powerhouse. He spent 1968 there as a high-school student and found Hong Kong was inculcating a very different set of leaders.

"I went to [Hong Kong International School]...it was a school with rich kids...I didn't recall a kid from any tech firm except IBM. The rest were from banks, raw materials, pharmaceuticals, textiles, trading, shipping, and airlines...Very few local entrepreneurs were interested in long-term capex when they were making money hand over fist off real estate."

Mok began his career as a banker in California, where he developed relationships with tech companies and investors. He took this with him to SVB, which he joined in 1989. We'll learn more about the SVB story later, as it will play a key role in Asia's VC industry. For now, it's useful to know that SVB specializes in the niche business of lending to VC firms. The top management was interested to explore whether the business could expand abroad. It tapped Mok to set up its PacRim Group, and Mok then spent a few years making connections in Asia.

Although the initial tech opportunities were in Taiwan, and Hong Kong was the region's leading financial center, Mok found himself drifting to Singapore.

ANG KONG WAH AND NATSTEEL

Unlike the *laissez-faire* business culture of Hong Kong, where the colonial administration abhorred anything like economic planning, Singapore's government coordinated with its industrialists to advance Singapore up the value chain in technology. The problem of funding this transition loomed large. Singapore could throw money at building factories, but this wasn't going to change the economy.

One of the first people to act on this was Ang Kong Wah, who today is chairman of Sembcorp Industries, an energy and engineering company. He is also chair of the investment board of the Government Investment Corporation, Singapore's sovereign wealth fund.

Ang made his career as a banker and industrialist in "Singapore Inc." He was part of the management team of DBS (then known as Development Bank of Singapore) when it was founded in 1968. From 1974 until 2003 he served as CEO of NatSteel (now known as NSL).

This combination of finance and manufacturing made him aware of the need for the means to support local innovation and develop new industries.

"It was Ang's idea to use the US-style venture approach to develop an electronics industry in Singapore," says Joo Hock Chua, who is today managing partner at Vertex Ventures, a prominent homegrown VC.[2]

Back in the 1980s, Joo was a junior engineer who got transferred to the Economic Development Board, a statutory board under the Ministry of Trade and Industry, where he was to help fund and train local companies. These were established companies, not startups, but Joo liked shining a light beneath the hood to see how their engines worked. The job was mostly administrative, however, so when Ang's NatSteel offered him a role in its nascent investment department, Joo jumped at the chance.

By the 1980s, VC was established in Silicon Valley and attracting notice abroad. "NatSteel pioneered it in Singapore," Joo says. "It was already doing angel investment, but not in a structured way."

Joo was the junior member of a team that visited Silicon Valley to understand venture investing. "I met Don Valentine [of Sequoia Capital] and we became friends," he recalls. "NatSteel began investing in VC funds and set up its own venture arm. Chairman Ang was very involved. He was the first one here to take Silicon Valley VC-style risk."

ADVENT ENTERS ASIA

At this time, no VC in Silicon Valley would have attempted to try investing in Asia. The VC business is steeped in personal networks.

Knowing who's who is vital within an ecosystem of tech-savvy entrepreneurs and the capital markets to provide an exit, none of which existed in Asia.

Except...who else but Peter Brooke from TA Associates? We met him in Chapter Three, fired by his dream of using VC as a Marshall Plan-like catalyst for economic development, but finding European ground infertile.

In 1981, an ambitious staffer at the International Finance Corporation (IFC) named Augustin "Toti" Que sought Brooke out for help. The IFC is the private-sector arm of the World Bank Group. It helps develop industries in emerging markets by co-investing in projects with private enterprise. Toti, a Chinese Filipino, was keen to get private capital to back startups in the "Asian Tigers" of Hong Kong, Singapore, Taiwan, and Korea—to support local companies as well as to enable technology transfer from Western multinationals.

The Asian Tigers were the region's dynamos, having copied Japan's model of rapid growth through supporting export-driven industrialization. Taiwan had already taken the lead by investing in its talent. Singapore's Lee Kuan Yew was also looking for ways to move his country out of low-cost, low value-add assembly and create a high-tech, science-based economy.

Brooke and Toti Que toured the region and noted Singapore's modern roads and other infrastructure, in contrast to its neighbor. "Other countries really lagged," Brooke wrote, noting that Kuala Lumpur was connected to its airport via a dirt road. What passed for factories in Malaysia were just Quonset huts in the countryside.[3]

Although Singapore had promise, it wasn't rich. Advent Capital had survived in Europe because European families and institutions had the money to use to invest in US tech companies, providing an anchor as the business sought to invest in European startups. There was no such pool of capital in Asia.

But with the IFC ready to support an Asian VC fund, Brooke agreed to give it a shot, provided he could find some local financial backers. TA Associates was using a British merchant bank, Morgan

Grenfell, to drum up investors, but Brooke knew the foreigners didn't have the right on-the-ground connections—until he met NatSteel's Ang Kong Wah.

"[Ang] was aware of Silicon Valley and Route 128, having invested in the US," Brooke wrote. "He would convince DBS to come in if I fired Morgan Grenfell."

LAUNCHING SEAVIC

That switch enabled TA Associates to launch SEAVIC, the Southeast Asia Venture Investment Company, in 1983—the first VC firm in Southeast Asia, established as NatSteel was formalizing its own.

Brooke's biggest challenge at the time was convincing his partners at TA to support the move. "My partners hated this," he wrote, because Asia VC was such a risky and complex move. The partners preferred to concentrate on backing startups in the US. The 1970s had been tough to VC in America, with high taxes and economic malaise. In Boston, where TA Associates was based, the industry was only now becoming mature, yet ARD's success with DEC's big IPO remained its sole hit. The partners insisted Brooke de-risk his overseas gambits, so he promised to get locals to finance and manage them, and not burden TA Associates.

But finding people to staff a VC fund in a land where the concept was unknown proved difficult. Toti Que was too brash for conservative Singapore, so a DBS banker was installed; while the chairman of another local investor, food-and-beverage company Yeo Hiap Seng Group, was named chairman of SEAVIC. The fund had to somehow apply American risk-taking skills within a safe "Singapore Inc." team.

Next: find deals. SEAVIC's mission was twofold: invest in Asian startups and facilitate US and European multinationals to outsource manufacturing and transfer technology to local outposts run by low-cost Asian laborers. Global companies were keen to exploit this arbitrage, but they lacked local knowledge, and didn't know who to trust. A VC firm could bridge the divide—in theory.

Brooke struggled. SEAVIC lost money on its multinational deals. Outside of Singapore, governance was poor, rule of law was iffy, and cronyism was rife. This made it difficult to structure transactions that met the standards of foreign multinational corporations (MNCs). The only way to get deals done was for SEAVIC to fund offshore subsidiaries that would in turn form JVs with MNCs and local partners.

EARLY SUCCESS, TOUGH CALLS

The fund did better by investing in Asian companies. "Cold calling didn't work," Brooke wrote. "Relationships were everything."

The first investment was in 1984, to Venture Manufacturing Singapore (VMS), a contract manufacturer of electronics components. The deal made money, but Brooke realized the company would fail if it didn't outsource more to Malaysia. This led to tensions with the company's managers, and SEAVIC ended up replacing them—a risky move in Asia, and a cold-blooded, rational decision that only a US-style investment firm could make in a relationship-dominated culture.[4] Brooke got his way because VMS was in Singapore—the only country in Southeast Asia at the time with robust contracts law.

Venture capitalism is not just about funding, or helping founders operate their business. It is also about ownership. The VC fund is an owner in the business, and it has a responsibility to its LPs to maximize that financial return. Good VC managers must be ruthless. The balance of power in venture's earliest days was held by the VCs, when capital was scarce. Sometimes a company outgrew its founders and needed more professional management.

Even in the US, where capitalism "red in tooth and claw" is the norm, these decisions can be excruciating. One of the most famous hard cases was Don Valentine of Sequoia Capital. In 1987 he took a 32 percent stake in Cisco, which had developed the routers needed to help websites communicate among one another. Cisco's growth rocketed but Valentine, who made himself chairman, decided different leadership was needed as the business changed. The original founders didn't fully understand the covenants in their funding agreement—but they learned what they meant when Valentine fired them.[5]

It was probably the right move: Cisco went on to new heights. Toughness worked for SEAVIC, too: VMS prospered under new management. It listed on SESDAQ, a secondary board of the Stock Exchange of Singapore, in 1992, achieving a market cap of S$25 million. Today Venture Corporation Limited, as the company is called, is a leading provider of technology to many Fortune 500 companies, and as of July 2022, it boasted a market cap of S$4.9 billion. It would have never existed without venture funding.

EXPANDING TO HONG KONG

Over time, SEAVIC would go on to find success, and it is active today. But for many years it struggled. Singapore, despite the government's interventionist approach, didn't have enough startups. Would the *laissez-faire* capitalist world of Hong Kong prove more fruitful?

Brooke met Victor Fung on a visit to the city in 1983. Fung and his brother William are the majority shareholders in Li & Fung, a venerable supply-chain management company based in the city. Fung was already an advisor to the Hong Kong administration on matters regarding economic development, and Brooke liked his interest in entrepreneurship.

They were also bullish on the emerging China story. China's new leader, Deng Xiaoping, was opening the country to foreign investors. Hong Kong is nestled on the underbelly of Guangdong Province, whose cities such as Guangzhou (formerly known as Canton) are longstanding gateways to foreign commerce in China. Shenzhen was then mostly farmland bordering Hong Kong, but Deng anointed it the first of five "special economic zones," with market-based policies and taxes favorable to foreign investors.

In Singapore, SEAVIC had dual missions: invest in local startups, and help multinational corporations set up joint ventures. But for Hong Kong, Brooke split these activities between two companies.

First, Advent International set up Techno Ventures Hong Kong, to facilitate technology-transfer deals for multinationals looking to get into China. As with Singapore, tech transfer in China proved difficult, although Techno Ventures did help Merck license products there—the start of the US Big Pharma company's presence in China.

Second, Brooke and Fung teamed up to co-chair a venture fund to invest in Asian startups, the Hong Kong Venture Investment Trust (HKVIT), which launched in 1985 with $22.3 million.

Fung recruited Chris Leong, a classmate of his from MIT, to run HKVIT. Other backers included HarbourVest Partners, a Boston-based PE fund of funds; Prudential Life Insurance; and Touche Remnant, an investment trust management company. Two years later, Fung would help set up the Hong Kong Venture Capital Association.

HKVIT enjoyed one big hit, investing in Multitech. This is the company founded by Stan Shih in Taiwan in 1976 as a contract manufacturer—which he would rebrand as Acer for its Taiwan Stock Exchange IPO in 1988.[6]

Overall, HKVIT delivered just modest performance, and Brooke says Victor Fung and Chris Leong were disappointed. Hong Kong turned out to be a difficult place to do tech investing.

Unlike Singapore, Taiwan, or Korea, whose governments were prepared to invest heavily in semiconductors and other tech programs, Hong Kong's British colonial administrators had no interest in such an outlay.

Hong Kong had been the first place to host US tech factories, since Fairchild set up operations there in 1963. The city was a bigger assembler of consumer electronics than the other Asian Tigers into the 1980s, until its manufacturing industry moved to mainland China. But its rulers opted to make the city into a pure financial center. And although one day it would host plenty of VC firms, it would only do so as a regional hub—not as a source of indigenous entrepreneurs.

Brooke lamented: "Hong Kong joined the lengthening list of places around the world where, I was discovering, early-stage venture investing of the kind that had succeeded in the United States could not be easily replicated."[7]

SINGAPORE SLING: CREATIVE TECHNOLOGIES

What Asia needed to produce was its own DEC: a startup that would list in the US and get everybody's attention. A company that could prove the VC model worked.

Taiwan was full of startups and had a small but growing VC scene, led by Walden International (Lip-Bu Tan), H&Q (Hsu Ta-Lin), and WI Harper (Peter Liu). But its companies listed on the Taiwan bourse, and these restless VCs were looking for the next new thing.

So was a handful of Singaporean VCs. NatSteel was backing SEAVIC. The government-backed Singapore Technologies, a new company that built the country's first wafer foundry, quickly spun off its internal investment team as Vertex Ventures—led by Joo Hock Chua, previously one of Ang's deputies at NatSteel. This being Singapore, Vertex wasn't established as a separate private company, but transferred to Temasek, the government's holding company for strategic companies.

(NatSteel had also co-founded a PE business called Transpac with DBS; Ang recruited Peter Mok from SVB to run it, so Transpac also dabbled in early-stage investing.)

Walden, WI Harper, and Vertex all ended up investing in the same company, which is both a testament to that company and a sign that the pickings in Singapore would be slim.

Two college buddies from Singapore's Ngee Ann Polytechnic set up a computer repair shop with just $6,000. Sim Wong Hoo, the co-founder, would go on to become CEO and chairman of their little company, Creative Technologies—and eventually become a billionaire.

They began in 1981 by customizing PCs for the Chinese language, trying to bring hardware solutions to something that AI would master 30 years later. Creative even produced its own PC that was also Mac-compatible and could talk. The initiative flopped, but their tinkering with audio led Sim's team to develop a sound card that allowed true audio reproduction—a breakthrough in the computer industry.

"Sim wasn't the first to come up with the idea, but he is a persistent guy," recalls Joo. "Creative had the better product and Sim could execute. He had spent time in the US. He knew both the product side—what customers would want—and the business side."[8]

GETTING ON THE MAP

The problem was that, while Sim might know the market, no one important knew Creative existed.

Bill Tai, today a wealthy investor, was then a young in-house banker for Creative. He had cut his teeth in San Francisco as an associate at Alex. Brown & Sons, one of the Four Horsemen of tech investment banking, and then helped TSMC establish its treasury. His antennae were tuned to find the next tech deal in Asia, and at that moment, his job was to help Sim secure the funding required to commercialize Creative's invention.

Tai knew the company had something special. The PC was taking over households in the rich world, but its adoption was held back by its lousy audio.

"Game developers wanted music and sound," Tai says. "But Microsoft's PC just went 'beep beep.'"[9]

Walden International backed Creative first, financing the development of its audio card, Soundblaster, and helping the company market it to the US. In 1988 Sim relocated to California, determined to find buyers. He knocked on Microsoft's door. The company had just released its Windows 3.1 operating system—the first to incorporate graphics, but still just going "beep beep."

Microsoft made Creative's Soundblaster audio card its standard in new PCs. "Microsoft changed their operating system configuration in their drop-down menu," Tai says, to rush the audio card into its new software.

"Microsoft's order rate surged something like 500 percent a year," Tai recalls. All the PC clone manufacturers had to respond. "Every

PC in the world now needed a sound card." By 1992, every game and sound card had to be "Soundblaster-compatible."

ASIA'S FIRST NEW YORK IPO

It was time for Creative to go public. Its soundcard tech had propelled it into the big leagues, but it faced many competitors and it would require a lot more capital to retain its edge. Sim needed Bill Tai to help the company find an underwriter.

Tai pitched them to DBS, figuring a Singaporean bank would help Creative list on the local exchange.

But he went in with the mindset he had honed while pounding the pavement as a tech banker in San Francisco. "I was used to placing a high valuation on tech companies, because they would grow into the valuation you had in mind," he says.

He told DBS that Creative should be valued at $400 million to $500 million.

The conservative DBS bankers didn't buy it. "Their offices overlooked Keppel Shipyard," Tai recalls. "They told me, 'Look out the window. That's what should be worth $500 million.' So I took Creative to the US instead."

Peter Liu of WI Harper, another VC backing Creative, says Goldman Sachs underwrote the deal. "Creative became the first Asian company to list on Nasdaq."[10]

It was also the top-performing IPO in 1992, listing at a market cap of $470 million—in the high range of Sim and Tai's valuation—and traded up to $1.5 billion.

ONE-HIT WONDER?

Creative would have its ups and downs, eventually relinquishing its Nasdaq listing when times got hard and moving to Singapore Exchange instead. Sim became Singapore's youngest billionaire when he turned 45. He remained CEO of Creative until his death in January 2023.

But Sim was an outlier. The same attitude that had made DBS spurn Creative's business was common in Singapore.

Sim even wrote a book in 1999 in which he accused Singaporeans of suffering from "No U-Turn Syndrome," or NUTS—a kneejerk deference to higher authorities before taking any decision. In the US, drivers can make a U-turn so long as there's no sign prohibiting it, but in Singapore, the rule is never make a U-turn unless a sign expressly allows it. The government said it was keen to foster an innovation economy, but its bureaucrats—usually the ones charged with making this happen—were in fact smothering entrepreneurs in red tape.

Sim and Creative were a huge success for Singapore, but also exceptions. The VCs operating in Asia quickly pivoted to China for their next hits. Creative had helped make video games more popular, but was it game over for VC and innovation in Southeast Asia?

THE GOVERNMENT WADES IN

Until this point, the Singapore government's focus had been on attracting multinationals to invest in the country. But the government came to realize that just building another foundry wasn't going to help Singapore climb the value-add ladder or become a center of innovation.

Whereas Taiwan's mandarins promoted talent, luring back the Chinese diaspora in Silicon Valley, Singapore focused on capital: using its growing wealth to establish influential institutional investing entities, and leverage their capital to turn the island into a hub for financing innovation.

"The real corner was turned when the government actively promoted startups to contribute to the economy and employment," Joo says.

To make it happen, the government turned to a commodities trader named Finian Tan—the same Tan we met in Chapter One talking about his investment into China's Baidu.

The year was 1997, a fateful one for Asia, which was about to suffer through an enormous financial crisis. Tan was trading commodities in New York when he got a call from back home. It was the Ministry of Trade and Industry.

"They wanted private-sector talent," he says. This was unusual. The government recruited the top university talent and only promoted from within. "It was almost like a priesthood," Tan says.[11]

But the mandarins were self-aware enough to realize they might have a groupthink problem. The same frustrations that were driving Sim Wong Hoo NUTS were becoming evident in the ministry, which was worried the country wasn't advancing up the value chain. By 1997, Singapore was rich. According to the World Bank, in 1997 it had reached per-capita income of $26,376—the same level as the UK. But the drivers of its wealth such as light manufacturing were disappearing.

Tan says: "We had achieved a high per-capita income, so the next stage of growth should be driven by entrepreneurs and innovation."

ENCOURAGING STARTUPS

In a break with precedent, the ministry asked Tan to join as deputy secretary—the most senior government role ever offered to someone from the private sector, Tan says.

The driver of this mission was Tony Tan Keng Yam (no relation), the powerful deputy prime minister who would later serve as the nation's President. A member of the innermost circle, Tony Tan championed the establishment of a new, US-style university focused on business and the development of an innovative ecosystem.

This was the environment in which Finian Tan joined the government. "The job was to make Singapore into the Silicon Valley of the East," he says.

Tan oversaw three initiatives. First, he proposed regulatory changes to support startups.

A major theme of these new rules was to take away the stigma of startup failures. The government revised bankruptcy laws to differentiate between failures due to business risks versus failures due to mismanagement, and founders' capital losses in liquidated startups could be deducted from their taxes.

The government also eased listing requirements, used tax to encourage employee stock options, and expanded foreign work visas. Last, the government allowed tech-focused entrepreneurs to use their homes as offices—a nod to the startup-in-a-garage ethos of Silicon Valley, which was hard to replicate in Singapore, where most citizens live in subsidized government housing.

"We wanted to make it cheap to start a business and easy to fail," Tan says. These measures may seem routine, but at the time, Israel was the only country experimenting with ways to support startups and VC. "This was in the 1990s. Other countries are doing this today."

FUNDING VENTURE

The second initiative was to establish Singapore Management University, fulfilling the ambition of Tony Tan, the deputy prime minister.

The third was to create a $1 billion Technopreneur Innovation Fund (TIF) to invest in VC businesses. Set up under the auspices of the Economic Development Board, TIF was designed to attract Silicon Valley VCs by allocating them money if they had a presence in the city; later its rules were tightened to require recipients to also invest in Singapore-based startups.

TIF's record was mixed. As an allocator of capital, it didn't hit any home runs, and was eventually shut down. But it supported a small but dedicated industry of venture capitalists, allocating $1.3 billion to over 100 funds.[12] It had a Yozma-like strategy of allocating $10 million to $20 million tickets to VCs that raised their own money to invest locally.

But it wasn't just the money: it was also Singapore's approach to "fair play."

"By ensuring fair competition, VCs didn't get any benefits just because they were run by Singaporeans," says Jeffrey Chi, vice chairman and founding partner of Vickers Venture Partners, a Singaporean VC. "The rest of Southeast Asia is different: discrimination is baked into the regulations."[13]

ASIA'S INVESTMENT HUB

Some of the firms that got their start with TIF support include Granite Global Ventures (GGV) and GSR Ventures, as well as spinoff funds run by individuals who would go on to hold senior positions in Asia at Silicon Valley firms such as KP, Matrix Partners, and Sequoia Capital. TIF's own management team, led by CEO Jimmy Hsu, would also depart to establish their own PE business, Eagle Capital Partners.

"TIF played an instrumental role in creating a Singaporean Silicon Valley," Chi says.

Awarding Singapore with that label may be justified today, but at the time it was still aspirational. Larry Lopez, who in the mid-2000s was a managing director at SVB, notes that Asian VCs were reliant on local funding.

"No Asia VCs raised US LP money," he says.[14] Singapore lacked the depth of engineering talent so local VCs were set up by financiers, not technologists or founders. These people relied on government grants and money from corporations looking for strategic investments.

This meant that exits to the US capital markets were mostly closed. Creative Technologies had been lucky that it had been backed by Silicon Valley-based funds like WI Harper and Walden International.

"Access meant having to go through Silicon Valley," Lopez says.

But Singapore was assembling the building blocks of an innovation economy, and the government was willing to play a patient game. Singapore's true achievement was not in creating a wonderland for startups, but for building the institutions of capital that could look for deals anywhere.

Edmond Ng, founder and managing partner of Axiom Asia Private Capital, a fund of funds established in 2006, credits this period for helping create an Asian VC industry.

"During the dotcom era, the Singapore government wanted to establish the innovation hub of Asia," Ng says. "They pursued many of the VCs in Taiwan to set up shop, and many did. And they got a few Silicon Valley firms too."[15]

The most notable of these was DFJ ePlanet—the fund managed by Finian Tan, who exited government service in 2000 to set up DFJ's Asia arm. It was to be the first of two major VCs founded by Tan, the other being Vickers Venture Partners with Jeffrey Chi.

But these VC pioneers were not finding many great startups in Singapore. Tan, as we know, made his reputation by investing in China's Baidu.

Ng says, "Singapore's initiatives were not successful [in building local startups], but it did put Singapore on the map. Singapore has done a lot to win talent. But people here realized that Southeast Asia was not the story. The opportunity was in China."

7

SILICON VALLEY: THE TRIUMPH

A HANDFUL of venture capitalists in Asia rightly saw China as a massive opportunity. It would take their peers in the US longer to open their eyes.

Before that happened, Silicon Valley would go through a bruising encounter with Japanese competition. It's a useful history to visit, because it reveals a lot about two themes about VC's globalization. First, can innovation flourish in markets without a strong VC culture? And second, how important is the role of government in fostering innovation?

Today, China looms as the only geopolitical rival to the US, and it is basing its power on technology. Understanding the US-Japanese tech battles of the 1980s can also put into perspective the current Sino-US competition—in which VC has become entangled.

In the next two chapters, we are going to catch up on the evolution of VC in Silicon Valley. This chapter looks at the rise of the iconic firms in West Coast venture investing, followed by a look at the Japanese challenge to American tech dominance and VC's role in Tokyo's defeat. Then we'll be ready to tell the China story.

THE US MODEL

Innovation has been the heartbeat of the US economy. It's more than just a way to sell things. Innovation is the lifeblood of modern societies. But what is it, how does it happen—and does it matter who does the innovating?

For most of the twentieth century and the beginning of this one, the unparalleled leader in innovation was Silicon Valley. "No other major financial center in the world has ever generated companies of consequence and prominence that are so large and visibly successful," said the late Don Valentine, founder of one of the Valley's mightiest venture investment firms, Sequoia Capital.[1]

Today the idea of innovation is popularly embodied in the Silicon Valley star entrepreneur: an iconic person like Steve Jobs or Mark Zuckerberg, whose vision creates world-beating companies that transform our lives.

The bold, sometimes reckless tech entrepreneurs are the ones who found and lead companies that drive the innovations that impact our lives. They are often regarded (in the United States, at least) as the embodiment of the American character, for good or ill: as rule-breaking visionaries who create enormous wealth and disrupt hidebound institutions.

They don't even have to be American-born, so long as they fit into Valley culture: Sabeer Bhatia, founder of Hotmail, is Indian; Melanie Perkins, founder of graphic-design platform Canva, is Australian; Sergey Brin, co-founder of Google, was born in the Soviet Union. All of these companies were financed by VC.

When such behavior becomes embedded in a society, it becomes transformational. Innovation is the commercialization of ideas and learnings into new products and services. When the forces of innovation are unleashed, they become a perpetually renovating energy that keeps people and businesses focused on the new. This dynamism drives economic growth and underpins a nation's influence.

Such dynamism is rare. Silicon Valley emerged as a locus in the 1960s around the invention of the transistor. Although the Valley has had its ups and downs, it has undoubtedly driven much of the American economy since the 1960s.

THE FINANCIER

The entrepreneur is, however, only part of the equation. Along with the founder is the financier—people like Don Valentine. Innovation requires funding, and it is the financier—not the inventor—who bears the risk of turning ideas into business realities. Money does, however, preoccupy entrepreneurs: the life of a startup founder is consumed as much by obtaining rounds of funding as it is by creating products and making sales.

Just as the Silicon Valley entrepreneur is regarded as an American institution, so too is the dominant form of funding them: venture capital, the professionalization of asset managers specializing in investing in startups and risky, privately held companies.

VC firms invest in privately owned startups in the hope that one of these companies will hit it—big—and knowing that most will deliver mediocre returns or fail outright. It is a style of investing that is deliberately risky. But that's what makes VC work.

Arguably, venture capital is also the one part of the financial services industry that fulfills its social function. Although finance has many uses, from providing deposits to loans and investments, the confluence of globalization, deregulation, and technology means Wall Street largely exists to enrich itself.

Famed investor Jeremy Grantham, co-founder and chief investment strategist at Boston asset manager GMO, puts it this way: "In my career in America, the percentage of GDP that goes to finance has gone from 3.5 percent to 8.5 percent. In a way, we're like a giant bloodsucker, and we have more than doubled in size, sucking more than twice the blood out of the rest of the economy."

But, as he told economist Tyler Cowen in late 2022, "I think whatever success we're going to have will be on new technology. And I am a great fan of American venture capital. It is, I think, the last, best American exceptionalism... It's very vigorous, and it attracts the best foreigners too."[2]

The number of VC firms in the US has grown rapidly. In the late

1960s, it was still a cottage industry, with the total pool of VC just a few hundred million dollars. Tom Perkins, one of the modern VC's pioneers, quipped that gathering the entire Silicon Valley industry would require only a "moderately-sized room."[3]

Today, VC is an established industry. As of 2020, the US boasted 1,965 firms managing $548 billion across 3,680 funds, according to the National Venture Capital Association.[4] It has an outsized impact unlike any other branch of financial services. It takes bets on the companies that shape our destinies.

It wasn't always so. VC is also a young industry, whereas people have found ways to finance change well before.

THE RISE OF LARGE COMPANIES

Commercialization of technology happened before the invention of VC. The Industrial Revolution was financed by private wealth. But these personal networks could not scale far, particularly in a nation as large as the US. The incredible inventions of the nineteenth century were developed by giant corporations, mostly in the US, Britain, Germany, and France.

The electricity industry is a good example. It began when Thomas Edison invented the incandescent light bulb in 1879—a venture backed by the banker John Pierpoint Morgan (investing his own money), as well as the Trask and Vanderbilt families.

Innovation in electricity, telephones, steel, and automobiles set the foundation for large-scale industries that required increasingly large amounts of capital. America's "golden age" of inventors outstripped the earlier cottage industry of families, financial agents, and entrepreneurs. Now inventors like Edison had to be absorbed into large corporations to access the resources they needed.

Such companies, however, could spawn an entire cluster of smaller, innovative peers. Cleveland became one such entrepreneurial hotspot. The Brush Electric Company was founded in 1880 by inventor Charles Brush at the urging of local investor George Stockley. Brush built electric street lighting systems that displaced gas lamps, and at one point his company commanded 80 percent of the national market.[5]

Brush attracted entrepreneurs in related businesses of iron, steel, and machine tools, which were needed to support Brush Electric. A band of wealthy Cleveland families helped pull inventors and businesspeople from around the country.

THOMAS EDISON AND THE CORPORATE LAB

Brush Electric couldn't compete with Edison for research labs, however, and soon the company's know-how was diffused into the market. By 1889, the company was merged with Edison's company, which formed the genesis of General Electric. But it wasn't a merger of equals: by 1896, Brush's factory was shut.

Edison had a firmer grasp of how to protect his industrial secrets—his IP. One reason for America's rise as an industrial powerhouse was its patent system, and Edison was prepared to defend his patents in court.

European patent systems charged inventors high fees to file in return for monopoly rights. The US Constitution's Article I, on the other hand, mandated Congress to establish a patent and copyright law to foster "the progress of science and useful arts."

The US patent system was cheap enough for ordinary people to apply for one, and it granted powerful but temporary protections. Moreover, it was more focused on identifying an innovation's "true inventor" rather than granting monopolies to whoever was first to file.

By 1810, the US was approving more patents than Britain on a per-capita basis. Many of these patents, such as those for the technology to build canals, were granted to people of modest means living in rural areas. The US also developed a secondary market in patents (that is, licensing), which gave inventors a way to raise additional capital.[6]

FINANCING SCALE BEFORE VC

Another advantage in the US was the growing diversity of its finance industry. American industry quickly outgrew its scrappy, proto-VC roots. Increasing scale required the kind of funding that only banks and stock markets could provide. Industrialists, when they got big enough, founded their own banks to finance their expansion.

Such institutions, however, were not looking to fund risky startups. They invested in established businesses with predictable pathways.

For example, banks were ready to lend to big companies in industries like iron, steel, chemicals, and pharmaceuticals. By the 1880s, such companies were in the vanguard of what Carlota Perez called the Age of Steel, Electricity and Heavy Engineering (1875 to 1920). Technology was going through another wave that was transforming the world, and required a different path to commercialization. These industries evolved from a combination of many technologies and required the sort of research labs that only giant companies could muster.

The leaders among these new industries succeeded in establishing competitive advantages that kept out startup competitors. Whatever the initial spark, these organizations were built to last beyond the lifetime of a founder. In such organizations, managerial skills were far more important than the next iteration of a technology; and they could often rely on retained earnings to invest in research.

Like modern-day startups in disruptive industries, these businesses succeeded by achieving economies of scale, which drove down costs for consumers. But eventually the science behind their products yielded no more discoveries. The chemical industry was created in the 1880s and 1890s by companies such as Du Pont (explosives), Dow (electrically produced chemicals), and Monsanto (fertilizer) in the US; and by German and Swiss leaders such as BASF, Bayer, Hoechst, Ciba, and Geigy.

By the 1920s, the chemical industry's leaders had been established, and they remain there today; the industry ceased being "high tech" by the 1950s and focused on product, marketing, and operational efficiencies.[7] But this combination of scale and predictability made such companies attractive clients for banks.

FUNDING RAILROADS

Such examples stand in contrast to disruptive industries with risky outcomes. Railroads, from Perez's Age of Steam and Railways (1829 to 1874), epitomize uncertainty. Banks couldn't work out the impact of the next innovation on a company's business prospects. Likewise, telegraphs, transatlantic cables, and the precursors of the electronics industry, especially electricity and radio, required a very different approach to financing.

Disruptive industries like these needed what today we'd call an "ecosystem," a social infrastructure of related technologies and businesses to get a technological idea off the ground. Electricity, telephones, and the internet required transmission lines and a host of consumer applications to work. Some conglomerates tried to create and own the entire value chain, such as RCA in radios and TV. For the most part, however, the ecosystem required investment into many new companies and technologies—a need that went far beyond what America's proto-VC industry or its wealthy families could meet.

US railroads were instead funded mostly by British investors and the London money markets. Eventually these companies listed on US exchanges, but even so, railroads were constantly losing money. This was an industry that kept driving transportation costs so low that it bankrupted itself, leading to a painful financial crisis in 1890.

In response, investment bankers such as Morgan pushed for institutional reforms on Wall Street to mitigate against speculative risks. That ambition wasn't realized, but it did lead the New York Stock Exchange in 1914 to change its listing rules to accept only high-quality companies. It introduced audited reports that gave investors the tools to analyze companies, as well as a clearinghouse and daily settlement, to make trading cheaper, safer, and more transparent. Meanwhile it set up a secondary board, the Curb

Exchange, for smaller companies that couldn't meet NYSE's blue-ribbon standards.[8]

These reforms made NYSE a credible venue to raise capital for large-scale, high-quality enterprises. But soon the stock market would begin to play a leading role in the biggest tech craze of the early twentieth century.

RADIO AND THE STOCK MARKET

In the 1920s, NYSE became a player for the first time in financing innovative startups, including in automobiles and aviation. But the stock market really came into its own with the radio industry, with a boom in radio stocks on NY Curb that resembled the dotcom boom of the 1990s. The number of IPOs prompted quips about there being more radio stocks than actual radio receivers: "A new radio stock a day," crowed boosters.[9]

Guglielmo Marconi invented radio (for which he won a Nobel Prize in physics) and set up his business in the UK, in 1897, to commercialize it. He proved a better inventor than an entrepreneur, as the industry was too marginal to attract enough capital, and no ecosystem emerged to support it—until the US government introduced public broadcasting, in 1920.

This sparked a rush of companies to produce broadcast tubes and receiving sets. In 1922, the industry sold 1 million tubes and 100,000 receivers; in 1929, it sold 69 million tubes and 4.4 million receivers. Making radio equipment didn't cost much money, so it attracted lots of companies, and there was little patent protection on the underlying tech. Most of these companies financed themselves by going public, riding waves of hype.

This financing mania supported many companies that would never make a profit, and the whole thing crashed in 1925. But just as the excesses of the 1990s dotcom boom also led to the birth of Amazon, the radio boom launched RCA.

RCA AND THE BIRTH OF CONSUMER ELECTRONICS

The Radio Corporation of America (RCA) was set up in 1919 as a partnership between General Electric, Westinghouse, AT&T, and United Fruit Company at the urging of the US Navy, which wanted a national champion to win the emerging battle for telecommunications.

RCA was a precursor to the Information Revolution. It would dominate consumer electronics until the late 1970s, first in radio and then in television.

The reason that RCA had so many competitors in its earliest years is the same reason why it could scale so rapidly: the equipment required was straightforward. Whereas a chemicals company relied on complex combinations of many scientific learnings, radio just required hardware to transmit and receive, and a means to process the message. In this regard, radio was the heir to Edison's phonograph and the forerunner of the transistor.

RCA was meant to be a marketing arm of General Electric and Westinghouse, but the parent companies couldn't keep up with demand, so RCA went into manufacturing. But it didn't rest there: its first CEO, the brilliant David Sarnoff, also set up two private broadcasting networks to develop and carry radio programs. These were National Broadcasting Corporation and American Broadcasting Corporation, which both evolved into TV networks. RCA then developed color TV.

Sarnoff also bought his way into phonographs and convinced General Electric and Westinghouse to give him access to their research in return for expanding their equity in RCA. By 1958, RCA had 70 percent of the market for consumer electronics.[10]

Radio galvanized the stock market into becoming a means of financing startups—a boom that eventually left most investors bust, but one that helped fuel consumer demand.

RCA was self-funded by big corporate parents, and it would go on to dominate the industry, to the extent that no startup would dare take it on. RCA set the scene for the next-level innovations that would give birth to Silicon Valley, but that transformation would need a new means of financing: the modern venture capital firm.

FROM RCA TO APPLE

We've already related the origins of VC, first in Boston and then in California: Georges Doriot and ARD in Chapter Two, and Arthur Rock, the "Traitorous Eight," and Intel in Chapter Three. As VC was finding its feet, the world of consumer electronics had changed. The days of RCA as a mega-corporation had given way to personal computing, and it would need a different way to get funded.

Arthur Rock would play a key role in this too. He has come to epitomize a style of venture investing: the networked financier. His Rolodex helped the "Traitorous Eight" find a corporate backer, and then his contacts with wealthy families let him quickly find the money to create Intel.

Rock would go on to a third iconic deal. A former Intel marketing executive, Mike Markkula, had retired early to enjoy his money. Markkula met two hippie techies, Steve Wozniak and Steve Jobs, and lent them $300,000 in return for an option for one-third of their venture. But the new company needed more capital to get off the ground, so Markkula asked Arthur Rock to invest.

"I met Jobs and Wozniak, and I didn't think I wanted to be involved," Rock recalled to an interviewer. "They were very young. Jobs had just returned from six months in India with a guru. They didn't appear well. They were bragging about [an invention] to steal money from telephone companies. I didn't like that."[11]

The buttoned-up Rock didn't care for the phone-freaking blue box that would later excite Bill Tai (see this book's Foreword) and other hackers. But Markkula convinced the financier to visit a computer show in San Jose where Rock realized Jobs and Wozniak's computer was on to something. He backed them, hoping Markkula would keep the other guys in line—and Apple was born, with Rock on the board.

SCALING APPLE

Rock would continue to play an important role by bringing in professional CEOs. Most failed. "They had to put up with Steve Jobs," Rock explained. "He was a very disturbing force."

Rock recruited John Sculley, previously president of PepsiCo, a marketing genius. Sculley had created the "Pepsi Challenge" ads, and Jobs recognized his talent. At Apple, Sculley would create a famous campaign pitting the independent Macintosh PC against an Orwellian Microsoft.

But Jobs wanted Apple to compete against IBM for business customers, while Sculley's vision was for the consumer market. Rock helped Sculley oust Jobs from the company. Jobs founded another computer company, NeXT, and co-founded Pixar, to develop computer graphics for George Lucas's film company, before returning to run Apple in 1997, launching the iPod, the iPad, and then in 2007, the iPhone.

By now Arthur Rock's time at the company had come to an end. Apple's aggressive marketing crossed a line for him when the company took out advertisements about how its new chip, co-designed with IBM and Motorola, would kill Intel. Rock was still a board member at Intel, so he left Apple. He had by now become not only Silicon Valley's first successful venture capitalist but also the financier who backed a change of guard, from semiconductors and business computing to software and PCs.

But as Silicon Valley matured, it would need VCs with more than just a Rolodex and a nose for a deal. It would need financiers who were themselves technologists—people ready to get stuck into the startup's operations.

KLEINER PERKINS AND GENENTECH

Until Apple, founders were hardware people with a lot of experience, like Noyce. But Jobs and Wozniak were different: rebellious, and most of all, young: Jobs was 21 years old when he co-founded Apple.

Technology was changing. The physicists who drove semiconductor companies gave way to visionary computer salespeople and software designers: from businesses about atoms to ones based on bits.

But this new generation still owed debts to the original Silicon Valley firm, Fairchild Semiconductor, not least because Fairchild spawned two other people who formed VC's triumvirate of pioneers. Eugene Kleiner was a Fairchild co-founder who would go on to set up KP. And Don Valentine, a Fairchild salesman, would establish Sequoia Partners.

Eugene Kleiner and Tom Perkins set up their firm in 1972 (officially called Kleiner, Perkins, Caulfield & Byers) on Sand Hill Road, an artery in Menlo Park connecting many Silicon Valley companies and other VCs. Both men were technologists. Kleiner was a physicist. Perkins, after studying at Harvard under Georges Doriot, worked at HP, helping the company get into minicomputers to compete with DEC.

KP has backed many of the most important tech companies in the world, including Amazon, Compaq, China's JD.com, Google, Netscape, Square, Sun Microsystems, and Tandem Computers.

But the firm is probably best known for Perkin's role in the creation of Genentech, the first biotech company. Giant pharmaceutical companies such as Eli Lilly dominated the industry and did their own research. However, at the University of California at San Francisco, geneticist Herbert Boyer saw the potential to reengineer E. coli bacteria to clone human insulin. Perkins put $100,000 into Genentech in 1976 and served as its chairman. The startup created the first recombinant DNA technology.

As Genentech hit one milestone after another, Perkins helped raise additional rounds of funding, each with a higher valuation. Progress was so impressive that Eli Lilly, scared of losing its hold on the insulin market (its version relied on insulin derived from animals), decided to license Genentech's products, paying the company $500,000 plus a royalty on sales. That deal helped Genentech go public in 1980.

KP did more than just make money on the IPO: it helped lead the company, thanks to Perkins's hands-on involvement. Moreover, a VC firm had played a central role in helping a startup invent an entirely new industry.[12]

This degree of involvement in a startup is unusual for VCs, but Tom Perkins's role in Genentech remains the poster child for an investor having deep domain knowledge of the industry, as well as an active role in the governance of the company.

MARKET PLAYER: DON VALENTINE AND SEQUOIA

If Arthur Rock is the networking banker and Eugene Kleiner and Tom Perkins are technologists, then Don Valentine represents a style focused on identifying promising markets and finding the entrepreneurs who fit the bill.

Valentine set up Sequoia Capital in 1972, initially as the venture arm of Capital Group, one of America's biggest fund management companies and, unusually, based in California instead of the East Coast. The experiment didn't go as planned and Valentine went on to lead Sequoia as an independent company.

Today it is Silicon Valley royalty, having invested in startups such as Apple, Atari, Google, Oracle, Nvidia, Stripe, YouTube, and WhatsApp. It is also unusual in having given birth to one of China's leading VCs, Sequoia Capital China.

Valentine was interested in creating companies that could grow and scale, but he realized that innovations by themselves might not succeed. A company with a new technology needed suppliers, distributors, and consumers willing to buy something new. Valentine fostered the idea of "aircraft carrier" investing. An aircraft carrier requires a fleet of supporting vessels to sustain its missions, defend itself, and project firepower. Valentine's strategy was to pick an anchor company with a unique innovation and invest in the necessary peripheral companies.

Valentine's best-known "aircraft carrier" was Apple, which was poised to launch the personal computing revolution. Valentine invested in companies that could speed this up, such as startups that could sell Apple better memory chips.[13]

"My interest was investing in companies that addressed large markets and solved a specific kind of problem," he told an interviewer.[14] "It's much easier to build a new startup company in an environment where the market is large, than to develop a market for a new technology with no obvious solution."

More than anyone else, he realized that the scale and returns that VCs needed were going to come from high tech and consumer electronics, not from other fields. With biotech the exception, the entire VC world became linked to the growth of the US computer industry, initially in hardware and then software.

THE ASCENT OF VC

VC's role in the 1960s was limited. The venerable firms were founded in the late 1960s and early 1970s, but it would take time for them to make their mark. The 1980s would see VC first enter the popular consciousness for the first time.

This first generation was also led by people who came from technology, rather than Wall Street. Eugene Kleiner and Tom Perkins were physicists. Don Valentine cut his teeth selling microprocessors. Even Rock was steeped in the tech from his earliest days, even if he wasn't interested in the "mumbo-jumbo," as he called it. These were founder VCs who, like good entrepreneurs, were motivated by building something rather than get-rich-quick schemes. (Although they did indeed become rich.)

"We don't think of it as investing," Valentine once said, "but as building companies or even building industries. It's an entirely different mentality than the idea of buying and selling things. Here you don't buy things, you participate in founding teams."

Silicon Valley was built thanks to the availability of this risk-taking capital, with financiers like Valentine willing, and even happy, to back entrepreneurs who had failed in their previous endeavors.

"I once tried to explain this to the deputy prime minister of Singapore," Valentine recalled, citing the visit by Tony Tan arranged by Finian Tan, whom we met in the previous chapter. "Silicon Valley is a state of mind. You can't take it with you. [Singapore] would have to move your people here, have their DNA changed, so when they moved back to Singapore, they'd take risks."[15]

That wasn't the Singapore way: despite the government's readiness to emulate Silicon Valley, it had more success building investment teams than finding startups at home. In Japan or Germany, few people would start a company because the shame of failure was too great. Worldwide, including most of the US, people would never risk leaving a good job to try starting their own business.

But in Silicon Valley, the VC community was prepared to support people who had failed once, so they didn't have a big ego, but still had fire in the belly. This made the Valley a unique cauldron spinning out one significant company after another.

That commitment was about to be tested—by Japan.

8

JAPAN: THE CHALLENGE

IN 1970, the American high-tech industry bestrode the world. By the mid-1980s, Japanese competitors had eaten the Valley's lunch, as they like to say on Wall Street.

Silicon Valley and Washington wrestled with ways to counter Japan's state-organized assault, including attempts at a US industrial policy. In the end, it was VC-backed startups that revived US technology and blindsided Japan's corporate behemoths. Japan, meanwhile, has struggled to foster a meaningful VC industry—and therefore has little in the way of innovative startups.

It's an epic story of triumph and failure that highlights VC's role within geopolitical struggles and the conditions in which VC thrives or dies.

Let's go back to Silicon Valley circa 1970. US semiconductor companies, all launched with VC backing, enjoyed 90 percent of the global market, led by the likes of Intel, Fairchild, Advanced Micro Devices, and National Semiconductor.

The only place US companies didn't have dominant share was Japan—which, ironically, was where the first microprocessors were sold commercially, to local tabulator companies. Despite their head start, US firms had only 25 percent of the Japanese market, and no European players exported there.[1]

DIGITAL TSUNAMI

By 1989 US companies' 90 percent market share of chips had whittled down to 35 percent. Similarly, their lead in data-processing equipment had declined from complete dominance to 57 percent.

Instead of Intel and its peers, the biggest semiconductor companies were now all Japanese: Fujitsu, Hitachi, NEC, and Toshiba. Several iconic Valley firms such as Fairchild Semiconductor had vanished.

This was true of other technologies up and down the value chain, including microprocessors and specialist chips such as microcontrollers and application-specific integrated circuits (ASICs). All of these were critical components in developing the next generation of tech, and these markets had fallen under Japanese dominance.

Perhaps the biggest American defeat was in DRAM chips. Microprocessors built with millions of dynamic random-access memory chips are used to power digital electronics that need a lot of cheap memory, such as personal computers and video game consoles. The US share of the DRAM business crashed from virtually 100 percent to a mere 8 percent by 1988.

In the words of Andy Grove, Intel's boss, Japan had unleashed a "digital tsunami."[2]

THE RISK OF CEDING GROUND

The Valley could take cold comfort in the argument that they were moving up "the value chain" and letting the Japanese focus on the less lucrative aspects of production.

It's true that US firms like Intel focused on the high end of microprocessors, leaving the more commoditized aspects of chips such as memory to the Japanese.

But losing these businesses meant shutting plants and firing engineers. From 1989 to 1993, Silicon Valley's electronics industry shed about 200,000 jobs, as manufacturing shifted to lower-cost regions or countries.[3]

By ceding the low end of chips and data processing, Silicon Valley was also falling into "the innovator's dilemma," even if that term had not yet been coined. In 1997 Clayton Christensen, a Harvard professor, published his book of that name, arguing incumbent companies lose market share because they focus on the highest-value products. New companies, catering to the least-loved segments of a market, are left to keep innovating, to the point they can overthrow their established rivals.

That was how the Japanese had unseated the US giants.

THE FALL OF RCA

The Japanese tsunami may have felt like a shock to the US, but it was a long time in the making. The rise of the Japanese challenge can be traced back to the hubristic fall of America's first great consumer tech company: RCA.

RCA was the first big company in consumer electronics. From the 1920s to the 1960s it dominated radio and television, from manufacturing to phonographs to broadcasting. Only IBM enjoyed an equivalent primacy, in business computers.

RCA self-destructed due to a series of disastrous management decisions, mostly concerning attempts to broaden into new markets. It tried to take on IBM in business computers, then it moved into businesses that had nothing to do with electronics, like sporting goods.

By the 1980s, RCA was in terminal decline, and its management hastened the end by selling off assets, including licensing its IP—to the likes of Taiwan's UMC, as we learned in Chapter Five. By 1986 RCA was gone, its last remains bought by General Electric.

Its collapse left a vacuum in consumer electronics that Japanese companies rushed to fill. For the Japanese, however, this was just part of a bigger strategy: to take on IBM, Intel, and the core of America's tech industry.

MATSUSHITA: MARKETING INNOVATION

The Second World War had destroyed the industrial bases of Germany and Japan. The US sheltered both countries under its military umbrella and invested heavily in their recovery. The Japanese tech industry was quicker to get back on its feet, supported by the nexus between its bureaucrats, politicians, and corporate families (grouped as *keiretsu*, with interlocking business relationships and shareholdings).

Japanese companies like Matsushita, Sanyo, Sharp, and Sony were able to dominate their own market in electronics and compete successfully in Europe. Most of these companies were no more than clever copycats (a label later applied to Chinese software companies), but Matsushita and Sony were something more.

Matsushita was founded in 1918 as a manufacturer of electrical appliances, including radios—which it produced thanks to licenses it acquired from RCA. Then came the devastation of the Second World War. Konosuke Matsushita, the company's founder, rebuilt the company. Through joint ventures and acquisitions, including RCA's phonograph business in Japan, Matsushita acquired enough know-how to build a powerful industrial base.

Konosuke Matsushita's flair was not in tech or manufacturing, however, it was in marketing. He built crack sales teams in Europe and the US that pushed brands such as Panasonic as low-cost, high-quality alternatives to Western makers.

Most of Japanese electronics companies were not innovative. They licensed American or European tech, and then relied on cheap labor and government protection to mass produce at cutthroat prices. It was part of a national strategy of economic catch-up, steered by government agencies such as the Ministry of International Trade and Industry (MITI)—a powerful bureaucracy that guided industrial policy, funded research, and directed investment.

VCR WARS

Matsushita's crowning achievement was in the nascent market of video cassette recorders, which allowed consumers to play ready-made videos (movies) and record TV programs. Japanese companies had been developing VCR technology since the 1950s. By the mid-1970s, Sony's version, Betamax, had focused on the video rental market by promoting the best viewing quality.

But Matsushita, through its subsidiary JVC, bet that what customers wanted was longer recording times—long enough to record a sports game on TV. This insight outcompeted Sony's superior technology.

Winning the VCR wars showed that Japanese companies had come a long way from mere imitation. They were now inventing entirely new categories in consumer electronics. By the late 1980s, JVC's standard (called VHS, for Video Home System) dominated sales in the US, Japan, and Europe.

In an ironic twist that showed who had come to dominate consumer electronics, RCA ended up licensing the VHS technology from Matsushita to produce its own VCRs. But RCA, like Sony, lacked the ideal balance of screen quality and recording time.

Sony, meanwhile, threw in the towel on Betamax in 1988, although it did successfully adopt its technology for new products and services in video recording.

SONY'S INGENUITY

Despite losing the VCR wars, Sony went on to dominate the 1980s. It was a truly innovative company, perhaps reflecting its history as a maverick within Japan, outside of the *keiretsu* system. Akio Morita co-founded the company just after the war, funded by his partner's family, and licensed transistor technology from Bell Labs to produce tape recorders.

This led to a string of consumer products that Sony invented, including pocket radios, VCRs, and next-gen color TVs that began to outpace anything made by RCA. The company's triumph was the introduction of the Walkman, a device that made music portable and became an icon of the 1980s.

Perhaps more impressively, however, was Sony's further work that digitized sound and video. In a joint venture with Philips of the Netherlands, it introduced portable compact-disc players, the DVD, and digital graphics processors for PCs.

It would invent new markets again in the 1990s with the PlayStation for video games. US innovators such as Atari (founded in 1972 with Sequoia money) invented video game programs. But today Sony and Nintendo dominate video games consoles.

WHY JAPANESE COMPANIES SUCCEEDED

The Japanese assault commenced in the 1970s, coordinated by MITI, which directed Fujitsu and Hitachi to enter the premium markets for mainframes, and NEC and Toshiba to attack the middle market. These companies were fierce competitors at home, but outside Japan they followed MITI's blueprint.[4]

Their playbook was to license US technology and then poach talent. Luck could play its part: Fujitsu was able to secure the man who had designed IBM's System 360, Gene Amdahl, who wanted to start his own company. Fujitsu financed him and began making Amdahl's new products, and "IBM became an open book in Japan," says business historian Alfred Chandler.

The biggest weapon the Japanese brandished was access to cheap capital. Conglomerate-linked banks provided bottomless loans at low interest rates. Japanese tech groups were paying 6 or 7 percent to borrow money, while US companies were paying interest rates in the high teens, and in the early 1980s, more than 20 percent.[5]

Given chipmakers needed to constantly establish new factories to meet the diktat of Moore's Law (smaller, cheaper, faster), the need for capital was intense. Cheaper funding not only allowed the Japanese groups to sustain losses, but it also supported research that designed superior chips. As US companies closed or moved out of consumer electronics, they ceded more innovation to the Japanese.

The Japanese didn't just copy. Again under MITI direction, Japanese companies commercialized the DRAM memory chips that Intel had invented in 1971. The next year, Japan's four major players had 5 percent of the world market for DRAM; by 1979, they had 71 percent; by 1982, there were no more US companies producing DRAMs.[6]

This reflected a broader rout of classic corporate America, from automobiles to industrial manufacturing to retail. Post-war American business was corporate, conformist, and hierarchical. Titans like AT&T, RCA, IBM, and General Motors had prospered in an era when Europe and Japan were rebuilding from the war, while America could rely on its continental size, abundant resources, and the mass education of its population.

Japanese and German companies could play at that game, with some government assistance. These countries didn't need to be innovative; they just needed to direct their national wealth away from consumption into education, savings, and supporting national champions.

CAN'T OR WON'T: AMERICAN INACTION AGAINST JAPAN

American corporate activity, meanwhile, became unmoored from patriotism. The 1970s ushered in globalization and a trend toward financializing US society (meaning the finance sector's size and influence began to outpace its size and role in the economy). Companies became transnational, driven as much by financial flows and international tax considerations as by any mission to manufacture and sell things.

The rise of free-market evangelists Ronald Reagan and Margaret Thatcher legitimized the new cult of maximizing shareholder returns, espoused by corporate leaders like Jack Welch of General Electric. This turn toward *laissez-faire* policy led US tech companies to complain that the Japanese were winning because they didn't play fair—ignoring their own willingness to license their IP to foreign rivals, or the better quality of Japanese chips and consumer products. Fair or not, it was true that the Japanese weren't focused on maximizing profits: they wanted market share.

If the foreigners weren't playing by market rules, then how should US industry respond? The quintessential analysis of MITI was by analyst Chalmers Johnson, whose studies labeled Japan a "developmental state," with strategic government direction, regulation, and planning. Other influential academics and writers accused Silicon Valley of being too short term, too greedy, too myopic. Chalmers advocated an industrial policy to fight back.

US tech companies had relied on the government for contracts in their formative years, but they were otherwise on their own. Washington wasn't coordinating who did what among Intel, IBM, and HP. The Pentagon's Defense Advanced Research Projects Agency (DARPA) research was focused on innovative ideas, not specific businesses or technologies. By the 1970s most tech companies had already shifted to the lucrative commercial market anyway.

The semiconductor industry for the first time formed an association to lobby for tariffs. The Department of Defense (DoD) attempted to cajole US manufacturers into a consortium, meant to pool the costs so they could compete against the Japanese. One attempt focused on flat-panel screens. Another, called Sematech, was meant to coordinate 14 US semiconductor companies. These failed almost instantly: it was one thing for tech companies to lobby for government money, and another for companies to put in their own capital.[7]

The US system was simply not geared to coordinate companies as in Japan and Europe. Its companies weren't ready to pool decision-making or money because it wasn't good for their shareholders.

The Reagan administration did browbeat Japan and Germany into coordinating a weakening of the dollar, to curb US imports (an agreement known as the Plaza Accord). But Americans kept buying foreign cars and electronics.

The Plaza Accord also failed to transform the Japanese and German economies to favor domestic consumption: they remained committed to industrialized exports. But it did have one unexpected outcome: the Bank of Japan had been slashing Japanese interest rates to stimulate the domestic economy, but the only things that really took off were real estate and stock prices. An apocryphal story has it that the single square mile of the Imperial Palace in Tokyo was worth more than the entire California real estate market.

When the government tried to cool the market in 1990 and 1991, it triggered a massive bust. Neither Japanese stocks nor property prices would ever recover, and the country was burdened with a debt that would lead to decades of slow obsolescence.

AMERICAN PHOENIX: VC REMAKES SILICON VALLEY

But the biggest reason why American fears of Japanese domination were overblown is that just as Japanese companies were launching their assault, American innovation was moving from top-down corporations to venture-backed startups in Silicon Valley.

By now, the area, powered by the research labs and commercial instincts of Stanford University and University of California, Berkeley, had cemented its importance, especially to the military. Unlike Boston's Route 128 companies, Silicon Valley firms were unstructured, freewheeling, and prepared to snub government ties if the commercial market beckoned.

This brazen drive to get rich made Silicon Valley startups the perfect vehicle for VC. It's also what attracted other key ingredients, namely talent, from around the country and soon from around the world. The VC firms populating Sand Hill Road were notorious for their provincialism: Don Valentine of Sequoia famously said he wouldn't look at a startup that he couldn't reach by a quick car ride. But if Silicon Valley wasn't interested in going out to the world, the world was certainly interested in coming to Silicon Valley—a phenomenon that would jumpstart the export of the VC model to other countries later.

THE RISE OF PERSONAL COMPUTING

VC money backed the creation of Intel in 1971 and thus the commercialization of the microprocessor, or IC: a computer on a chip, capable of processing millions of functions per second. This miniaturization made possible the PC, and later the cellphone.

Apple launched in 1976 to commercialize a PC designed by Steve Wozniak, with production taking place in Steve Jobs' garage. With money from venture capitalist Arthur Rock and Sequoia, Apple Corporation was established in 1977, and Rock took a seat on the board.

Apple was adept at finding ideas from elsewhere, such as the mouse (developed by Xerox), and commercializing them. But it was a pioneer in graphics, and it maintained independence by developing its own operating system. It was this integration of hardware and software that made it unique and enabled it to survive.

Microsoft was founded in 1975, probably the last great Silicon Valley company that didn't rely on VC because it was profitable so early. It did, however, accept a $1 million check from Technology Venture Partners (TVP)—partly to provide stock options to reward staff, partly to put TVP's older "adult in the room" on the board; and to help Bill Gates' nervous co-founders and employees lock in the equity he had promised.[8]

Bill Gates and Paul Allen were hobbyists who came up with a program to run on another early PC, the Altaire 8000. Successful demos won contracts, but the breakthrough was to sell their operating system, called MS-DOS, to IBM, which was looking to enter the PC market.

IBM got into PCs to prevent Apple and other startups from winning the market. But it made two concessions. First, Microsoft insisted on keeping the licensing rights to MS-DOS, so it could sell it to others. Second, IBM had to license its PC technology to anyone. This meant that almost overnight there were around 200 other companies licensing their own PCs—companies like Dell and Compaq, which were all launched with VC backing. And they all incorporated free-to-use MS-DOS software, with the hardware powered by Intel chips.[9]

These legal failures are a strange oversight for a company that obsessively dominated other markets. Perhaps IBM was used to competing against different kinds of players in the mainframe world: either the Japanese, or European state-backed companies like Bull (France), International Computers (UK), and Olivetti (Italy)—which all failed. IBM hadn't learned the lesson of being blindsided by a VC-backed startup like DEC, and now it would fail to win the PC market. But its mistake, by freeing the MS-DOS operating system, also catalyzed the PC industry.

Another winner from the rise of the PC was Intel. The semiconductor company had taken the painful step of exiting the DRAM market. Its last bastion of competitive advantage was microprocessors—logic chips that executed computer programs. This was a niche market, until IBM came along looking to contract out chips for personal computers.

Thus, Intel and Microsoft came to quickly dominate the PC world, even if the hardware came from all over the place. They remained the innovators, while others competed on marketing or price, with just Apple as the creative outlier—indeed, Microsoft copied Apple's graphics capabilities to solidify its lead in PC software.

CASCADING INNOVATION

The rise of PCs led to the need for them to communicate. This ushered in networking devices, with Cisco (backed by Sequoia) commercializing the router and Novell (Safeguard Scientifics, a VC in Pennsylvania) providing networking software. Then came companies providing packaged software, such as Adobe, Oracle, and WordPerfect, all launched with VC money.

VC also played a critical role in backing companies that linked hardware and software. To make PCs ubiquitous required making them useful to people. The original "killer app" was VisiCalc, an electronic spreadsheet created by VisiCorp, another Venrock-backed company that helped Apple sell PCs.[10] IBM's PCs were similarly driven by spreadsheets designed by Lotus, which was funded by Ben Rosen Funds, a Texas-based VC that was influential in the history of the PC.

Microsoft would eventually develop Word and Excel, wiping out VisiCalc and Lotus; and later its Windows operating system would do the same to Novell for networking. But the internet was a phenomenon that not even Microsoft could dominate.

THE INFORMATION SUPERHIGHWAY

The idea of linking computers to be leveraged by many users began with DoD projects in the 1960s. The first networks involved university labs. The DoD's research arm, DARPA, funded the creation of a protocol to communicate between networks, called Transmission Control Protocol/Internet Protocol, which allowed data to be sent in packets—groups of digital information that could be packaged, sent, and read.

Meanwhile, in Europe, scientists at CERN, a giant physics lab in Switzerland, wanted to share information. In 1989, Tim Berners-Lee, a British scientist, came up with the protocol that became known as the World Wide Web, using a series of hyperlinks to link disparate "intranets," or closed networks. The US Congress passed legislation in 1991 pushed by Senator Al Gore to open the DoD-backed networks into a commercial "information superhighway."

It would take VC-backed Silicon Valley companies to commercialize these building blocks—which is to say, to make them relevant outside of a narrow set of users. Websites were beginning to pop up: at universities, at labs, and among hobbyists. But there was no practical way to connect them, until Netscape, the first company created to exploit the internet's business opportunities.

Jim Clark and Mark Andreessen, backed by KP, founded Netscape in 1994 as an online gaming company. They pivoted to an online browser, called Mosaic. Netscape achieved a blockbuster IPO in 1995 that was like firing the starting gun on the new internet, or dotcom, boom.

Mosaic was not destined for success: Microsoft acquired another browser and bundled it into its Windows 95 release as Explorer. Given Microsoft's domination among all non-Apple PCs, its browser soon won out, helping it become one of the most entrenched monopolies in US corporate history.[11] But Netscape had shown what was possible, and Andreessen would go on to become one of Silicon Valley's leading venture capitalists.

BIOTECH

It's worth bracketing another innovation that came out of Silicon Valley that also bypassed both the Japanese and the Europeans: biotech.

The pharmaceutical industry was one of those nineteenth-century creations that had long since stopped being considered high tech. But change was coming: the discovery of DNA's molecular structure by Francis Crick and Thomas Watson in 1953 opened the possibility of genetic engineering.

This possibility became reality as researchers at Stanford and the University of California at San Francisco (UCSF) discovered how to recombine DNA. In 1978, Robert Swanson, a partner at KP, and biochemist Herbert Boyer, a professor at UCSF, founded Genentech as the first company to commercialize these advances. Tom Perkins served as the company's chairman.

Genentech focused on niche applications, splicing human genes to generate a human-based insulin developed in E. coli bacteria, versus the existing products that were based on animal DNA. The results were so successful that Eli Lilly, one of the biggest pharmaceutical companies, licensed the technology.

Biotech quickly exploded into a new industry, helped by a 1983 federal statute that granted a seven-year monopoly to companies that commercialized drugs for uncommon life-threatening diseases. These so-called "orphan drugs" were too niche for a big pharma company to invest, but the legislation made it financially possible for VC-backed biotech companies to attempt a cure.[12]

As a result, biotech companies launched in quick succession, many of them ultimately absorbed into the big Swiss, German, or US pharmaceutical companies. These companies would use recombinant DNA to develop new drugs to fight anemia, alleviate chemotherapy, and develop vaccines.

The mapping of the human genome and the development of gene editing is opening a new set of doors for biotech companies: the industry's potential was made obvious with companies like Moderna, a Cambridge, Massachusetts, biotech whose work on messenger RNA led to the rapid creation of vaccines against Covid-19 in 2020. (Moderna actually got its start in 2013 with a $25 million investment by DARPA.)

VC had taken the risk of backing companies like Intel, Apple, Netscape, and Genentech. At first, VC was not a substitute for the sort of funding that long-term, capital-intensive businesses might require—that remained the preserve of deep-pocketed corporations like IBM, or the government. But with changes to America's pension laws, it became possible for institutional investors to allocate more to VC, creating a huge pool of capital that VCs could draw on to give startups access to something like permanent capital.

FROM HARDWARE TO SOFTWARE

The rise of VC in Silicon Valley is partly related to the nature of the tech itself. The arrival of software required a lot less capital: Microsoft was founded by two nerds with hardly any money. VC also came to prominence as tech companies became less dependent on government contracts, which led to a divergence of agendas between the companies and the military, as the Sematech fiasco made clear.

The rise of VC as a force of funding innovation also enabled the rise of the PC and the internet—two massive trends that caught the Japanese by surprise. It wasn't just that these were new innovations. It's that they required a synthesis of hardware with software that Japanese companies couldn't muster.

Why? First, much of Japan's prowess in the 1970s and 1980s was a consequence of its rebuilding effort rather than developing a culture of innovation.

Paul Krugman, in an influential article in 1994—published amid the peak of America's panic over Japanese competition—argued that Japan, like the Soviet Union of the 1950s, was very good at mobilizing resources. It educated its workforce, invested heavily in its infrastructure, and instead of letting its people become wealthy consumers, diverted its wealth into overseas lending and investment. Japan's growth was less about tech-driven efficiency and more about smart but one-off boosts to its capacity to grow.

"If there is a secret to Asian growth," Krugman wrote, "it is simply deferred gratification, the willingness to sacrifice current satisfaction for future gain."[13]

Second, its *keiretsu*-bureaucracy nexus, which proved so good at overtaking the US in consumer electronics and chips, was blind to new innovations. It was the old guard, companies like Fujitsu and NEC, that had MITI's ear, and they had no clue about what was brewing in Silicon Valley.

Even Sony was caught off guard. K.O. Chia, a veteran venture capitalist based in Hong Kong, says, "Sony was the first to call itself a 'lifestyle' company, but it couldn't manage the software side." He says Sony's hardware devices were never integrated, and that its software efforts always lagged the hardware. "Apple saw it," Chia said. "If Sony could have learned to manage software, there'd be no Apple, and there'd be no iPod."[14]

Third, although Japanese companies dominated consumer electronics and aspects of hardware, they could not match Intel's microprocessor. Perhaps had the PC not emerged, Intel would have faded into irrelevance, but it created a moat that no competitor could bridge. Other US semiconductor companies survived by ceding DRAM and other chips to the Japanese while following Intel into microprocessors.

This is not to say that Japanese companies failed. They were expert followers, and they largely achieved what they set out to accomplish.

It's just that the goalposts moved, and to keep up required a massive ecosystem that would link risk-taking VC and gutsy entrepreneurs out to make a lot of money.

JAPAN'S VC FAILURE

Why didn't Japan also develop a VC industry to nurture its own startups?

The first domestic VC was established in 1972 in Kyoto, a charming but economically marginalized city, whose elders looked to ARD as a model for revitalization. Their fund, Kyoto Enterprise Development, flopped over an overly bureaucratic investment committee and a paucity of Kyoto-based startups.

Later that year, Nomura Securities set up Japan Associated Finance Company (JAFCO), which would prove a success and remains today one of the country's biggest investment funds—but it eventually abandoned early-stage equity investing in favor of PE.

The domestic VC scene didn't begin to take off until the 1990s, in line with the dotcom boom in the US. By 2000 it recorded ¥1 trillion of assets. The Ministry of Economy, Trade and Industry (METI), MITI's successor, announced a plan to create 1,000 university spinoffs. Japan's universities boasted top-notch engineering and scientific research, and METI passed regulations to encourage these capable people to go into startups.

But the dotcom bust of 2001 decimated Japan's VC industry, whose asset size wouldn't recover until 2005.[15] Moreover, most of the IT and biotech startups emanating from universities were poorly managed. By 2008, Japan had 591 VC funds but, aside from JAFCO and a handful of others, they remained small and on average generated internal rates of return of 4.5 percent—well below US peers.

VC IN NAME ONLY

Japan has cutting-edge capabilities in robotics, supercomputing, healthcare, and other high-tech industries. It has a tradition of small-business creation. But it didn't develop an ecosystem to rival Silicon Valley, for three main reasons.

First of all, most VC funds, like JAFCO, were sponsored by investment banks and insurance companies, and staffed by people seconded from the parents. Most ended up operating as corporate VC, which meant they were investing to meet company objectives rather than for purely financial returns. The professionals staffing these funds then returned to the parent, rather than making their careers as venture capitalists.[16] This inexperience meant Japanese investors rarely got involved in a company's operations or provided advice or connections.

Second, these funds hardly counted as VC: more often, they disbursed capital as loans, not equity. This was for two reasons. The VCs themselves were usually capitalized by corporate parent debt, so they owed interest—and therefore they needed to match that with income. This limited their upside—no home runs here—so their appetite for risk was also capped. The other reason for debt was that the entrepreneurs themselves preferred it, because they didn't want to give away a lot of equity. They wanted to build family businesses they could pass on to the next generation.

Third, Japanese culture was antithetical to risky startups. Peter Brooke from TA Associates, still globe-trotting, set up a US-style VC fund in Japan in 1984, with a view to facilitating technology transfer. It failed: relations with his local partner soured, the language barrier was significant, and small companies couldn't operate independently of their big *keiretsu* customers. But the problem went deeper.

"Working for a small company was seen as a sign of failure," Brooke wrote. And for anyone brave enough to do so: "There was no culture of frank and direct communication." A US VC needed to conduct due diligence and ask tough questions, and it would expect the same from the founders it backed. But the culture in Japan was to avoid criticism so no one had to lose face.[17]

ISLAND MENTALITY

Although there was plenty of goodwill in Japan toward the idea of fostering VC and startups—including government support and corporate investments—the social environment was simply not conducive.

A big part of that environment was insularity. Japan was rich and boasted powerful corporations that attracted its best engineers, so its people didn't feel the need to work in the US. They didn't learn English. Very few foreigners tried to work in Japan, and those who did could never advance far. Japan's talent missed out on the informal networking in Silicon Valley, leaving their companies blindsided by the PC revolution and the internet.

For a time, Japan's rise in the 1970s and 1980s seemed unstoppable. But catch-up growth without a dynamic innovation machine would eventually sputter, particularly after the Japanese bubble burst, damning the economy to decades of retraction—a trend worsened by its aging demographic profile.

THE IPHONE CONQUERS JAPAN

Japan's loss of innovation was brought home in 2008 with the arrival of Apple's iPhone.

If there was one area where Japanese innovation should have won over the world, it was cellphones. Led by local telecom NTT DoCoMo, Japan was a decade or more ahead of Apple, and 20 years ahead of WeChat.

Japan's clam-shell cellphones came with GPS, games, TV, music, and video downloads. They supported videophone, mobile payments, contactless sharing of data, and voice or fingerprint identification. Japanese phones were at the heart of consumer lifestyles.[18] The iPhone didn't offer these; its camera couldn't focus on the ubiquitous QR codes used to launch websites. It didn't even support emojis!

All the iPhone had was its touchscreen face, the popularity of the

Apple brand—and the incredibly ambitious SoftBank as its carrier network.

SoftBank's CEO, Masayoshi Son, was already a legend by this point, having made his fortune with a big investment in Alibaba, among other things. SoftBank, his holding company, had gone into the Japanese telecom business by acquiring the number-three player in 2006. Lagging NTT DoCoMo and KDDI, Son was eager to help his friend Steve Jobs—and find a way to boost SoftBank Telecom.

Son convinced Jobs to tweak the iPhone to suit the Japanese market—and Jobs made this rare accommodation, even adding emojis. But the key was brute force. SoftBank blanketed Japan with TV ads, print ads, and pricing giveaways. Son pitched the iPhone as cutting edge, even though in Japan it was an inferior product. The blitz worked, and by 2010, three out of four smartphones in Japan were made by Apple.[19]

VC: MORE IMPORTANT THAN EVER

When Tokyo hosted the Winter Olympics in 2021, visitors noticed that Japan's digital services were decidedly old-fashioned. The nation that gave us the *shinkansen* (high-speed trains) was still working on clunky drop-down menus, forms to be filled out on paper—or by fax. Only 7.5 percent of government procedures can be conducted online, and the paperwork is so regressive that it hampered Japan's Covid-19 vaccine rollout.[20]

It's not all bad news. Foreign VCs in the 2010s have done well in Japan, particularly in video games. The aging population has made the *keiretsu* reconsider the merits of lifetime employment, and a younger crop of entrepreneurs has emerged that wants to master market forces instead of putting up with hidebound corporate life. There is also a large domestic stock market with both the main board in Tokyo as well as several smaller bourses aimed at startups.

In 2020, Japanese IPOs had their best year since the 1999 bubble burst, with investors eager to snap up the latest tech names. Companies in AI, image recognition, and internet-of-things development showcased a new breed of VC-backed startups. Of the 94 companies that went public that year, 70 percent went to Mothers, one of the startup-friendly listing venues.[21]

But 2020 was a bubbly year for tech startups worldwide, and Japan's entire IPO raises totaled $3.3 billion—a measly number compared to the $51 billion raised in Hong Kong or the $181 billion in New York.

Chalmer Johnson's "developmental state" had fallen into a state of arrested development. Japan still has incredible talent, powerful companies, and areas of cutting-edge technology. It also now has a more resilient, if still small, VC industry that is supporting startups. It will need to rely more on VC, particularly VC's global ties, to keep pace with the next wave of innovation. But for now, those waves are not emerging from Japan. They are to be found in the US—and China.

9

CHINA: THE AWAKENING

BY the mid-1990s, pockets of venture capital had been established in a handful of places outside the United States: Israel, Taiwan, Singapore. In each case the government played a catalytic role.

Israel's Yozma project jumpstarted venture investing in Israeli startups. Taiwan and Singapore both sought to climb the value chain, evolving beyond assembly of simple electronics.

Taiwan lured back talented citizens working in the US while the government played midwife to the establishment of the chip foundry industry.

Singapore's attempt at building semiconductor companies was also in full swing, although this would eventually fail. The government, however, focused on making the island nation a hub for multinational companies and for capital formation.

These promising moves drew a few daring venture company funds in the US, such as Walden and DFJ. But it was, to say the least, early days. Israel and Taiwan were too small to be more than interesting auxiliaries to Silicon Valley; Singapore was a nascent financial center but lacked an entrepreneurial culture.

DOTCOM BOOM AND BUST

Meanwhile the consumer internet economy in the US had gotten ahead of itself. Software companies overtook hardware makers as the technology leaders, and by the early 1990s the Japanese threat had been vanquished. A boom in funding and runaway valuations, along with loads of hype, generated the dotcom era.

In the US, venture funding became easy to secure. Retail investors poured into tech stocks. Loss-making dotcoms went public on grandiose visions, not on sound revenues: by October 1999, the market cap of the 199 internet stocks tracked by Morgan Stanley was $450 billion but their combined annual revenues were a mere $21 billion; the sector's collective losses were $6.2 billion.[1] VCs regarded profits as a barrier to getting a better valuation that would lead to a blockbuster exit via IPO.

The internet hype peaked in early 2000 when 17 dotcom companies bought ads they couldn't afford for the Super Bowl. Two months later, in March, a teetering market finally collapsed on news that a US court found Microsoft guilty of anticompetitive behavior. Markets fell; by the end of 2000, dotcoms began to go out of business and most internet stocks had declined in value by 75 percent from their highs, wiping out $1.75 trillion in value.

In the US, the tech bust set in motion a general market downturn, which was accelerated by rising interest rates, accounting scandals, revelations of fraud at Enron, and in the following year, the September 11 terrorist attacks.

The prolonged agony caused many venture companies to close shop. Funding for startups evaporated and many startups went bust once their funding ran out. Silicon Valley had never experienced such a financial shock—although those startups that scraped through, such as Amazon and eBay, would help define the new era of technology. Indeed, only 48 percent of dotcom companies founded in 1996 or later survived the market turmoil[2]—if they had enough VC cash already banked, and enough of a real business to hang tough.

The boom had other benefits, particularly in infrastructure: telecom companies invested heavily in laying fiber optic cable and wireless networks in expectations of internet growth. After the bust, much of this capacity went unused—providing cheap bandwidth for the next generation of software companies.

THE DOTCOM BOOM IN ASIA

The emerging tech hubs of Asia were not immune. New stock markets had emerged, modeled after Nasdaq to attract tech companies, including Hong Kong's Growth Enterprise Market, and the DAQs: Kosdaq in Korea, Mesdaq in Malaysia, Sesdaq in Singapore. The region's investors were just as tech-crazy as Americans, and they got scorched just as badly.

The one place that got hit hardest, though, had no "DAQ." Its primary bourse had only been operating for a decade. This was China.

China was just emerging from decades of self-imposed isolation and the tragedy of the 1989 Tiananmen Square crackdown. It developed a small but enthusiastic coterie of internet entrepreneurs. A decade after Tiananmen, a few of China's internet darlings struck it big time with listings on Nasdaq. China was caught up in internet fever, but the 2000 bust didn't just kill a bunch of companies: it nearly wiped out its entire internet sector.

China's story also began with VC, but VCs in Silicon Valley had no interest in China. Anyone paying attention knew that China was going to be a goldmine for investors, but financiers in Silicon Valley were focused on easy wins close to home. To them, China was an impoverished land of peasants in Mao suits.

China's one billion-plus population—brimming with maverick entrepreneurs hungry for success—and its emergence on the global stage was a once-in-a-lifetime chance to get super rich. Taiwan and Singapore were tiny opportunities in comparison. Indeed, it would be the VC pioneers in these peripheral markets that took the first steps toward investing in Chinese startups.

TWO BOMBS, ONE SATELLITE

China wasn't the tech wasteland it may have appeared to be.

Mao Zedong was quick to link the survival of the Communist Party regime to technology and innovation in the military sphere. Despite 1960s China being a poor, rural, isolated country, the Party under Mao succeeded in developing nuclear bombs and missiles.

Under the slogan "Two Bombs, One Satellite," Mao relied on mass mobilization and a marshalling of what resources the state possessed—plus leveraging plenty of Soviet know-how—to produce a Chinese atomic bomb in 1964.[3]

The political and organizational management of this project was copied to achieve later state-led science and technology goals, including the Shenzhou manned space flights and landing rovers on the far side of the Moon.

Mao gave China the bomb, but otherwise his rule was terrible for science and innovation. The country founded a semiconductor research lab in 1960 and produced transistor radios, and in 1965 Chinese engineers figured out how to make an IC.[4] But Mao's radicalism and the Cultural Revolution he launched made it impossible to attract foreign investment, which wouldn't have been welcomed anyway.

Mao died in 1976, by which point the rest of North Asia was firmly on a course of state-led development, prosperity, and integration into trade and technology flows. China was still reeling from self-inflicted wounds such as the Great Leap Forward and the Cultural Revolution. But Mao had left his successors an opening, by thawing relations with the US.

DENG XIAOPING'S PIVOT

Deng Xiaoping came to power in 1979 determined to redirect Mao's military-focused technological base toward developmental goals. He waged a long campaign to transform military research into quasi-corporate organizations.

Once the People's Republic of China was founded in 1949, the Party nationalized all industry and agriculture, banned all private enterprise, and introduced centralized planning.

In some regards, the "Two Bombs, One Satellite" campaign wasn't different from what the US had done during the Second World War: a mass mobilization of scientific and state-led resources to harness technology, to win a hot war, and then a cold one against the Soviet Union.

But the US success was clearly based on a decentralized ecosystem of startups, university research, and corporate labs, with a freewheeling culture that welcomed global talent. The US military was the biggest customer in the earliest days of semiconductor companies like Fairchild, and federal government funding supported universities. But these private entities were also free to pursue their own commercial goals, which gradually took precedence over government projects.

Deng's developmental goals sought to replicate this success as he began to liberalize Chinese markets and businesses. Starting in 1982, he launched science and technology programs that leveraged the national security infrastructure built by Mao and aimed to lay down foundations of science and research. These included basic research projects funded by the Ministry of Science and Technology and the National Natural Science Foundation, while the strategic weapons program was oriented to high-tech R&D.[5]

But state infrastructure wasn't enough: China needed new ways to foster commercialization and innovation. Deng set up several programs, including ones to attract Chinese working abroad, especially in Silicon Valley. And there was something called Torch.

TORCH

Launched by the Ministry of Science and Technology in 1988, Torch's mission was to foster high-tech entrepreneurialism. It was, in effect, a startup incubator and accelerator program. Of all the Deng-era science and technology initiatives, Torch was given the most bureaucratic leeway, so it could keep pace with the explosion of private-sector growth galvanizing the country.

Torch's objective was to recreate Silicon Valley-like clusters of technology and innovation. This was hugely ambitious, considering at the time only Taiwan, Israel, and Singapore had attempted this with any success. The question was whether China could create indigenous clusters that would become sustainably competitive.

Under Torch, China created dozens of industrial parks, the most important of which was Zhongguancun Science Park in Beijing—which is now recognized as "China's Silicon Valley." Other parks around the country were established with a particular focus, such as medical devices or integrated circuits. Shenzhen, for example, was selected for telecommunications.

These parks were usually associated with nearby universities and local businesses, and many of them established startup incubator programs, offering workspace and access to technology developed by universities in return for seed funding. By 2011, there were over 1,000 incubators across China, hosting nearly 60,000 companies.[6]

Torch was designed to generate companies that would attract private investing. By the 1990s the first venture capitalists had set up shop. They were looking for startups: the government was incubating them. Some of China's biggest technology companies emerged from Torch-backed incubators, including Huawei (telecoms), Lenovo (consumer electronics), and Suntech Power (solar panels).

Although universities did foster the first private startups, the engineers who worked at companies like Huawei did not go off to create their own startups.[7] Whereas Taiwanese companies from UMC to Acer generated successive waves of entrepreneurs, the university-tied companies were too wedded to government relationships. The ones that survived usually did so by becoming conglomerates, rather than specialized tech companies. The lesson is that when the state tries to drive tech business, picking winners and losers, it doesn't lead to a startup ecosystem.

EARLY "VC" IN CHINA

But authorities, aware of the failure but not sure why, decided it had to do with the lack of private funding. The laws didn't recognize anything akin to venture capital. So the science ministry created two types of licensed VC: those funded by local governments, and those funded by universities.

It was the mid-1990s, and VC in China was still perceived to be a form of government funding. This evolved from local initiatives to national ones: in 1999 the State Council—the chief administrative arm of the government—launched the Innofund (Innovation Fund for Technology Based Firms), the first of many state-backed funds designed to finance tech companies in preferred sectors.

State-backed venture investing had a poor track record. Innofund followed a previous attempt at central-government venture investing: in 1986 the Ministry of Finance had backed a "China New Technology Venture Investment Corporation," which flopped.

China's talented engineers and hard-driving entrepreneurs were being let down by the country's poor, barely functioning capital markets and banking system. The Shanghai Stock Exchange and the Shenzhen Stock Exchange were only opened in 1990, with the government deciding what companies could list, and when. The government likewise controlled the banks, be it at the central, provincial, or city level, and banks existed to lend to SOEs. Lenders had no understanding of credit assessment or risk.

This lack of understanding of finance extended to VCs and their backers. Managers didn't know how to weigh up a company. There was no concept of fiduciary responsibility or corporate governance, and only the haziest idea of limited liability. Shareholders wanted high returns but at zero risk. There was no legal system to back up a contract. Corruption always lurked. As a result, most Torch funding went to existing state-affiliated companies, not private startups.[8] These were VCs in name only.

The biggest problem for a would-be investor was the lack of exits.

The stock markets existed for government-controlled companies, not for private startups.

CHINAVEST

But in 1990s China, the rewards were too great. If anything, the barriers could justify outsized payouts for those brave—and smart—enough to figure out how to work around absent regulation and the weak financial system.

Two Americans working in China set up the first private indigenous funds. One was Bob Theleen, an investment banker who had been visiting China since the 1970s. In 1981 he set up ChinaVest in Shanghai, the first onshore VC funded by global institutional investors.

Theleen became an insider, leveraging his way to become a director of Beijing Enterprises, an SOE that cobbled together the capital's utilities and infrastructure assets to get listed in Hong Kong. Over the next three decades, ChinaVest would allocate $500 million to over 50 startups. Theleen died in 2021, but ChinaVest continues to operate under the guidance of his wife, Jenny Hsiu.

IDG CAPITAL

Another American, Patrick McGovern, was a media entrepreneur. He had founded International Data Corporation in 1964, in Massachusetts, which became a publisher of techie magazines like *Computerworld* and *PC World*. On a visit to Beijing in 1978, he caught the China bug. He returned in 1980 and, with government blessings, forged a publishing joint venture to bring *Computerworld* to China.

IDG grew quickly, expanding into all kinds of publishing deals. These included representing other US brands like *National Geographic*, but media is a broad term that can include entertainment, including games and the internet. McGovern wasn't done. In 1992, he set up IDG Capital in Boston as a VC firm, and the following year it entered China.

Being the top foreign media baron gave McGovern's venture business a unique network. IDG Capital would go on to become one of the biggest VCs in China, with early-stage or Series A round investments in iconic tech companies such as Baidu, Tencent, Ctrip, Xiaomi, Meituan, and Qihoo 360.

"These were the early internet companies that transformed online e-commerce and gaming," says Simon Ho, who is today IDG Capital's chief financial officer in Shanghai.[9] "Partnering with them gave us access to more entrepreneurs. And if an entrepreneur had a side business, we'd also partner with them."

Ho adds, "The IDG brand helped companies because we're from the US, so we can bring capital and an overseas network to them, to help companies expand their business in the US."

But by Silicon Valley standards, IDG Capital was small, and there was a limit to the capital it could deploy. Its model relied on capital from US-based LPs, not Chinese investors. It would later partner with Accel, a top-tier Silicon Valley VC, to share deal flow.

McGovern died in 2014 but the IDG Capital he left behind is a major player. In 2019, IDG was the third-largest investor in Chinese unicorns, with 25 under its belt—behind Tencent and Sequoia Capital, according to The Hurun Report.[10] It's gotten even bigger since. In 2022, at a time when international venture funding was halting new China allocations, IDG Capital raised $900 million for a new fund to back Chinese startups. By now it had invested in over 1,300 companies, with 400 successful exits.[11]

WALDEN INTERNATIONAL

But such success was not obvious in 1990s China—or rather, the idea of success was there, but the path to achieve it was paved with mystery and high risk.

Other than a few maverick Americans with existing businesses in China, the entry of VC came from the pioneers in Taiwan and Singapore.

One of these was Peter Liu, who left Walden International to set up his own venture business, WI Harper, which he founded in 1993 to invest in the US and Asia. Liu was literally born to make this shift: not only was he the great-nephew of Taiwan mandarin KT Lee, but he also had family connections in mainland China: he had, in fact, been born in Beijing but his family fled the Communist takeover to Taiwan. Those relations were now asking him to bring Silicon Valley-style venture investing to China.

"The Lius are a seventh-generation family in Beijing," Peter Liu said. He had a cousin, Liu Zhongli, who was finance minister in 1992. "I have given him a lot of advice. I told him venture capitalists and technology pioneers need incentives."[12]

In an environment in which *guanxi* (relationships) are required, Peter Liu had them in spades. Relationships, however, may open doors, but they don't deliver deals. He began by courting the ministries he'd need to back his desire to bring private investment to China. Even so, navigating China required exercising different muscles.

"China is bureaucratic," Liu says. "You can meet the top guy and he'd endorse us, but then you must deal with all of his subordinates. It takes a lot of time to get to know everyone."

Sometimes it didn't matter what the top of a government agency agreed. Liu says the rank and file bristled at the notion of sharing profits with the private sector. "It needed a lot of hand-holding—a lot of wining, dining, and exchanging gifts," he says.

Liu initially brought WI Harper to Shanghai, but when a deputy mayor he was courting as an investor insisted on taking control of the fund, Liu immediately closed shop and reopened in Beijing. "My US partners could never understand why," he says.

WI Harper, like other VCs in Silicon Valley, was backing dotcom companies. Liu struck gold with a US internet company called CommerceOne. It was an early iteration of a B2B e-commerce company. It wasn't a true online platform connecting buyers and sellers—the platform model didn't exist yet. But CommerceOne used online auctions to connect businesses with suppliers.

Liu hadn't heard of B2B e-commerce before, but he liked the idea and pumped money into it over multiple rounds. The company had a massive IPO in July 1999 but would end up a casualty of the dotcom crash, closing its doors in 2004. But in that time, it would seed ideas from unexpected places.

ALIBABA'S ORIGINS

In 1998, one year before the IPO, Liu visited a young entrepreneur in Hangzhou named Jack Ma. Ma had been an English teacher who parlayed his language skills into a visit to the US, where he had discovered the internet.

He was determined to bring this marvelous invention to China—this was 1995 and there were no Chinese-language pages on the World Wide Web. Ma bootstrapped a company called China Yellow Pages, working with software developers and translators in the US to build those pages while Ma tried to convince Chinese companies that they should advertise on this newfangled thing to attract global customers.

Peter Liu says Jack Ma got the idea for business-facing e-commerce from CommerceOne. "He was just getting started by selling ads in the online yellow pages. It was the first global trading search engine. CommerceOne led to Jack Ma."

Jack Ma didn't take WI Harper's money, however. He wasn't ready, and like most entrepreneurs unfamiliar with VC, he couldn't imagine giving away equity in his business.

CHINA YELLOW PAGES

Building out the business was a hard slog as there were still no direct dial-up connections in China, but as the major cities began to build basic digital infrastructure, China Yellow Pages could make some money.

The internet was taking off in China. The portals Sohu.com and Sina.com had launched in 1998. The first Chinese online gaming company, Shanda, got started in 1999.

But Jack Ma got muscled out of business. China Yellow Pages

instantly attracted hundreds of copycats, and unfortunately one of those was Hangzhou Telecom, which had deep pockets and political connections. They bought China Yellow Pages, and Ma, unhappy, didn't stick around for long. He experimented with a new startup in Beijing that was owned by the government, but that too didn't work. Ma was restless to find a way to become an internet entrepreneur—on his own terms.

He launched Alibaba from his home in 1999 with a group of employees from his previous businesses. Ma had the idea of leveraging internet ads for China's private companies, not its SOEs or well-connected conglomerates.

That meant he'd need funding. An internet business was expensive to get off the ground. Ma knew now that money alone wasn't what mattered: who gave it to you—that's what mattered.

Ma had an innate showmanship. He had known how to get attention, like by winning the contract to take *China Daily*, the government-controlled newspaper, online. Plenty of local investors pitched him, but he declined. Ma needed investors that could help take him places.

ALIBABA'S FIRST ANGEL: GOLDMAN SACHS

In the heated dotcom environment, the biggest investors were Goldman Sachs and Morgan Stanley. The two US investment banks were not known for venture capital. But at this stage in China, there were no defined lines within financial structures, and almost zero professional VCs. There was just a landgrab, and the two rival banks were taking Sina and Sohu to list in New York.

Goldman has a unit called Principal Investment Area (PIA), which is its in-house investment unit. PIA enjoys a broad remit, able to invest in anything the partners think will make money.

Shirley Lin was a partner at PIA scouring China for deals. It was gritty work, sifting through thousands of business pitches in an exciting but opaque and raw environment. She led deals in the three portals, Sohu, Sina, and NetEase, as well as in hardware companies like Semiconductor Manufacturing International Corporation (SMIC)—at the time one of dozens of chip startups, but today China's semiconductor champion.

Amid this chaos she met with Jack Ma. China Yellow Pages was nothing special, but she took to its founder, who had vision, pizazz, and acumen. He was also a true local but one who spoke good English.

Ma wanted to raise $5 million for 10 percent of Alibaba. In Lin he met a far more experienced and hardnosed negotiator. He ended up with his $5 million—for 50 percent of the company.[13] Although he later felt buyer's remorse, Ma knew that he needed the global cachet of a name like Goldman to take the business to the next few levels.

Lin's partners were wary of the deal, though. For a group like Goldman $5 million was too small, the payoff was too distant, and Alibaba didn't have anything unique about it, on paper. The investment was signed on October 27, 1999, with Goldman reducing its principal in this tiny startup, bringing in Fidelity Growth Partners Asia to take up the slack: from the get-go, the firm began to hedge its bet.

A few months later the dotcom crash began to wipe out Chinese internet companies, and almost took Alibaba with it. Once Lin left Goldman in 1993, the partners were eager to wash their hands of the startup. In 2004 they sold out completely, netting a $22 million, a 7× return. Not bad!

But Goldman misread some pretty obvious tea leaves. No sooner had the ink dried on its investment than Jack Ma sat down with a new suitor: Masayoshi Son.

ENTER MASA

Son was the hard-driving founder of SoftBank. He blended venture investing with SoftBank's corporate ambitions to lead the internet revolution. In later years, he changed VC by creating huge funds designed to take late-stage startups to market at huge valuations, but in the 1990s and early 2000s he knew how to turbocharge small but dynamic tech startups.

Masayoshi Son—"Masa"—was a Korean-born Japanese entrepreneur. Being a Korean in Japan made him an outsider, a status that Son decided to own instead of shun. From a young age, he ditched the sanitized Japanese surname his family had adopted. He would be a Son—a son of Japan.

After studying at Berkeley, where he made a bucket of money selling video game machines to college hangouts, he founded SoftBank to distribute software to all of Japan's biggest corporations. This was 1981, when Japan Inc. was riding high but its giants were ignoring the software and PC revolution.

But Son was a hustler and a gambler. He had a vision of bringing the internet to Japan, and he didn't care how. In 1985 Tokyo decided to break up its telecommunications monopoly. Son, ignoring his board of directors, ploughed SoftBank's money into acquiring one of the spinouts and investing heavily in data networks.

Ten years later, Son got the internet bug. He had been elected to the board of Cisco in 1995, which gave him a bird's eye view of networking on top of his expertise in software. "Masa then was one of the few people who could see what was happening globally," recalls Gary Rieschel, who worked at SoftBank's venture arm before founding his own VC firm, Qiming Venture Partners.[14] "He knew Yahoo! would be big in Japan."

Son wooed Jerry Yang and David Filo, the co-founders of Yahoo!, an early search engine in the US. SoftBank began acquiring shares and by late 1996 owned more than 30 percent of the company.[15] Son would oversee Yahoo! open shop in Japan, with a view to the coming integration of cellphones and the internet.

This was the background to Son visiting China to find internet entrepreneurs. By now he was the richest man in Asia. Morgan Stanley bankers eagerly lined up the cream of the crop in China's high-tech sectors, including the founders of Sina and Sohu, to curry favor with SoftBank.

SOFTBANK: GO FOR GROWTH

Son and Ma hit it off: game knows game. Ma didn't need money, as he had just sewn up $5 million from the Goldman-led consortium. Son pushed him to take $30 million for 30 percent, which would be enough to give SoftBank de facto control. In return he dangled a vision before Jack Ma: don't be the biggest in China. Be bigger than Yahoo!.

Ma bargained Son down to $20 million for a smaller stake that would leave him in control, but the die was cast.[16]

In the US, software had already become the darling of venture investing, eclipsing hardware. It led to the rise of a new class of entrepreneur: founders who were young and internet-savvy, rather than experienced technicians steeped in transistors and microprocessors. A software founder could grow a scalable business out of their house; a semiconductor foundry needed a multi-billion dollar factory.

Most of all, software companies didn't have to be in Silicon Valley. The talent could be a young team pretty much anywhere—so long as they had a market to scale into. This is why the US continued to attract the most global talent: the US offered both a mature ecosystem and a big consumer base.

China, with its vast population, entrepreneurial spirit, engineering chops, and (almost) anything-goes business environment, was the only place in the world that could provide the same scalable opportunity as the US—if it could get right some key problems around finance and markets.

But China wasn't the same as the US. As Shirley Lin had discovered, there were tons of startups all doing the same thing. Even Son hedged his bet: after sealing the deal with Jack Ma, that same day he met another Chinese internet startup called SparkIce and made the same deal, $20 million for a 20 percent stake. SparkIce failed but Alibaba succeeded.

"There were dozens of startups but there is only one Jack Ma," Rieschel says. "Masa could see that e-commerce would be significant in China, either selling from there or within the Chinese economy."

There was also at the time only one Masayoshi Son, urging

founders to take bigger sums of capital in order to rapidly scale. Son would later expand this notion to late-stage investing, along with hedge funds such as Tiger Global and Coatue Capital. This would end disastrously with the SoftBank Vision Fund, a $100 billion fund launched in 2017, which we'll look at in our closing chapter.

But SoftBank's influence reached back to early-stage funding rounds. In 2000, Son formalized his interest in China's tech future by setting up SB China Venture Capital (SBCVC), led by Chauncey Shey, who had been Son's right-hand man during his meetings with Alibaba and other startups. It remains a major investor in Chinese tech, telecom, media, and healthcare companies.

"Internet adoption in China was very rapid," Rieschel says. "There was a rapacious desire to get online. The energy in its internet cafes was phenomenal."

NO EXIT

The Goldman PIA team ignored this when it decided to cash out of Alibaba. Although Alibaba was struggling in the wake of the dotcom crash, it survived thanks to SoftBank's capital. The penny dropped in New York when, a year after Goldman exited, Yahoo!'s Jerry Yang invested $1 billion into Alibaba, for a 40 percent stake.

Alibaba wouldn't IPO until 2014, listing on the NYSE, raising $25 billion—the largest IPO in world history. Goldman was one of the bankers, collecting a fee, but it was no longer a shareholder.

When Lin was Alibaba's first angel investor, however, there would have been good cause for skepticism. Not just about Alibaba, but any tech company in China. The foreign investment scene in China at the time was a messy free-for-all.

In the US, the industry had long since divided itself into neat lines: angel investing for seed-stage startups, VC for startups with the beginnings of a product and market fit, and at the bigger, more mature end, PE—which was focused on restructuring existing companies, usually through leveraged buyouts (taking on debt to acquire a company).

But the finance markets in China were too immature, so angels, VCs, and PE got blurred. At this time, a $5 million deal was considered big, and it didn't matter what people called it.

Leveraged buyouts didn't exist in China—no matter what a contract might say, no CEO was going to accept foreign control, and there was no legal system for foreigners to lean on. Even VCs found it difficult to explain to a founder that they would have to relinquish one-third to half of their equity to accept foreign money.

This made China much harder to navigate than Taiwan, but the rewards were also going to be far greater—if foreigners could learn how to make investing work.

"The fundamental problem with investing into any private company, whether it was through VC or PE, was the lack of an exit strategy," says Stuart Schonberger, a managing director at Beijing-based PE firm CDH Investments, one of the first Chinese PE firms, founded in 1998.[17] Without a path to an IPO, investors weren't going to generate the kind of returns they expected for such high risks.

The other potential exit was a strategic sale of the business, but China's market was so dominated by SOEs that there was little domestic M&A activity. On top of that, foreign investors in a business—be it a startup or a restructuring—were constantly surprised in China by the ability of multiple domestic copycats to appear almost overnight. This complicated efforts to sell companies because it was hard to make them stand out.

LEGAL PERSON SHARES

But IPOs in China were also off the table.

Of course, the fact that Communist China had stock markets was already quite novel. Deng Xiaoping realized the country needed private markets to guide its economic reforms. But he was not about to let finance run free of Party control.

The stock markets in Shanghai and Shenzhen were opened for the purpose of listing SOEs or large private conglomerates that the

Party nonetheless could influence. The government dictated which companies could list and when.

Moreover, the government would not allow Chinese companies to be majority owned by foreigners. Anyone entering the market had to do so through joint ventures. This was a hurdle for overseas investors, but as we'll see, they found ways around it.

A bigger challenge was ideological. The critical element to allowing stock markets in a Communist country was the government's decree that "the people" must own these assets. The government established two types of shares: common stocks, similar to what traded in other markets; and Legal Person Shares, which were meant to represent public ownership. Any restructuring or new listing had to convert about 80 percent of equity into Legal Person Shares, but they were not tradable.

Legal Person Shares were only phased out starting in 2008, so for a long time, China's stock market was illiquid, with limited free float (the portion of a company's equity available to trade). This meant that domestic investors could not get rewarded via an IPO: even if their company was approved for a listing, they couldn't sell most of their shares. Meanwhile, the small supply of common stock—what became known as "A Shares"—traded like crazy. Domestic VC and PE investors could only watch jealously as the bulk of their investments sat inert while the markets boomed.

An early generation of Western financiers tried to take IPOs offshore. They attempted to buy majority stakes via a special purpose vehicle in an offshore haven such as the Cayman Islands. But these were Chinese companies, with local managers who were shut out of the soaring valuations of the offshore company, which could IPO or sell overseas. Local managers were being told to work hard to make foreigners rich.

The result? The management walked out and formed a new company, and the foreigners found themselves owning an empty shell. Financial games didn't work when investors weren't backing company management—and so foreigners got justly punished for violating this core tenet of VC.

"It was China that got tagged as a 'Wild West' by foreigners," says Schonberger, "but it was the foreigners behaving like cowboys."

The situation wasn't working for China, either. The government had established stock markets to help companies raise money, so they didn't have to depend on government handouts or loans. The government also wanted foreign shareholders to inject better governance and technology, and help Chinese companies become more competitive. It was already discovering that Mao-style mobilizations didn't work with technologies like semiconductors.

CHINA FAILS AT CHIPS

China's industrial policies have had mixed success. Since Mao, the state has thrown resources at many strategic industries. Most of these efforts are hobbled by competition between central and provincial governments, corruption, and misallocation of capital to SOEs. But in areas such as telecommunications, the strategy paid off, helping establish national champions that advanced homegrown technology and growth.

One of the first areas of focus was semiconductors. From 1956, led by the State Council, China launched a series of initiatives—factories, university labs—to make chips. Initially, China's level of sophistication, while low, was probably ahead of Japan, Taiwan, or South Korea.[18] But China's state-run system hampered the diffusion of knowledge that is vital to establishing a technology cluster. The Cultural Revolution of 1965–75 put a stop to any progress.

Under Deng, the State Council attempted to revive China's semiconductor industry, with a strategy to import secondhand manufacturing technology and to consolidate research into a handful of factories. The approach failed, however. By the mid-1980s, outsiders judged Chinese chips to be 10 to 15 years out of date.

In the 1990s, the government allowed chip factories to enter joint ventures with foreigners, but these efforts likewise failed. Meanwhile, China's growing economy made it an increasingly large consumer of chips: in 1995, China made up only 2 percent of the global chips market, but by 2005 it was 25 percent.[19] This would invigorate future efforts to develop a homegrown chips industry—one backed by private capital.

GOING MOBILE

In the meantime, however, China was leapfrogging the developed world in mobile telecommunications.

"China in the 1990s needed infrastructure," says K.O. Chia, president of the Hong Kong Venture Capital Association, whom we met in Chapter Eight. "Just like the US in the 1800s needed railroads."[20]

The People's Liberation Army owned all the bandwidth, but Deng was determined to liberalize the industry. According to Chia, Beijing was advised by the World Bank and other experts to lay cables and build telephone exchanges, and recreate America's infrastructure.

But this was an expensive proposition. In the US, cable was laid along roads; China hadn't built highways yet. Instead, China invested in wireless technology. This was regarded as a poor man's, retrograde option. The US, Europe, and Japan had their separate standards so there wasn't a clear roadmap for China to follow. "But this meant China could leapfrog the others," Chia says.

At the time, the focus wasn't on overtaking the West, but just getting a basic phone service up and running. Cellphones were clunky and slow. The best available in China was 2G, or second-generation telephony—but it worked, and it enabled the first text messaging, called Short Message Service (SMS).

China began by buying cellphones from foreign companies like Motorola and Nokia, while Ericsson and Siemens helped build the networks. Even migrant factory workers could afford to send an SMS, whereas placing a call via a landline was prohibitively expensive, and no one owned a PC.

EMBRACING SMS

K.O. Chia says China's tech story found its unique path by embracing mobile early. Chia, a Malaysian Chinese, was a hardware engineer specializing in microwave-length communications. He became a product manager at HP, where he learned how to take products from an idea on a blueprint to the market, first in Scotland and then the US. In 1984, HP sent him to Asia.

"If the job had been in Silicon Valley I would have stayed in the US," he says, "but they wanted me in Colorado Springs, and after Scotland, I didn't want to be in cold weather."

Once in Asia, Chia jumped to Apple to help it launch the Macintosh PC, navigating between the wants of corporates in California and consumers in Asia. But in 1991, Chia joined a startup called Premisys Communications to run Asia operations.

Premisys was an OEM, the type of company making components for others' end products. Premisys was a US company backed by VCs including Walden and Vertex. This gave Chia his first experience of a VC-backed startup, which IPO'd successfully in 1995, giving its investors a handsome payoff. Walden's Lip-Bu Tan recruited Chia to represent Walden in Asia ex-Taiwan.

With his diverse background, Chia soon came to realize that China's mobile story was going to be huge. "From 1995 to 2000, SMS took off in China, while the rest of the world was still laying cable," he says.

"SMS-based services have no potential in the US. But when VCs rushed to Asia, they didn't understand the context of wireless business. This is what created the split between how the internet would develop in China versus the West. People in the US thought China should follow in their footsteps and didn't realize that China was leapfrogging them."

SMS led to messaging and—crucially—mobile payments. These would be the backbone of China's consumer internet in the 2010s. Later, when the rest of the world would marvel at companies like Alibaba and Tencent, they would see businesses transacting vast amounts over proprietary mobile networks at mind-boggling scale. But, Chia says, "Mobile payments in China aren't an overnight phenomenon. It took time."

But now, as mobile services and handsets became increasingly affordable, Chinese companies such as Huawei (infrastructure) and Xiaomi (handsets) can upgrade their networks with relative ease. Today China has already shifted from 4G to 5G, which represents a huge shift in latency (the time it takes to send and receive a message) and up to 100 times faster download speeds, and its leading companies are already fixed on 6G.

That has implications for breakthroughs in AI, autonomous vehicles, virtual-reality applications, and military intelligence and communications—any environment that relies on devices to share data with one another.

In the US, 5G rollouts have been hampered by poor infrastructure and an uncompetitive market dominated by AT&T and Verizon, but consumers' lifestyles are also less tied into their cellphones (believe it or not). Today, Chinese lives are lived within the mobile ecosystems of Alibaba and Tencent's WeChat: food, transport, finances, entertainment, shopping, gaming—everything revolves around these ecosystems. The same is true for small businesses, which rely on mobile services for everything from ordering supplies to managing their working capital.

"America is far behind in almost every dimension of 5G while other nations—including China—race ahead," warned former Google CEO Eric Schmidt and Harvard professor Graham Allison in a recent *Wall Street Journal* op-ed.[21]

RED CHIPS

Although mobile and SMS would provide the foundations for a tech boom, fostering startups still faced the financial problem of Legal Person Shares and the lack of a viable IPO market.

This led to a pair of innovations: the Red Chip, and an offshore-ownership structure called Variable Interest Entity (VIE). The first companies to use these were state-owned telecoms—and VC-backed internet portals.

China's leapfrog began with the commercialization of its technology companies, which was made possible by reforming the financial rewards for its entrepreneurs and investors.

At the SOE level, investment bankers developed Red Chips: Chinese companies with some degree of state ownership that incorporated in Hong Kong, where they could list. Red Chips began to appear in the early 1990s, and Hong Kong investors were eager to purchase these stocks to participate in the economic boom unleashed by Deng Xiaoping.

Until the 1990s, Hong Kong's capital markets focused on Asian arms of European businesses, with old-school British merchant banks handling most deals. But now the city was taken over by "Red Chip fever."

The trend is associated most closely with Francis Leung Pak-to, a Hong Kong banker. From 1988 to 2008, Leung and his partner, Philip Tose, ran a boutique investment bank based in Hong Kong called Peregrine Investment Holdings. They rode the Red Chip trend all the way, turning Peregrine into Asia's biggest dealmaker.

Their deals included Beijing Enterprises, which involved mashing together a variety of assets owned by the city's government and listing them in Hong Kong in 1997, for $240 million.[22]

For China's government, Red Chips were only partly to help amass offshore fortunes. The real benefit was to transform the incentives within SOEs once they were incorporated as offshore, public companies.

SOEs proved impervious to reform, however, and minority shareholders had little real power to effect change. Lip-Bu Tan initially considered investing in SOEs because they were the only game in town, but he quickly realized their managers weren't interested in submitting their empires to the whims of private market forces.

Walden began to back private companies wherever Tan could find them. For example, he invested in Newave, China's first private semiconductor company, founded by Howard Yang, a US-educated returnee from Silicon Valley. The company didn't IPO but it did get acquired, by a Silicon Valley firm, in 2002 for $85 million. This convinced Tan that the only way forward in China was to support entrepreneurs who were steeped in the Silicon Valley mindset.[23]

Red Chips peaked later that year with China Mobile—a $4.2 billion blockbuster underwritten by Goldman Sachs and China International Capital Corporation, a new Beijing-based investment bank joint venture, with Morgan Stanley a shareholder. China Mobile listed in both Hong Kong and New York, and the deal succeeded in the teeth of a gathering storm: the Asian Financial Crisis.

THE ASIAN FINANCIAL CRISIS

The crisis began in July 1997, three months before the China Mobile IPO, when the Thai baht broke its peg to the US dollar. The region's companies had been borrowing in dollars at a furious rate to speed their growth, but their businesses were mostly domestic, and their revenues were in local currencies. Their central banks relied on accumulating dollar reserves to manage their currency exchange rates.

Inevitably many companies over-borrowed and blew the proceeds on speculative investments like real estate, instead of productive or innovative businesses. Foreign bankers actively encouraged these groups to borrow from them—and then complained about "crony capitalism" when the exchange rates collapsed and swaths of Asian businesses were insolvent.

The damage was severe across Southeast Asia and Korea, and it tanked the Hong Kong property and stock markets. Peregrine went bust, having lent $260 million—one-third of its capital—to an Indonesian taxi company, only to see the rupiah collapse.[24] Red Chip fever burned out. But the China investment story had only just begun.

Red Chips were a success and the deal pipeline would eventually resume. But they didn't address the core problem at home: these entities' domestic listings (the A Shares) were still mostly illiquid Legal Person Shares.

THE VIE STRUCTURE

Foreigners were restricted from owning tech, education, and media companies in China. But these companies needed foreign investment to get off the ground. Attempts to simply incorporate offshore didn't work because it left local entrepreneurs out in the cold.

Multinationals made the first attempt to get around the obstacles to foreign ownership. Companies like AT&T and SingTel attempted joint ventures structured as China-China-Foreigner (CCF). This involved three parties in a joint venture, with one of the Chinese entities indirectly controlled by the foreign company—usually by entrusting it to someone's relative or friend.

This was an obvious attempt to dodge Chinese bans on foreign control, but the Chinese market was large enough to tempt a few companies to try it. The Ministry of Information Industry (today known as the Ministry of Industry and Information Technology (MIIT)), prohibited it.

Rocky Lee, now the Silicon Valley office managing partner at law firm King & Wood Mallesons, was then a young lawyer in Shanghai working on these deals. He says the collapse of CCFs threatened a broader regulatory crackdown, but instead it gave birth to the VIE.

VIEs solved the exit problem by creating a series of contracts that let the entrepreneur license their operations to an offshore entity. It was CCF but with an important twist: the entrepreneur maintained control, and worked with VCs and investment bankers to list these offshore entities.

"A company listed on Nasdaq doesn't own the China asset," Lee says. "Foreigners can't own these assets but they can indirectly control them. Every internet company relies on VIE."[25]

No one knew if regulators would squash VIEs, but now venture investors were willing to give them a try. These structures might not last for long, but young internet companies were not considered a strategic industry, compared to a telecoms company—the government was willing to also take a risk on these structures.

In 1999, though, investors were less concerned about the government and more focused on trying to convince founders to accept US-style investments.

"Chinese entrepreneurs didn't understand standard, early Series A term sheets," Lee says. "They'd ask me, 'Is this for real? Why would anyone give us free money for our equity? What's the con? Do I have personal liability?'"

What usually won them over was the understanding that if a founder took foreign VC money and they died, their family could keep the money. "I'd say if the spend doesn't fit the business, you might have to give it back," Lee says. Eventually Chinese entrepreneurs embraced VIEs when they saw how wealthy these deals could make them.

Say an entrepreneur sets up a Cayman Islands company that has a license for the mainland domestic business. The offshore entity has $10 worth of assets, $10 in earnings, and a 1× book value of $10. To sell the company via IPO, the entrepreneur would only be able to raise from the market the book value, $10.

But the entrepreneur works with a VC or PE firm, which decides the company is actually worth $40. Why $40? It's a typical VC tactic: being a tech company with bright prospects, investors argue it will grow into that heady valuation.

Now the entrepreneur is being offered a price/earnings ratio that's 4× book value. The entrepreneur only has to list 25 percent of the equity to raise $10. The entrepreneur now owns 75 percent of the offshore company, while still controlling 100 percent of the onshore business—and they've got $10 in their pocket, which they can use to fund options for their team, acquire other businesses, or buy a yacht.

So long as the transaction involved transfers of money (as opposed to shell games exchanging paper ownership), it was...well, not strictly legal, as the Chinese government would never bless the VIE. But they tolerated it.

SINA.COM GOES IPO WITH VIE

Sohu.com was the first company to plan on a Nasdaq listing using VIE, but Sina.com's chief operating officer (COO), Hurst Lin, caught wind of this and pushed for his company to be first.

Sina's founders were the first to exit this way. The company was taking a regulatory risk. The deal almost never saw the light of day—although this was because of internal strife and cultural clashes rather than government interference.

Sina.com was the result of a merger of separate Chinese-language internet portals. One, Sinanet, was set up in Silicon Valley by three Taiwanese (including Hurst Lin) to target the Chinese-speaking community there. The other was Beijing-based SRSNet, focused on developing the mainland market. In 1998 the merged entity made California its headquarters as neutral ground, so as to recruit American executives to smooth the way for a Nasdaq listing.

This led to a messy clash around where to grow the business and how to handle the IPO. Goldman Sachs, an early seed investor, was supposed to underwrite the deal. In the end, the Taiwanese and Beijing founders ditched most of the US executives and agreed to focus growth on mainland China—where they had about 1 million users, a number they knew should grow not by 10× but by 100×. They even fired Goldman and retained Morgan Stanley for the deal.[26]

The founders had to be more focused on managing the domestic political risk. They didn't want to see the VIE get canceled. "This took foresight and strategic planning," says an investor in Sina. "We had to develop relationships with the State Council and the Premier [Zhu Rongji], who had to sign off."

He notes that one reason the government was willing to allow Sina.com and its brethren to list in the US was because data was not understood to be a strategic asset. It wasn't a sensitive issue. Today data is at the heart of problems with Chinese tech companies listed overseas, but in early 2000, the government was open to risky ideas to support indigenous innovation.

For investors, getting the VIE to work meant China was now

creating the kind of opportunity that had never existed outside of the United States. "We realized that China's economy was burgeoning, and that digital adoption was leapfrogging the US with mobile," the investor says. "In the top cities, even then, more people used mobile apps than in America's cities."

Another advantage for investors was that capital was scarce. The investor says, "We saw the biggest players in Chinese tech come to us for financing, both startups and traditional companies. Everyone knew that the consumer market was about to explode. It was the right time and the right place."

LEGACY OF SINA'S VIE

Sina.com listed on Nasdaq on April 13, 2000, raising $68 million. NetEase and Sohu followed in June and July, despite market turbulence as the dotcom crash gathered steam.

This proved the viability and the necessity of listing in the US. By incorporating overseas, tech companies had recourse to US legal and financial institutions, they could override internal cultural or personal disputes, and they could easily network with Silicon Valley companies to ensure Chinese firms stayed on top of everything new in tech.

Sina.com would go on to new heights, eventually hitting that 100 million users. In 2009 it launched Weibo, a Twitter-like microblogging site, further adding to its popularity. The portal integrates news, sports, finance, entertainment, fashion, and other services for Chinese-language users both at home and abroad.

At the time of Sina's listing, the VIE was considered a short-term measure: with China about to enter the World Trade Organization (WTO), financiers expected China would liberalize foreign-ownership rules. That didn't happen, though, and the VIE matured into the de facto structure for every major China tech IPO in the US: Alibaba, Tencent, Baidu, and more than 100 others eventually relied on VIE.

There would be moments when the tech industry feared the government would pull the plug on VIEs. But the stakes continued to rise, as more companies listed successfully in the US. By 2006, there was $100 billion in public equity based on VIEs. By 2020, there would be $4 trillion.

Over the years there has been an occasional fear that MIIT will declare VIEs illegal, but China has been a huge beneficiary, using VIE to leverage foreign investment to build its own innovation economy. When Beijing launched a painful restructuring on the tech industry in 2020, it used brutal measures such as cybersecurity laws to punish US-listed companies like ride-hailing pioneer Didi Chuxing—but it hasn't rescinded VIEs.

EQUITIES REFORM

Both Red Chips and VIEs provided tax havens that made entrepreneurs and foreign financiers rich. This was uncomfortable for a Communist regime. But these structures injected capital and expertise into the Chinese economy, so regulators allowed it.

Eventually Chinese authorities realized that VIEs had drawbacks. Once a big company like Alibaba was listed overseas, China had no mechanism to force it to pay tax on those earnings. The best companies were rushing to the US instead of listing at home. The Legal Person Shares issue had to be resolved.

In the mid-2000s, the government began to transition Legal Person Shares out of the system, and gradually boost liquidity in A Shares. By 2008, authorities began to authorize renminbi-denominated VC and PE funds. Ultimately, China's innovative companies still preferred to IPO abroad, but these reforms set the stage for Shanghai to become Asia's biggest stock market. In today's environment, marked by hostile relations between Beijing and Washington, the A-Share market is starting to welcome home some of these companies.

Solving exits opened the door in China to VC, and the New York listings of Red Chips like China Mobile and of internet companies like Sina showed the country's potential.

The Asian Financial Crisis and the dotcom crash put activity on pause, but it didn't stop venture capitalists from entering China. They would continue to rely on VIE structures, because of restrictions on foreign ownership of Chinese-domiciled companies. The question was: where did these VCs come from, and what did they bring to China?

TAIWAN'S DECLINE

The first source of VC was from firms with experience in Taiwan, including Walden, WI Harper, and H&Q Asia, as well as the venture arms of Taiwan's successful tech companies, such as Acer.

Taiwanese entrepreneurs and investors flocked to China and took much of Taiwan's manufacturing base with them. They started with the most labor-intensive businesses, such as assembling keyboards and scanners, but soon all aspects of producing a PC had moved across the Straits—mostly to Dongguan, a gritty town between Hong Kong and Guangzhou. The more sophisticated Taiwanese businesses, such as those managing the entire supply chain to produce notebooks, migrated to Shanghai.

This was a structural change. Businesspeople were relocating with their families. By 2000, there were 200,000 Taiwanese-born residents in Shanghai alone.[27] Taiwan still had the world's leading OEM and chip design companies, but they had shifted their supply chains to the mainland.

Taiwan had placed electronics at the heart of its economy, becoming expert at semiconductors and equipment, from circuit boards to laptops to compact disks. But rising costs at home, mainly due to a shortage of labor, and mainland China's explosive growth, was too attractive for Taiwan's businesses to ignore.

Taipei was wary of seeing its industry hollow out—or of giving away its advantages to a hostile government. But in 1990 the government allowed investments on the mainland, provided the money was routed through companies in other jurisdictions (which usually meant Hong Kong). After China joined the WTO, Taiwan lifted most investment restrictions.

Taiwanese investment on the mainland boomed, averaging $7.3 billion annually from 2001 to 2009, with the two economies becoming intertwined. Whereas in 2000, China imported relatively little from Taiwan, by 2010 Taiwan was the second-biggest exporter to China.[28]

Fears of hollowing out proved only partly true. It did see GDP growth and per-capita GDP growth slow, starting in the 1980s. Real wages declined and economic inequality widened. Many OEM factory jobs moved to mainland China, and Taiwan's technology sector was squeezed by peer competitors in Korea and Japan, and by low-cost upstarts across the Straits. The Taiwan Stock Exchange was soon eclipsed by Hong Kong.

Taiwan was a victim of its own success, with its middle class losing out to the same forces of globalization that undermined blue and some white-collar jobs in the West.

Eventually, Taiwan's model would prove to be resilient. While OEM manufacturing moved to China, the IP and value-add stayed in Taipei. Taiwan was able to sustain a vibrant market of mid-sized companies.

And then there were semiconductors. TSMC went on to become the world's dominant foundry. By 2020 it commanded over half of the world's orders for specialized chips. Although rivals dominated DRAM chips, TSMC enjoyed a 90 percent market share in the most advanced logic chips. But even in semiconductors, Taiwan's ecosystem was broader than just TSMC, with 247 listed companies related to chipmaking generating total revenues of $108 billion.[29]

But in the early 2000s, the mood in Taiwan was grim, as its capitalists and businesspeople decamped for the bigger market opportunity in mainland China. The country was overly dependent on exports and US ties, but its leadership under the KMT was keen to integrate economically with China, leaving its small domestic market to stagnate. For Taiwan's venture capitalists, the direction was clear. The money to be made in startups was no longer in Taiwan.

Yet these pioneering investors, once they set up shop in Beijing and Shanghai, were not the only game in town when it came to VC in mainland China. Their influence would soon be eclipsed by a different wave.

SINGAPORE'S DIASPORA

The bigger source of VC expertise came to China from Singapore. The Lion City had developed itself as an investment hub but with little homegrown tech to show. And while Singapore's VC community was prepared to take risks, Singapore's bureaucrats kept the place buttoned-up. But Singapore's VCs were attracted to China for the same reasons as Taiwan's. And after the dotcom crash, Singaporean funds were desperate to find ways to make money.

One of the first Singaporeans to make their way to China was Thomas Ng, who co-founded GGV Capital in 2000. The practice was based in California but Ng soon recruited other Singaporeans to run the business in China. These included Jixun Foo, formerly from DFJ ePlanet; and Jenny Lee, a US-trained engineer who had done stints at Morgan Stanley and JAFCO, the Japan VC firm. Foo and Lee helped get GGV established in Shanghai, and would go on to be early backers of Alibaba, Didi Chuxing, Xiaomi, Toutiao, and, in Singapore, Grab.

DFJ also led to Finian Tan setting up his own firm with four partners, Vickers Venture Partners, based in Singapore. Another investor from the DFJ family, Fan Zhang, would end up co-founding Sequoia China with Neil Shen, a Chinese tech entrepreneur.

Another cluster of investors came out of the Singapore TIF that Tan had helped set up while serving at the Ministry of Trade and Industry.

Veterans of TIF included Tina Ju and David Su, who set up their own VC firm, Venture TDF, in 1999. They moved to Shanghai in 2000, and would end up backing the likes of Alibaba, Baidu, and Ctrip. Later, in 2008, TDF China was acquired by KP, the venerable Silicon Valley firm—although disputes among the partners nearly sank this effort.

Vertex Ventures as well as Government Investment Corporation of Singapore also established offices in China, with Vertex launching bespoke funds.

Together, these Singaporeans provided the most talent to China's nascent foreign VC community. They all knew one another, and often co-invested in the same companies.

ATTRACTING AMERICAN VCS

But by the early 2000s, VC in China was still limited to Asian firms, or a handful of Silicon Valley firms whose outposts were run by ethnic Chinese. None of the big names from the Valley had shown interest. Sina and other IPOs had won some attention, but the dotcom crash killed whatever appetite may have existed to try investing outside of the US. The real money and the depth of experience was still within an easy drive from VC offices along Sand Hill Road.

China's industry needed those big names. The leading VCs in America brought with them connections to the LP base—the pension funds, universities, and other big institutions that invested in VC. And US firms knew how to help foreign companies expand operations or connect with the lawyers and bankers critical to going IPO and managing stock options.

Asia had nurtured the embryo of a native VC industry but it was far too small to support the kind of tech story that China promised, let alone the region as a whole.

Something had to be done to bring US venture capital to Asia. And that's exactly what happened—only the catalyst wasn't a VC firm. It was a bank—but not an investment bank doing tech IPOs, like Goldman or Morgan Stanley. Into this void stepped SVB.

10

CHINA: THE CATALYST

THERE are few moments in history when a single event marks a "before" and an "after." One such moment did happen, though, to turbocharge Asia's VC ecosystem—and transform Silicon Valley into a global industry. That was when Silicon Valley Bank led a delegation of the Who's Who in VC to Bangalore and Shanghai.

The visit opened the eyes of American investors to the idea that Asia's mega-markets—each with a population greater than 1 billion and governments keen on liberalizing their economies—were going to enable the growth of durable, massive, world-class tech companies.

That there was going to be another Silicon Valley out there—and maybe more than one.

VENTURE DEBT: SILICON VALLEY BANK

SVB fills a niche role in the story of funding startups. VC is about equity, taking stakes in startups to fund their next step, and delivering a share of the returns to VCs' institutional investors. It's a high-risk, high-return business model that relies on a handful of massive successes to paper over the duds.

Banks are ill-suited to lending to startups. They only extend credit to companies with a track record, a history of financial statements, and a credit rating. Startups lack these things. Banks are obsessed with getting their money back, rather than earning a huge return. Startups are more likely to burn the cash and go bust. VCs exist because banks won't touch startups.

Nonetheless, two California-based banks, Bank of America (BofA) and Wells Fargo Bank, began to experiment with lending to the emerging tech industry in the 1970s, focusing on the capital-hungry hardware and semiconductor companies.

Harry Kellogg, who would go on to become SVB's vice chair, got his start in West Coast banking at this time, at Wells Fargo. He recalls the bank made one bad loan to a startup. "We lost $6 million and the San Francisco office shut us down," he says. "They could have owned the venture-banking business, but they withdrew."[1] So did BofA.

He bounced around other West Coast banks and noticed how VC firms were proliferating, and then joined SVB in 1986. SVB was a new business, founded in 1983 to accept deposits from businesses financed by VC.

Another former managing director at the firm, Larry Lopez, describes the business this way:

> We were trying to find transformational companies, but you can't lend on that. A bank can't lose half of one percent of its capital without risking going broke. No, you have to be made whole, which means there's limited upside. We had a high net-interest margin in the US, but low RoA [return on assets] because our companies rarely borrowed from us.[2]

SVB got itself into the center of VC deal flow. By being the rare institution willing to lend to VC firms and their portfolio companies, SVB captured most of the market. VCs, in turn, came to realize that if they allowed SVB to take a loss on loans extended either to the VC or to its portfolio companies, the relationship would be tainted and they'd forever lose access to debt.

SVB structured its loans to ensure it was on top of the borrower's capital structure. "In a liquidation, we're ahead of the VCs," Lopez says—if a startup closes shop, SVB is a secured lender; and if it decides to foreclose on a failing company, it has legal rights to its IP. "We treated IP as an asset, almost a hard asset," Kellogg says.

But the preference was to avoid a foreclosure and get the bank's money back. "We banked multiple companies of Sequoia and Venrock, and they weren't going to screw us over a deal," Kellogg says.

"Default was a bad outcome for VCs, so they made sure we got paid back," Lopez says. "And we'd remember those VCs that tried to do a runaround in court."

On the other hand, VCs benefited from having a bank willing to extend bridge loans and other forms of credit to their portfolio companies. By enmeshing itself in VC ecosystems, SVB developed unique insights that gave it the comfort required to lend to risky businesses.

LENDING OVERSEAS

SVB had senior bankers from overseas as well, and these became champions for extending the bank's horizons. These included Peter Mok, who ran a Pacific Rim transaction group, and Daniel Quon, a junior banker who wanted to push for China. Two Silicon Valley-based bankers, Larry Lopez and Harry Kellogg, were doing trips to Israel and beyond. They noticed several Singapore-based VCs opening offices. The Pacific Rim group began to feed these relationships to SVB in Silicon Valley, where it could provide foreign VCs with a beachhead and a bank account, so the VCs could bring their startups to the US. Once a foreign startup had a US presence, SVB might lend to it.

"For foreign VCs, the path to exit was in the United States," and an IPO in New York, says Lopez.

FIRST ATTEMPT: JAPAN

The bank noticed that some of the Asians working in the Valley were keen to return to their home countries to launch venture funds or tech businesses. Shouldn't SVB discover which startups abroad might become clients?

SVB also was unusual in that it had several senior American managers also interested in the rest of the world, with several culturally fascinated by Japan.

Among them was Ken Wilcox, SVB's president and CEO from 2001 to 2011. He helped expand SVB's business overseas. This generated the same kind of resistance that Peter Brooke experienced at Advent 20 years earlier: the other partners were making good money in the US, where they had a tight relationship with the big VCs. Lending to companies outside of the network, especially in markets without a clear legal system or a track record of innovation, was too risky. SVB didn't even have banking licenses in these countries.

"I believed that tech is a global industry," Wilcox says. "If you're in tech, you have to be concerned about every innovation center. You can't be cutting edge in one place and not another."

As it turned out, some Japanese were fascinated by SVB. In 2000, Masayoshi Son and SoftBank led a consortium to acquire Nippon Credit Bank, an insolvent Japanese lender. Son relaunched the bank as Aozora Bank with the idea of dedicating it to lending to the internet economy.

Son had even pitched SVB to participate in the deal, recalls Ken Wilcox, who was SVB's president and CEO at the time. "Aozora then wanted us to teach them how to lend to cashflow-negative startups."[3] In turn, SVB wanted Aozora to bank US tech companies in its portfolio, because foreigners found it difficult to obtain banking services in Japan.

The deal didn't go anywhere—Wilcox says Aozora never set up a single account. "Every time I asked why, they made me drink a lot of sake before telling me it was 'very difficult,'" he says.

Masa lost interest too: SoftBank sold out of Aozora in 2003, and SVB looked for opportunities elsewhere.

SVB GLOBAL

SVB decided to consolidate these overseas efforts into a single division, SVB Global, which would go abroad as a VC group, not as a bank. It seemed better to use its information edge to set up its own funds, or seed local VCs, rather than engage in risky lending.

SVB, like many VC firms with international ambitions, learned that putting every market into one division, SVB Global, wasn't efficient. The tech might be global, but investing in startups varies among markets, and relies on local relationships, not a global P&L.

But the global division did launch SVB into multiple markets, with initial offices being opened in Bangalore, Shanghai, Tel Aviv, and London. These offices would expand upon the Pacific Rim team's early investments in local VCs in Taiwan, Korea, Australia, and Israel.

"It was all about building relationships," says Kellogg. "We needed to leverage people who understood the local market," which is why the bank repositioned Ash Lilani to lead a coordinated global effort. Lilani was appointed head of SVB Global and ran it from 2002 to 2006.

One reason for an arm's-length relationship was that no other country had the ecosystem of Silicon Valley. No other center had the capacity to ramp up a company like Google into a behemoth. Ecosystems take time to develop, involving universities, investors like family offices and pension funds, lawyers and other service providers, and a spectrum of financial specialists, from angel investors to VCs to growth-stage players and PE. Perhaps more importantly, the ecosystem needed to be open, collaborative, and inclusive. Silicon Valley, with its influx of skilled workers from around the world and a culture that rewarded the diffusion of knowledge, was unique.

But perhaps the conditions that made Silicon Valley special could be nurtured elsewhere—with a little help.

"After 18 months of being hired, I get a coffee with Greg," Ash Lilani recalls, referring to Greg Becker, then the firm's COO (and later its CEO). "We talked about India and China. I said, 'We need an ecosystem. Normally Silicon Valley Bank follows the VCs. Let's lead them there, for a change.'"[4]

Thus began a project to bring America's top VCs to India and China, to meet their local counterparts—to catalyze the ecosystem. SVB led two pioneering delegations: one to Bangalore in 2003, and then to Beijing in 2004. "We had to get the VCs there and show them what's happening," Lilani says. "We globalized the VC industry."

EXPLORING INDIA

India wasn't ready for foreign VC. Some of the Americans recoiled at the experience.

Peter Mok, who had founded SVB's Pacific Rim group before SVB Global was established, recalls, "India was too scattered for Don Valentine, it didn't capture his attention."[5]

"I've seen people's reactions to India," Lilani says. "Your senses are assaulted by the unique smells, sounds, visuals. India is very transparent. There's poverty, it's crowded. China, on the other hand, is clean, beautiful, there are no beggars. India required patience. But everyone speaks English, and some people appreciated the warmth of India, of having local VCs invite us into their homes."

The country was known for IT outsourcing, not software, but companies like Cisco, Intel, and Motorola were opening offices, and Bangalore was developing a reputation as an open, progressive city with good weather.

SVB's first trip hosted 23 VCs from the US, who met 29 Indian investors and companies. SVB brought in the IT giants like Infosys and Tata Consulting to give the meeting credibility, but the foreigners were more interested in finding startups, not working with landed family conglomerates.

SVB's pitch to the US firms was to set up a desk in SVB's office, which formed a co-working hub. From there they could find a local partner to franchise the VC's business or form a joint venture. In the end, 19 US firms committed to doing business with SVB in Bangalore, although most left. It would take a few years for the first US-backed VCs to open their doors.

But for the handful that stuck around—always because the US VC had an ethnic Indian partner who wanted to champion the country—they were keen to invest in Indian startups. "Their partners had made time for India and they wanted to do deals, and we sourced flow," Lilani says.

SVB GOES TO CHINA

We'll soon turn to the India story, but the biggest impact SVB had was in China. The market was more developed. It was ready. But that's not to say it was large.

Thomas Tsao, co-founder of Gobi Ventures, was one of the Chinese VCs invited to the SVB event in Beijing. "The original idea had been for the top 20 VCs in the US to meet the top 20 VCs in China. But everyone in Silicon Valley wanted in, so they raised the number to 25. But there weren't 25 VCs in China. So we sent two people, because they just needed bodies."[6]

Tsao had set up Gobi in Shanghai in 2002 after a career in investment banking, first in New York and then in Hong Kong. He was second-generation Taiwanese-American—"I'm a New York Islanders fan"—and found his Chinese language skills gave him an asset on Wall Street. He helped Merrill Lynch and Dresdner Kleinwort Benson (DKB) underwrite Chinese privatizations and sovereign bond issues.

He ended up running tech, media, and telecom deals for DKB, helping set up investor roadshows in Silicon Valley and New York. The dotcom bust put deals on hold, but by now Tsao could see China was going to be a huge tech story—if it could recreate the Silicon Valley flywheel. And that meant finding exits in the US using VIE structures, because there was no way to get paid doing domestic IPOs.

But for a China-based VC, taking companies to the US was difficult. No one in the US knew Gobi—or cared.

"The SVB trip was a seminal moment," he says. "The smart money was beginning to come to China, but there was a 'before' and an 'after.' That trip opened the floodgates."

"THE AVENGERS" OF VC

The US contingent represented the most venerable figures in the business: Don Valentine from Sequoia; John Doerr from KP; Don Dixon from DCM; Jim Breyer from Accel Partners; and other senior executives from the likes of Bessemer Venture Partners, GGV, Lightspeed Venture Partners, NEA Capital, Sierra Ventures, and some corporate VCs such as Walt Disney Corporation's Steamboat Ventures.

This led to some diplomatic challenges. Valley titans were used to traveling by private jet, which wasn't possible at the time for China. Everyone was booked everyone on a commercial flight.

This led to a battle for who got the coveted first-class seats.

"It was like The Avengers of the venture world coming to China," Tsao says, referencing the superhero collective. "Who got to sit in first class got hugely political."

Lilani adds, "Whose bags got lost? Don's."

On the China side were homegrown firms such as IDG, represented by Hugo Shong, and ChinaVest; as well as the Singaporean crowd (including Tina Ju from Venture TDF) and firms that cut their teeth in Taiwan like Walden International, which was represented by Lip-Bu Tan.

The room also included a few of China's internet founders, including Neil Shen, founder of Ctrip, an online travel booking site that took the Expedia playbook and tweaked it for China's new legion of tourists and business travelers.

The two delegations met formally at the Beijing branch of the Hong Kong Jockey Club. Valentine represented the Americans, and Tan the Chinese.

Tsao recalls that Tan made a rousing speech about the need to access US capital, but then Valentine bluntly said Sequoia would never invest in any company more than a car's drive from his office.

"Chopsticks dropped," Tsao says.

MUSICAL CHAIRS

But Michael Moritz, the British-born Sequoia Partner who made his name in the firm in 1999 with a $12.5 million investment in Google, was keen and took up the reins in China.

Both the India and the China trips led to matchmaking between the US and Asia firms. The deals in China happened almost on the spot: Accel and IDG, Sierra and Gobi. Other relationships were set in motion that would blossom later, such as KP and Venture TDF. Despite Valentine's skepticism, Sequoia opened its doors in China in 2005 by recruiting local investors and entrepreneurs to run it.

For local firms, these partnerships were gold, because now they had connections to US investors. They could leverage their US partner to source dollar funding from US endowments, pension funds, and family offices. For US VCs, providing those LPs with China access opened a new wave of money. Those with the strongest China commitment would demand that LPs in the US invest in their China fund if they wanted access to their coveted fund at home.

Tsao says, "That China trip opened up people's eyes. The old assumption that all the entrepreneurs were in the Valley gave way to the understanding that venture capital was going to go global."

VC might go global, but it would turn out that VC firms don't globalize easily. Tech is universal but companies are local, and so are investors. Attempts to create transoceanic investor teams didn't work. Having to get a local investment thesis approved by partners in California was usually a recipe for failure.

It was up to the people on the ground to invest in the companies of the future. India's industry would not gather pace for another decade, but China's tech founders were already transforming the country—and the world.

11

CHINA: THE GOLDEN AGE

CHINA is the first country to develop an innovation engine comparable to America's.

It did so by combining American capital with Chinese startups, within an environment that appeared open and freewheeling, but in which the Communist Party maintained the ability to guide, manage, and intervene when it needed to—in a manner far more abrupt and decisive than elsewhere.

Despite this political difference, Beijing was keen to nurture a VC-backed technology sector; and it succeeded, catapulting Chinese companies into the top global echelon within a decade.

Look at the ten biggest publicly listed companies ranked by market cap for March 2001, March 2011, and March 2021 shown in Figure 1. And then look at the age of each region's largest public companies shown in Figure 2.

Figure 1: Global leading companies by market capitalization (companies funded by venture capital in bold)

2001

Rank	Name	Headquarters	Primary industry	Market value ($bn)
1	General Electric	US	Conglomerate	372
2	**Microsoft**	**US**	**Software**	**327**
3	ExxonMobil	US	Oil and gas	300
4	Wal-Mart	US	Retail	273
5	Citigroup	US	Finance	255
6	Pfizer	US	Healthcare	249
7	**Intel**	**US**	**Computer hardware**	**203**
8	BP	UK	Oil and gas	201
9	Johnson & Johnson	US	Healthcare	198
10	Royal Dutch Shell	Netherlands	Oil and gas	190

2011

Rank	Name	Headquarters	Primary industry	Market value ($bn)
1	ExxonMobil	US	Oil and gas	417
2	PetroChina	China	Oil and gas	326
3	**Apple**	**US**	**Consumer tech**	**321**
4	ICBC	China	Finance	251
5	Petrobras	Brazil	Oil and gas	247
6	BHP Billiton	Australia	Oil and gas	247
7	China Construction Bank	China	Finance	323
8	Royal Dutch Shell	Netherlands	Oil and gas	226
9	Chevron	US	Oil and gas	216
10	**Microsoft**	**US**	**Software**	**213**

2021

Rank	Name	Headquarters	Primary industry	Market value ($bn)
1	**Apple**	**US**	**Consumer tech**	**2,050**
2	**Microsoft**	**US**	**Software**	**1,778**
3	**Amazon**	**US**	**E-commerce**	**1,558**
4	**Alphabet**	**US**	**Internet search**	**1,395**
5	**Facebook**	**US**	**Social media**	**839**
6	**Tencent**	**China**	**Consumer mobile**	**767**
7	**Tesla**	**US**	**Electric vehicles**	**641**
8	**Alibaba**	**China**	**E-commerce**	**615**
9	TSMC	Taiwan	Semiconductors	613
10	Berkshire Hathaway	US	Finance	590

Source: *Financial Times*, Wikipedia ("List of public corporations by market capitalization").

Figure 2: Age of largest public companies, 2021 (companies founded by venture capital marked in bold)

United States

Rank	Company	Market cap ($bn)	Year founded
1	**Apple**	**2,050**	**1976**
2	**Microsoft**	**1,778**	**1975**
3	**Amazon**	**1,558**	**1994**
4	**Alphabet**	**1,395**	**1998**
5	**Facebook**	**839**	**2004**
6	**Tesla**	**641**	**2003**
7	Berkshire Hathaway	590	1839
8	JP Morgan Chase	469	1799
9	Visa	463	1958
10	Johnson & Johnson	429	1886

Europe & UK

Rank	Company	Market cap ($bn)	Year founded
1	Nestlé	328	1866
2	Roche	300	1896
3	LVMH	220	1765
4	Novartis	213	1857
5	Total	197	1924
6	L'Oréal	179	1919
7	SAP	169	1972
8	ASML Holding	154	1984
9	Novo Nordisk	149	1923
10	Prosus NV	149	1915

Asia-Pacific

Rank	Company	Market cap ($bn)	Year founded
1	**Tencent**	**767**	**1998**
2	**Alibaba**	**615**	**1999**
3	TSMC	613	1969
4	Samsung Electronics	500	1969
5	Kweichow Moutai	385	1999
6	ICBC	277	1984
7	Toyota Motor	252	1937
8	Ping An Insurance	236	1988
9	**Meituan-Dianping**	**224**	**2010**
10	**Pinduoduo**	**218**	**2015**

These rankings are not stable; company valuations go up and down, sometimes in short periods, and tech companies suffered a market rout in 2022. The list in ten years' time will be led by different companies from different industries. But look at the big picture.

First, in 2001, the US dominated the top-ten list of global companies, with the UK and the Netherlands also represented.

Silicon Valley was the unparalleled leader in innovation. "No other major financial center in the world has ever generated companies of consequence and prominence that are so large and visibly successful," said the late Don Valentine, founder of Sequoia Capital.[1] Since then, China has taken its place as the second-biggest source of world-beating companies.

The second conclusion from the changing list of the biggest public companies is that nine out of ten of the companies in 2021 got their start with VC backing. The VC model, it turns out, has funded all of the transformational companies that dominate today's business world and have changed our lives.

The question is whether VC-backed companies will continue to dominate the charts in, say, 2031. Even if there's not an explicit "tech" flavor, however, it is likely that traditional industrial leaders will dominate by adopting the innovations created by VC-backed companies, such as AI.

VC continues to support the emergence of an even bigger wave of innovative companies. The industry is awash with capital: US VCs alone closed 2020 with a record $151 billion in "dry powder," money in the coffers poised to back the next startup.

Increasingly, the biggest startups are also being built outside of the US, and the first truly big competitors have emerged in China, where more startups are achieving unicorn status. China has even given the world its first "hectocorn," Bytedance (the company behind TikTok), which was valued at $140 billion in November 2020 by CB Insights.

Along with unicorns galore, China is the only country to develop a complete VC industry to back them.

Chin Chou is a managing director at Morgan Stanley in Hong Kong. He runs the firm's PE funds investment team for Asia-Pacific. "Equity returns do not equate to an economy's performance," he says.[2] "But for the past 40 years in the US, equity returns have been driven by new businesses—not by old businesses."

Michael Moritz, Valentine's successor at Sequoia, agrees, saying the two best places in the world to start a company are now Silicon Valley... and China; with India and Southeast Asia on the rise.

"When I started [at Sequoia], Silicon Valley and Boston had 100 percent of the market share of the most valuable technology companies," Moritz told an audience at Stanford University. "That's changed. Investments are now often outside of the US."[3]

It's not just that the US and China are great places to launch innovative companies: it's also that other countries are often not. Pierre Omidyar, the (French) founder of eBay, told an audience of his compatriots in 2005 that he couldn't have launched the company in France.[4]

BENIGN BACKDROP

China's VC-led tech boom benefited from favorable conditions. Within China, Deng Xiaoping had begun to remove the shackles from private enterprise. He used his 1992 "Southern Tour" to Shenzhen, then mostly farmland bordering Hong Kong, to emphasize the "reform and opening-up" program in the wake of the 1989 Tiananmen Square disaster that had frozen progress. This is when Deng made his famous statement that it didn't matter whether the cat was black or white, so long as it caught the mouse—a signal that pragmatism, not Party ideology, would shape economic policy.

The US, meanwhile, supported China's entry to the WTO. The fall of the Soviet Union had ushered in a feeling of optimism in the West. The new "information superhighway" promised to unleash a billion Chinese voices that the Communist Party could never control—or so the thinking went.

US-China relations were never easy. Taiwan shook off the dead hand of the KMT dictatorship and ushered in a new era of democracy in 1996, which triggered Beijing to fire missiles into the Straits waters because it feared Taiwan might declare independence. US President Bill Clinton sent two aircraft carriers into the area, forcing Beijing to acknowledge the US had the ability to defend Taiwan.

This left a bitter taste in both Washington and Beijing, but the September 11, 2001 terrorist attacks caused the George W. Bush administration to sidestep questions about whether China was a friend or foe. It opted instead for a vast level of political and commercial engagement with Beijing.

The 2008 Global Financial Crisis, epitomized by the collapse of US investment bank Lehman Brothers, was a further distraction for the West, and a chance for China's rulers to begin to advance their alternative vision of the world.

By now China's economic reforms had lifted hundreds of millions of people from poverty. Beijing had just hosted the 2008 Olympic Games, shrugging off concerns about its human rights record and presenting a confident image to the world. Its tech sector was thriving. This made for an attractive narrative for other emerging markets, particularly those that resented the US for its 2003 invasion of Iraq and the way Washington tended to intervene during times of financial turmoil.

This period saw the US and Chinese economies joined—if not at the hip, then symbiotically, as China became the manufacturing "workshop of the world" for buyers everywhere, notably the US.

China's entrepreneurs, in traditional industry as well as technology, initially came from "returnees," ethnic Chinese who had studied and worked in the US. Some were from Taiwan, others from the mainland. Many initially returned to China to work for big Silicon Valley firms—such as Intel, Microsoft, or Oracle—that had set up plants in China. Gradually more of these people would leave to start their own businesses. They'd all rely on VC to get off the ground.

VCs early to the game made fortunes that until now had only been possible in the US. It didn't matter how many bad deals an investor made because a single success in China could sustain an entire fund.

"Tons of startups failed," says Chang Sun, China managing partner at TPG, a US PE firm. "You could see the carcasses everywhere. But the successes were so huge, they dwarfed the failures: a 1 or 2 percent success rate was all you needed."

The SVB trip for US venture capitalists opened the floodgates for American capital to support Chinese tech founders. Brand-name

VCs from Silicon Valley began to set up shop in China, in some cases leveraging the partnerships struck with local players from the SVB visit.

SEQUOIA CHINA

The iconic success story is Sequoia China. The firm wanted to recreate the governance to support another Don Valentine, with local partners that could identify the market opportunity and then find the entrepreneurs to fill it—rather than try to have the partners in the US manage things, as others such as Lightspeed and DCM were attempting.

The firm hired two men to run it—one a known VC and the other a proven entrepreneur—and launched in China in 2005.

The investor was Zhang Fan, who had once been an analyst at Goldman Sachs before joining DFJ ePlanet Ventures. There he helped set up the firm's China iteration, TDF Ventures, and sat on the board of companies such as Baidu. Zhang had also led the firm's successful investment into Focus Media, a Shanghai company that specialized in outdoor digital advertising—a big business before the arrival of the smartphone.

The entrepreneur was Neil Shen Nanpeng. He had studied in the US and went into banking, becoming the head of Chinese capital markets business at Deutsche Bank. Most of the work catered to SOEs doing Red Chip deals.

He noticed two things. First, by the late 1990s, private enterprise was becoming a major force in China. Second, the rise of the internet was going to have as big an impact in China as it was already having in the US. While manufacturing or semiconductors required vast amounts of capital, the first batch of internet entrepreneurs, like Baidu and Alibaba, didn't need to have their own money. They could raise it from venture capital.

Shen set up Ctrip with three other co-founders in 1999. Online travel companies like Expedia were already rewriting the rules of how people booked hotels and flights in the West, and Shen bet that the same would happen in China. Ctrip was a huge success, winning a Nasdaq listing in 2003, just four years later.

Even before the IPO, Shen had moved to his second startup, Homeinns, a budget hotel chain—a novelty in China, but once again a market segment with massive latent demand.

Looking back, Shen reminisced, "In the early days of my career I felt it was less about choice than about going with the big trend, which is that China will become a global economic powerhouse. If you believe in that, if you're all-in on China, you will largely do well."[5]

Shen knew that his investment banking and entrepreneurial experience would make him the perfect fit for venture investing. He could have started his own fund, but he opted to franchise the Sequoia brand and bring a global VC name to China.

Shen and Zhang raised $1 billion for three US dollar-denominated China funds plus an additional Rmb1 billion for a local currency fund.

Sequoia China would go on to invest in the biggest tech names over the next 15 years, including Sina, Alibaba, JD.com (e-commerce), Meituan-Dianping (the biggest group-buying platform), drone manufacturer DJI, food-delivery service Ele.me, and Didi, the ride-hailing company.

After 2009, though, Shen became the sole managing partner: Zhang left under a cloud, having led a deal for Asia Media, an advertising company, whose founder resigned under accusations of mishandling the company's money; the business had to delist from the Tokyo Stock Exchange.[6]

HITS AND MISSES IN FRANCHISING VC

Other US imports were not as successful as Sequoia China. Two partners from TDF Ventures, the China spinoff from Singapore's state-led TIF, took the franchise for KP. These were Tina Ju and David Su. They were joined by another high-profile investor, Joe Zhou. The partners' collective CVs looked like KP would be just as big a winner in China as it was in the US.

KP's China business blew up within a year, though, with three partners exiting, including Zhou and Su, who left to set up rival VCs—a big loss of face for one of the Valley's most venerable investment firms.

Zhou set up his own business, Keytone Ventures, and negotiated to buy the investments he had made—and KP sold them at face value, making zero returns on the money invested (and minus the cost of capital). Su went on to run Matrix China, jumping to a major competitor.

Overseas firms focused on the quality of the investment team, but ignored local dynamics. "Everyone wants to do well and outperform the others," says an investor who was part of the original KP team. "But you need a leader, someone to stabilize the platform and resolve conflicts."

In KP's case, it was eager to ramp up by hiring locally, but the China partners had no experience with the firm in the US. They were removed from its culture. For a time the firm's China website even misspelled its own name: "Buyers" instead of "Byers."[7]

Eventually Tina Ju righted the ship, making investments in healthtech, computer technology, and e-commerce. She's still the firm's managing partner.

PERSONALITY CLASHES

And conflict was the norm in these young businesses. The partners were eager to do deals but frequently couldn't get them through the investment committee in California. Disappointed people would leave to start their own firm—as David Su did by quitting KP to run the China business at Matrix Ventures. He's still there today, having led investments into Baidu, Focus Media, Ele.me, and many other companies in healthcare, biotech, and media.

Sometimes the conflicts were personal.

An investor recalls working at a US-named fund run by two partners who are well known in the industry today. "They were smart people but the partner dynamics didn't work," he says. "They brought in a geomancer to advise on *feng shui* for the office." Such queries involve things like moving furniture around to generate favorable energy to make money.

"We did it because some people believe in *feng shui* and we wanted to strengthen the fund," the investor relates. "The master told us to move the fish tanks, things like that. But then one partner asked the master how he could be stronger than his partner. The geomancer wouldn't do it, but it showed the dynamics going on." A few months later the partners split up.

Such breakdowns were bad for the portfolio companies. The investment committee in the US usually had no idea what was going on—they could only see that the fund wasn't performing well.

US firms are no stranger to in-fighting or big egos. But in emerging markets, where teams are smaller and where the business challenges are greater, such divisions are starker and have a greater impact on returns.

There are also intangible differences that become very real when people's backs are against the wall. Kathy Xu had led Baring Private Equity's (venture) investment into NetEase in 1997. The company's founders were young and most of the employees were still working out of university dorms. The founder, William Ding, begged Xu to find him a CEO so he could focus on being the chief technology officer and avoid being distracted by management issues. Xu, herself only 30 years old, helped recruit a CEO and soon regretted the move.

"It was a big mistake," Xu recalled. "They didn't get along. The CEO had to bring a bodyguard to work."[8] NetEase would eventually list on Nasdaq during the IPO bubble, but suffered in the dotcom bust. Its board members wanted to sell the business and get what they could. Xu and Ding were the only ones who wanted to keep going: the business had $70 million cash in the bank and could ride out the storm. "I called every director—they're all 20 years old—and told them they have a fiduciary responsibility," Xu says. She and Ding won the day, and Xu would go on to an illustrious career running her own China VC firm.

NetEase was an example of a company in difficulty. The other problem that VCs faced in China was what happens when the startup is a success. "In Asia there is less appreciation for the role and the price of capital," says Jan Metzger.[9]

Today Metzger is head of Citi's corporate and investment bank for Asia-Pacific. He's used to dealing with companies that have already reached a large size. But in the 1990s he was part of a tech startup trying to market voice-recognition AI (the business was too early and failed), so he's familiar with small-scale entrepreneurs.

"If you go and invest $100,000 for 30 percent of the business, and the business succeeds, the owner won't give you the money," he says. "The owner says, 'I'm the one who did all the work, did I really give up one-third of the business?' If it's a cash-generating business, they'll steal the cashflow, there's a big fight. The founder tries to kick the VC out at a level that the founder views as a great return, or even a loss."

Founders may feel aggrieved, Metzger says, but they're ignoring the fact that they had to pay for their business model to work—they had to pay the VC. The US has many serial entrepreneurs who understand this, but VCs operating in a market like China (and, later, in other emerging markets) would face many boardroom battles over the value of their capital.

Therefore, whether local conditions were favorable or not, US venture firms only succeeded in China when they could establish a local team with autonomous local partners. The firm's investment committee in the US couldn't understand local disputes, internal or with founders, and if they tried to assert control over decisions, these local details would lead to bad investments.

HOMEGROWN HEROES

US firms weren't the only players, though. The domestic investment industry came alive with thousands of entities that called themselves venture capital. They promoted funds denominated in renminbi. Most of them were of poor quality, more interested in chasing short-term results than investing in long-term structures. They were run by amateurs with no access to foreign LPs.

But some serious professionals emerged to become industry leaders. After all, they knew the companies and they knew the regulations, and they didn't have to grapple with the politics of an overseas parent.

In these early days, the lines between VC and PE blurred. Some of the earliest firms such as Hony Capital and CDH were PE players that could reach down into late-stage startups.

But the trend could go the other way, as shown by the phenomenal rise of Hillhouse Capital.

LEARNING FROM SWENSEN

Hillhouse was founded by Zhang Lei, who had an unconventional streak: graduating from the prestigious Renmin University, he eschewed finance to go into mining. He did eventually go to the US to study at Yale, where he interned at the university's endowment, run by chief investment officer David Swensen.

Swensen is a legend in finance. Indeed, if we had to attribute the success of VC to just one person, it wouldn't be Arthur Rock or Don Valentine or Neil Shen. It would be Swensen, because he transformed the world of LPs almost single-handedly.

The received wisdom for institutional investors—pension funds, endowments, life insurance companies, and big family offices—was to allocate mainly to fixed income and public equities. This was done by selecting third-party mutual fund managers to do the actual investing.

But institutional investors did a bad job of selecting these fund managers, usually following the latest performance figures like lemmings. Three-year performance ratings are purely backward looking and don't predict future performance. Moreover, very few fund managers have the skill to consistently beat the market. So most institutions found themselves buying high and selling low to a revolving door of mediocre fund houses.

Swensen's insight was to buy and hold across a more diverse set of asset categories, particularly those that were volatile. The real driver of risk-adjusted returns was asset allocation, not picking fund managers. From 1999, he began to diversify Yale's endowment into what became known as "alternative investments": hedge funds, tech-focused firms, emerging-market stocks, and VC. From 1999 to 2009, the portfolio enjoyed an annual return of 11.8 percent, far outperforming traditional institutions—many of which then began to mimic the "Swensen model," pouring money into VC firms. A portion of this found its way to China and beyond.

Zhang Lei absorbed these lessons. He could see that China's tech industry was on the cusp of an explosion. In 2005 he hit the streets of New York to raise money for a fund. No one was interested—but Yale agreed to seed him with an initial $30 million check. Zhang went to Beijing and opened Hillhouse.

HILLHOUSE'S HITS

His first investment was prescient. The country was awash with messenger services, and US giant Microsoft's MSN was the prestige platform for businesspeople in the big cities. But Zhang noticed in second-tier cities, businesspeople were all using QQ, a chat desktop app operated by a Shenzhen-based startup called Tencent.

Tencent had already received initial VC money from IDG Capital and PCCW (a telecoms company from Hong Kong) in the form of $2 million in convertible bonds, but it remained desperate for capital. QQ was constantly burning cash to win eyeballs—even though Tencent's founders had no idea yet how to turn their userbase into revenues.

Zhang decided the VC market was wrong to discount Tencent and he made an all-in bet on the company, buying as many shares as he could. Tencent, as we'll see, would go on to become a behemoth in Chinese tech.

But it would be Zhang's investment into JD.com that would seal his reputation. JD.com was an e-commerce rival to Alibaba, with backers including Tencent.

JD.com's founder, Richard Liu Qiangdong, wanted to expand from being just a matchmaking platform to building his own logistics capabilities, to solve the last-mile issues that were always a problem in China. His other investors hated the idea, noting that Amazon had tried and failed to do this in the US.

According to analyst Lillian Li, Liu initially asked for $75 million. But Zhang told him he had to accept $225 million—take it or leave it. Zhang's insight was that last-mile logistics would have far greater value in China than in the US, so if JD.com controlled this, no competitor could stop it—not even Alibaba.

JD.com listed on Nasdaq in 2014, followed by a secondary listing in Hong Kong in 2020. It listed its logistics business separately in Hong Kong, raising $3.2 billion. The New York IPO turned Hillhouse's investment into $3.9 billion.[10]

THE BAT

Hillhouse is an investment firm. What sets China's VC landscape apart is the huge role that its own technology firms play—especially Tencent and Alibaba. US tech firms have their own corporate venture arms, such as Intel. But these have nothing like the scale of Chinese tech companies.

And in the US, there are many such corporate venture arms. In China, there are really just two. Although China has thousands of local and foreign venture funds, it's the investments led by Alibaba and Tencent that have come to define and dominate the entire industry.

Baidu was originally part of this triumvirate—known as the BAT, after the three company's initials—but the business committed some missteps and it was eclipsed by its rivals.

We've heard the story of investors backing Baidu and Alibaba. Tencent's story is the strangest, and probably the most important of them all. It's also a good way to introduce the behind-the-scenes nature of the government in China's tech scene.

PONY MA

Ma Huateng, nicknamed Pony, grew up in Guangdong Province, the economically dynamic province abutting Hong Kong. Its ancient capital, Guangzhou, had become the first major base for multinationals entering China, such as Procter & Gamble and Merck, thanks to its wealth, proximity to Hong Kong, and distance from Beijing.

This traditional city was quickly overshadowed by Shenzhen, anointed by Deng Xiaoping as China's first "special economic zone," which offered incentives including tax cuts, free trade, and cheap land to foreign investors.

Shenzhen, just across the Hong Kong border, was a farming village in the 1990s. It had a foreign investor community, oil riggers from Scotland and Texas, developing energy fields offshore, but was otherwise known to Hongkongers as a seedy place to buy knock-off handbags or to party.

Today it's China's fourth most populous city. Among its forest of gleaming skyscrapers and US-style industrial parks, visitors will find the headquarters of Huawei, drone maker DJI, and Tencent. It is also home to the Shenzhen Stock Exchange, with a market capitalization of $5.16 trillion in 2022. In 2018, Shenzhen's GDP exceeded that of Hong Kong.

Pony Ma and some friends from Shenzhen University founded Tencent in 1998 but without much of an idea of what to do beyond something in tech. Ma came across ICQ, the messaging chat service created by Israel's Mirabilis (which we met in Chapter Four) and copied the idea for China.

Although China's tech companies began by emulating foreign ones (Alibaba and eBay, Baidu and Google, Sina and Yahoo), the key to survival was adapting these for local tastes. Tencent faced hundreds of other messaging apps, at a time when fewer than 1 percent of Chinese had a computer. Tencent didn't develop its version of ICQ for everyone; rather it focused on a product to cater to the youth who accessed the internet in smoky cafes.

One thing Tencent didn't innovate on was branding: initially it called its service OICQ, and Mirabilis sued. Tencent retreated and renamed its messaging app QQ. Nonetheless, by tweaking the idea for a local audience, Tencent experienced explosive growth: by 2000 it had 100 million users.[11]

TENCENT AND NASPERS

Pony Ma was constantly scrounging for capital. In April 2000, he successfully pitched IDG Capital, which joined Hong Kong telco PCCW to take 40 percent of the company for $2.2 million. They liked the company's growth and Ma's business acumen, but they were concerned the company had no monetization strategy: QQ was given away for free.

Tencent was an interesting play but it was deep in the shadow of Alibaba, which had just received $25 million from Goldman and SoftBank, and Baidu, which had raised $10 million from DFJ ePlanet and IDG. Sina would raise $68 million listing on Nasdaq the same year.

So when the dotcom bubble burst later that year, Silicon Valley VCs were forced into survival mode. Alibaba and Baidu had cash to ride out the storm, but IDG and PCCW wanted out of Tencent. Pony Ma's company was burning cash and its runway was disappearing.

He then received an unexpected visit from a 21-year-old American named David Wallerstein, who was bumping around China trying to parlay his language skills into lucrative deals for global information technology and communications companies. Wallerstein had talked his way into being the man on the ground for Naspers, a South African telco that had recently gone IPO in its home market and had cash looking for investments. While sniffing around Shenzhen, he noticed everyone seemed to be using QQ: the service had leaped from the internet cafes into the business world.

In 2001, Wallerstein offered Ma $60 million for a controlling stake—a huge sum at the time, particularly given the market crash. Ma and his team refused to cede control. Wallerstein convinced

Naspers to accept a backseat role, but it ended up paying $32 million in cash for the largest shareholding.

PCCW and IDG each owned one-fifth of Tencent, but PCCW used this opportunity to exit, selling everything to Naspers, while IDG sold 12.8 percent and retained 7.2 percent (which it sold in 2006). The early backers made an 11× return, which at the time must have seemed like a pretty good outcome.[12] But Pony Ma was just getting started.

It is notable that China's authorities allowed foreign companies such as SoftBank, Naspers, Sequoia, and IDG to maintain large stakes in its leading internet champions. This was because in the early 2000s, regulators didn't consider the internet or data as strategic. That stance would change, but the regulators never forced these foreigners to sell. They would have a different way of asserting control—but that's a story for later.

LANDMARK DEALS: TENCENT'S HONG KONG IPO

Two deals demonstrated that China's internet story had become a huge deal on a global scale. The first was Tencent's overseas IPO in 2004. On the advice of a Goldman Sachs tech banker named Martin Lau, Pony agreed to list on the Hong Kong Stock Exchange instead of in New York.

Tencent was now expanding into mobile games. This drove revenues but was an early demonstration of how a Chinese company could begin to monetize a huge user base. The choice to list in Hong Kong was unusual: this was one of the first tech deals there, and the regulators and exchange listing committee had to be persuaded by Lau.

Hong Kong also meant a much lower valuation than what the company might have achieved in New York, and the IPO in June that year raised HK$1.4 billion ($180 million)—big but not a blockbuster. But Lau and Ma agreed Tencent needed to stay close to its userbase. After the IPO, Ma recruited Lau to join him as his right-hand man.

LANDMARK DEALS: ALIBABA AND YAHOO!

The next milestone was Yahoo!'s acquisition of a huge stake in Alibaba. Jack—the other Ma—was in a cutthroat battle with eBay, the US e-commerce site, to dominate China. In 2004, Alibaba achieved the largest-ever VC fund-raising round, receiving $82 million from TDF, Fidelity Investment Group, and GGV. SoftBank used the raise to also increase its stake.

Jack Ma used the proceeds to transform Alibaba into the digital backbone of China's blossoming small-business sector. These were companies that thrived by selling goods and services to foreign companies sourcing cheap goods from the "workshop of the world." Although these small and medium-sized enterprises (SMEs) were the biggest employer in China, individually they were too obscure to obtain funding from the state-owned banking system, and too small to afford a lot of marketing.

Alibaba and its various platforms gave them a way to showcase their wares, in a more sophisticated version of Ma's original China Yellow Pages. But Alibaba wasn't an ads platform, but a marketplace.

The key to its success was to build a trusted means of exchanging money for goods. China's financial system didn't serve SMEs. The banks didn't trust them to repay a loan, multinationals didn't trust them to deliver goods, and the small businesses didn't trust the multinationals to pay up. Their only option was a credit card, but few businesses had access to a Visa or Mastercard, and the charges for receiving overseas payments were too high for small fry.

Alibaba added an online payment that included an escrow account, with the platform serving as a guarantor. This established trust, which greased the wheels of commerce. Jack Ma later rebranded this service Alipay. Alipay charged a tiny transaction fee for payments made on its system. Later, as its trove of data on its SME customers grew into a mountain of information, Alipay deployed a credit rating system. The more transactions, the more data, and therefore the better insight Alipay had on the customer. Then it would offer them loans.

Alipay wasn't the one providing the capital to these SME borrowers. Instead it provided its ratings to a coterie of commercial banks and charged a cut to allow those banks to make the loans. The banks hated working with Alibaba because the internet giant had already cut them out of payments, but Alipay was an irresistible lending channel. Alipay's credit scores, based on real-time data on SME behavior, was better than anything the banks could source on their own, given the parlous state of China's credit rating bureaus.

The Alipay escrow service had already attracted such a huge pile of cash that the company restructured it into a mutual fund company that put most of it into a liquidity reserve. By 2010, it had overtaken JPMorgan as the manager of the world's largest money-market fund. Later, Jack Ma would rebrand this part of the business as Ant Financial—a fintech serving the millions of "ants," China's SMEs.

The initial focus of this hive of activity was to displace eBay in China, and this required a lot of capital—even more than the $82 million raised in 2004. The following year Ma executed a complicated deal with Jerry Yang of Yahoo! and Masayoshi Son of SoftBank, who was a shareholder in both. Yahoo! became the largest shareholder in Alibaba via a VIE structure, acquiring 40 percent of the shares (but only 35 percent of the voting rights), for $1 billion plus ownership of Yahoo!'s China assets.[13]

This deal valued Alibaba at $4 billion—a whopping sum. It united Alibaba with Yahoo!, which was then struggling against Google but was still a force. Alibaba coveted the search capabilities to make listings on its merchant platform easy to find—and free—whereas eBay continued to charge. Soon after, eBay quit China.

GOING MOBILE: XIAOMI AND QIMING

It took more than ten years for these tech giants to shift their emphasis from PCs to mobile. Gradually the investments China made into its mobile infrastructure paid off. This was the enabler for its internet companies to evolve beyond copycats and mature into leaders of global innovation.

"By 2010, you had a generation of experienced technology executives spun out from the portals, Alibaba, and the China operations of multinationals," says Edmond Ng, founder of Axiom Asia, a Singapore-based fund manager that invests in VC funds. "Some started tech companies and others became VCs, and that's when China really took off."[14]

One of these veteran tech leaders was Lei Jun, who had run Kingsoft, a Beijing-based software company that he shepherded onto the Hong Kong stock exchange in 2007. He soon decided his next move was in mobile, where things were stirring.

The MIIT granted three 3G licenses in 2009 to the leading mobile operators, and later that year Apple launched its iPhone in China. Lei saw that consumer mobile was about to take off with the same wild impulse as the internet had ten years before.

He founded Xiaomi Corporation with the intention of building apps for the Android operating system, taking aim at Apple's expensive and inflexible business model. Xiaomi quickly grew an enthusiastic userbase, but Lei understood that Tencent was going to be a formidable competitor. Moreover, Android-operated phones were clunky at the time.

Xiaomi seized its destiny by controlling its entire product line and branched into handset manufacturing. Its Mi line was at the low end of the market, only catering at first to 1.5G bandwidth. But this was enough for Chinese consumers, and Xiaomi became a $1 billion revenue business by 2012. In 2014, Xiaomi advanced into making its own smartphones, taking Apple on head-to-head.

VC was there for the entire journey. Qiming Venture Partners was both a seed and a Series A investor.

Qiming was at the forefront of a wave of venture capital firms opening in China. It was founded in 2006 in Shanghai by Gary Rieschel and Duane Kuang. Rieschel had helped Masayoshi Son set up SoftBank's China VC business and Kuang had led Intel's China investment strategy. The two could see the venture space was on the cusp of going from an obscure business to an institutionalized part of China's growth story.

"IDG was already there, but otherwise VC was mostly done by people flying in," Rieschel says. "Now it had to be done on the ground."

He credits his partner, Kuang, for going into Xiaomi from the start. "Duane insisted on doing the seed round," he says. Qiming led the Series A round with a $350,000 commitment and participated in the Series B and C rounds too. By the time of exit, the Xiaomi stakes returned $1 billion to Qiming.[15]

INVESTING LONG-TERM: CAPITAL TODAY

Qiming represented the institutionalization of VC in China that its partners had sensed was coming. Rieschel and Kuang set it up as a true partnership rather than as a personal vehicle, which was typical at the time. It even extended the same salary and carry compensation to new managing partners.

This was to ensure the firm could be a long-term investor. "We needed the best incentives for a team that didn't just revolve around Duane or me," Rieschel says. "Other firms ended up as a hierarchy beneath a king or queen."

But some of those monarchs also found ways to embed VC in the long-term prospects of China's tech industry.

Kathy Xu Xin is the rare female founder in China's VC industry who has become industry royalty. She started off as an investment banker and private-equity investor, first at Peregrine (the master of Red Chips) and then at Baring Private Equity, where she did the NetEase deal.

By 2005, she had a decade of dealmaking experience and hands-on involvement in her portfolio companies. She noted the firms investing in Chinese startups were based in Hong Kong, or were flying in from the US, with little on-the-ground presence. With the encouragement of an LP that promised to back her, she launched her own VC firm, Capital Today.

She made her reputation by investing $18 million in JD.com as its sole Series A backer in 2007. When she had met its founder, Richard Liu, the year before, they had talked about JD.com until two in the morning. The company was an e-commerce platform that was posting 10 percent revenue growth every month, but at the time was unknown compared to the mighty Alibaba.

Liu asked her for $2 million, but she said he needed at least $10 million if his cash-burning internet business was to expand quickly enough to secure a dominant position. Growth, not profits, was what mattered. She later flew Liu to her office in Shanghai to sign the investment deal, to make sure she kept him from meeting other investors.[16]

That sum turned into a $2.6 billion return for Capital Today when JD.com went IPO in 2014, a return of more than 150x. *Forbes China* declared Xu the "queen of venture capital," a label she hasn't disavowed.

INNOVATING E-COMMERCE

VC firms backed all of China's successful consumer technology companies, from internet to e-commerce to mobile. China was sharing in this global wave of innovation, but its founders were demonstrating creativity and hard work in developing solutions to meet local needs.

For example, one of the factors that enabled JD.com to succeed was Richard Liu's decision to go into direct distribution. In the US, Amazon invented e-commerce, but it could rely on FedEx or DHL to deliver goods to its customers. China lacked national logistics companies and delivery was unreliable. Customers laid the blame on JD.com. The company decided to build its own nationwide network of warehouses and a fleet of delivery vehicles. This was a massive investment that required the company to lean on its VC backers.

When it came to scale, though, no one could top Tencent and Alibaba.

Alibaba leveraged fintech into mobile applications such as gaming and messaging, but its crowning achievement was mobile shopping.

It created Singles Day, making 11 November an annual online extravaganza dwarfing any single shopping event in the US.

But Alibaba was really playing catch-up with Tencent. Pony Ma had long envied Alibaba's fintech prowess. From the beginning, Tencent had built one service on top of another—games, shopping—to create a lifestyle ecosystem. But QQ, its messaging backbone, was a desktop app. The rollout of 4G broadband services allowed Tencent to launch WeChat in 2012 as a mobile messenger, and pile its lifestyle apps inside.

Payments would also be the game-changer for WeChat, but it took Tencent a while to figure out the path to dominance. In 2014 it rolled out a digital version of *laisee*—the red packets with cash gifts that are a staple at Lunar New Year and other events. Tencent allowed users to give red packets either directly to someone else over the platform, or in groups. It added a casino-like element, varying the amounts inside. But all of this cash was moving around on Tencent's servers, just as Alibaba had captured small-business financing. Soon Tencent added investments and insurance to WeChat, with WeChat Pay—the payments business—underpinning everything.

Alibaba came to dominate mobile business and Tencent's WeChat became the indispensable service in people's lives. In the early years, they appeared complementary, but Tencent's move into mobile payments meant Pony was taking on Jack directly. From then on, the two internet giants became locked in a deadly serious competition.

And their biggest battle would be fought in the world of VC.

CORPORATE VENTURE CAPITALISM

For both companies, 2013 was the year they became VCs themselves. Tencent had two assets: its massive user traffic and its capital. Although the business had launched many business lines, not all of them made sense. For example, it had set up an e-commerce site designed to take on Alibaba's consumer platform. But Tencent's team weren't e-commerce experts, so Pony Ma decided to sell the business to JD.com, an erstwhile Alibaba rival, in return for a stake. Instead of trying to run the business, Tencent could simply invest, while sending its WeChat traffic to JD.com, helping it compete against Alibaba.[17]

Alibaba also began to make acquisitions, including overseas. It sought a broad range of companies that in some way would drive traffic to Alibaba's e-commerce businesses. It invested in media, games, soccer clubs, luxury fashion stores, dating apps, photo apps, news portals, logistics and delivery firms, and video content portals.

It spent about $2 billion in 2013 on two acquisitions and then around $5 billion in 2014 on 20 deals—followed by $18 billion across 29 deals in 2015, its most active year as an investor.[18]

Alibaba's spate of activity was initially geared toward boosting its profile ahead of its long-awaited IPO on the New York Stock Exchange. In September 2014, Alibaba raised a record-shattering $25 billion.

Tencent would set a record of its own in 2017, when it became Asia's most valuable company, hitting a market cap of $500 billion.

THE AIRCRAFT CARRIERS

The two became the biggest investors in Chinese tech, with war chests no one else could match. They competed fiercely to deny the other a valuable prize. Their rivalry fueled the next generation of startups, including Meituan (group buying), Pinduoduo (agricultural e-commerce), and Didi Chuxing (ride-hailing). Overall, Alibaba, Tencent, and Baidu capital accounted for three out of four of China's unicorn startups. This is a much bigger concentration of ownership than among US Big Tech companies, which never backed more than 8 percent of US unicorns.[19]

This was a double-edged sword for founders that sold to one of the giants. On the plus side, any startup brought into an Alibaba or Tencent network could access a vast userbase, which kept its cost of customer acquisition very low. On the other hand, this led companies to become lax about how much money they were spending. In other cases, Alibaba and Tencent acquired startups deemed a threat simply to keep them out of play, and the business would suffocate.

The sheer size of the duopoly became the most important determinant of what startups were going to succeed or fail. Back in the 1970s, Don Valentine built Sequoia on the idea of finding a market leader such as Apple and then investing in the companies that would support its various products and services. He had likened this to the armada that sails in tandem with an aircraft carrier.

In China, Tencent and Alibaba were the aircraft carriers, but instead of waiting for VCs to finance the ecosystem around them, they did it with their own money and userbases that dwarfed anything in the US. This prevented the emergence of a robust market for M&A, highlighting once again China's overall weakness in financial markets.

But a stake by Alibaba or Tencent sent a powerful signal that a good startup might become a major success. Traditional VCs co-invested in many of these deals. Indeed, partnering with Alibaba or Tencent was how VCs could open doors. It was one factor behind the move by many foreign firms to raise funds denominated in renminbi, which gave them the option to exit on domestic stock markets (although they still had to figure out how to repatriate the earnings back to the home country).

But foreign VCs had to be prepared to be aggressive if they wanted to keep up.

"Deals in China are done much faster than in the US," says David Lam, the San Francisco GP at Atlantic Bridge, a cross-border technology fund based in Europe. "That was the advantage of Chinese capital."[20]

COPIERS TO CREATORS

This phenomenon transformed China's tech industry from copycat to innovator.

Jing Hong, a Hillhouse partner who founded her own VC firm in Beijing, Gaocheng Capital, likens the transformation to "two time machines."

The first time machine involved the rapid learning from Silicon Valley. Thirty years of Valley history was absorbed and emulated by

Chinese entrepreneurs and investors in compressed time—about ten years. "Chinese companies learned from global peers, like a time machine we can leverage," she says. "Now it's the reverse: the innovation is coming from China."[21]

The second time machine (in her formulation) is the convergence of many cutting-edge technologies into new, China-created businesses. China skipped mass adoption of PCs and the use of email because it initially set out on a path of SMS and mobile messaging. WeChat and Ant reaped the harvest.

Now investors like Hong are backing companies they believe will drive change worldwide, not just at home. For example, Gaocheng is backing enterprise software companies using AI that are already making an impact abroad. Hong cites Tuya, a mobile, AI-enabled enterprise training software, which has more sales outside China than within. "Japanese insurance companies are now running on Chinese software-as-a-service [SaaS]," she says.

VENTURESOME CONSUMERS

How can China leapfrog like this? The country lags the US and other countries in many aspects of fundamental R&D. "We'll see more progress at the application level," Hong says.

What makes such companies competitive is their combining mobile with AI, riding on trends such as the internet-of-things (mass use of measurable sensors) and 5G telecom networks.

But there's another aspect to this beyond the tech itself: it's how it gets used.

While we usually think of innovation in terms of entrepreneurs and inventions, the VC industry demonstrated that innovation is also a function of access to funding and the prospect of a huge payoff. There's a third aspect to innovation, what the economist Amar Bhidé calls "venturesomeness," which is the appetite by consumers for a given technology.

Take the transistor, the invention that underpins the entire electronic world. It wasn't enough that the Bell Labs team invented it, or that Arthur Rock helped the Traitorous Eight go found Fairchild Semiconductors.

Companies like TI, RCA, and Sony integrated chips into radios—that realized their economic value, and along the way required those companies to undertake a lot of engineering work. It was no simple thing for a radio maker to shift from using vacuum tubes to transistors: it required an entire movement to reimagine design, marketing, pricing, and sales.[22]

Americans have long fretted about losing their competitive edge to foreign rivals. The rise of Germany and Japan in the 1980s as fierce competitors led to much handwringing about the paucity of American engineering and math students, Wall Street greed, or short-sighted company management. But the United States went from strength to strength—because of Silicon Valley's open culture, and because American companies kept buying and integrating new technology, whereas corporate Europe and Japan stuck to paper and tradition. American consumers (be they retail or businesses) were venturesome, willing to try out new products and services.

By this argument, a country will prosper even if it's not the one doing the inventing, so long as it gets to benefit from the sweat and ingenuity of others.

VENTURESOME CHINA

China's population has proved to be extremely venturesome. It has ridden more vicissitudes than most, from the Cultural Revolution to the reform and opening-up of Deng, and now superpower status, relative wealth, and an innovation wave. When Ant and WeChat arrived, life for nearly 1 billion people changed on a dime. The entire population downloaded a handful of apps and put the mobile phone at the center of their lives.

To get a sense of this scale, consider that in 2018, Apple Pay facilitated about 1 billion transactions a month—and WeChat Pay did 1.2 billion a day.[23]

China has two advantages: a venturesome population, and a big one, with 1 billion internet users and nearly the same number of smartphone users, making it the biggest smartphone market in the world. That generates a continuously rising mountain of data and raw material for constant innovation that no other country can match—except perhaps India, whose story we have yet to tell.

This means that, in theory, the experiences of Alibaba and Tencent and their peers in China are a harbinger of things to come in the rest of the world. Already Facebook (now Meta) is trying to copy WeChat Pay and TikTok (the contagious video-sharing app created by China's Bytedance, which was funded by Kathy Xu's Capital Today). Amazon is copying some of Alibaba's moves in streaming, online shopping, and offline, sensor-heavy stores. And the obscure but valuable companies in Jing Hong's portfolio are bringing Chinese mobile and AI capabilities to businesses overseas.

The world is transitioning through another of Carlota Perez's waves of innovation. She created the framework of tech-defined eras, from the Industrial Revolution to the Age of Steam and Railways, to today's Age of Information and Telecommunications.

This age had its own waves, beginning with the transistor that Silicon Valley turned into ICs and microprocessors. This was the first tech wave that was enabled by VC, and VC played a formative role in subsequent waves: the rise of software, the PC, networking, the internet, and the mobile internet.

Someone in the 1880s might have struggled to realize they were now in the Age of Steel, and that the epoch of steam and railways was over. After all they were still crossing the ocean in steamships and railroads were the fastest way to cross continents. Today we still feel as though we are in the Age of Information and Telecommunications, because the fruits of that age dominate our lives and its companies remain the most powerful in the world.

We don't know what era we are now in, but we do know that China will play a part in defining it. Britain dominated the Industrial Revolution; it wasn't until the 1880s that the US and Germany became the major drivers of innovation. The Information Age spread from the US to Asia, but was still an American-led story.

Partly within that trend, but also in resistance, China developed its own tech story. Although there are many reasons behind this rise, not least the size and depth of its brilliant entrepreneurs, a critical factor was its development of a mature VC industry.

"China is the only market other than the US to develop scale in VC," says Qiming's Rieschel. "It's the only market to prove VC firms can raise money, invest it, and realize their returns."

This is why China is going to play a leading role in the new age, and why VCs continue to pour time and money into its founders. Take the metaverse, a fuzzy concept championed by Facebook, which even changed its name to Meta. Some VCs see the Chinese consumer driving a different metaverse ecosystem—one that could become ascendant.

China has a huge gaming market, which is raw material for virtual reality applications developed by China's cutting-edge AI and internet-of-things companies. Chinese companies such as Huawei lead the world in 5G bandwidth, which means Chinese tech players can cram more power and features onto their mobile devices. If China lags the advent of cloud computing, it could catch up with quantum computing.

It's not a given that a US company will develop something beloved by global consumers. China could do it, based on its companies' vast userbase and culture of cutthroat innovation to please its consumers. And global VCs are still prepared to write the checks to make it happen.

It would seem there's nothing that could stop the Chinese tech juggernaut from overtaking Silicon Valley as home to the world's leading companies. The US can still do most of the R&D and inventing, so long as it's the Chinese who apply new technologies at scale, and set the standards defining consumer taste. Not even the animosity of the US can stop this process.

Nothing—except China itself. Bizarrely, that's what may have just happened.

12

CHINA: THE RECKONING

THE tech and VC world in China was on the cusp of a massive celebration. The dual-listing of Ant Financial on the Hong Kong Exchange and on STAR, a startup-focused board in Shanghai, was slated to raise $35 billion, valuing the company at $315 billion—the second time Jack Ma would break IPO records.

The deal represented the ultimate "liquidity event" for Ant backers. By now the company was too big and mature for VC, and its biggest investors outside Alibaba were giant PE firms such as Warburg Pincus, Carlyle Group, and Silver Lake; BlackRock, the world's biggest asset manager; Hong Kong-based Primavera Capital; and GIC, the sovereign wealth fund of Singapore.

These groups had poured a combined $10.3 billion into Ant in 2018 as part of an invitation-only pre-IPO fundraising into a VIE structure with no assets, and no recourse in the event the IPO didn't take place.[1]

But why would they doubt this? Ant had transformed how Chinese companies and people gained access to capital. Via its Alipay app, Ant had credit and other data on 1 billion users and 80 million merchants. It had significant stakes in many technology companies around the world, and Jack Ma was enormously popular both at home and abroad.

The IPO was slated for November 2020. Shortly beforehand, on October 24, Ma attended a high-level summit of Communist Party leaders, financial regulators, and bank executives in Shanghai where he extolled the virtues of data-led credit allocation—and took a direct swipe at the people in the audience.

He accused financial regulators' "old-people's club" of impeding innovation and said China's banks operated with a "pawnshop mentality" that was bad for entrepreneurs.

The response from the Party was swift and merciless. The Ant IPO was suspended indefinitely and the regulators told Ma and the Ant executive team that they would no longer enjoy lax oversight. Then came a slew of regulations that forced Ant to restructure and be regulated as a bank, and a monster $2.8 billion fine on Alibaba.

Jack Ma was a flamboyant figure and so was his transgression, which led many investors to believe the government's ire was mainly about putting Alibaba in its place.

As it turned out, however, the Party was just getting started. In the coming months it would transform China's domestic technology sector and assert blunt state control. The foreign investors backing Ant are out of pocket—Ant may be allowed to list in 2023, but at a much lower valuation—and investors in many other tech companies would soon lose even more.

For more than 20 years, foreign capital, led by US VCs, had financed the incredible rise of the Chinese internet economy, which in turn created an innovation powerhouse that rivaled Silicon Valley and spread its influence throughout global emerging markets.

That compact was coming undone.

KEN WILCOX: READING TEA LEAVES

From the start, it was clear to foreign investors that doing business in China was going to be different than doing business in other countries because of the role of the state. This role was never explicit. On the one hand, the government was happy in the 2000s to give tech startups a free rein. The sector wasn't considered strategic, and Beijing valued the benefits of innovation.

Ken Wilcox, the former CEO of SVB, moved to Shanghai in 2010 to oversee SVB's newly minted onshore business. "I had a fabulous four years," says Wilcox, who has also been chairman of the Asia Society since 2005—a non-profit educational organization dedicated to building bridges between the US and Asia. He would grow disillusioned by the experience, however.

The onshore banking license was baked into a government five-year plan, suggesting the authorities had a clear blueprint for supporting the innovation economy.

Upon arriving in Shanghai, Wilcox was pitched by the municipal authorities to operate a fund of funds managing city money, and suggested a few local funds. Wilcox noticed one of these fund managers had no experience. "There are a lot of successful VCs that are professional, but most are based on *guanxi* [relationships], and their main positive quality is they have good connections or are well regarded by the Party," he says.[2]

Wilcox was largely impressed by what he experienced. "The evidence is overwhelming that the Chinese system works. But in large measure, the Party determines the outcomes. It determines these because it controls anything it wants to control. That doesn't mean it does control everything. It means it can if it wants. The US government can't and doesn't aspire to do so."

PICKING WINNERS

For example, the Ministry of Science and Technology took an interest in the corporate venture activities of the tech giants. It encouraged Alibaba to invest in startups involved in building smart cities, and Tencent to back companies in computer vision.[3] Baidu has been similarly guided to invest in autonomous driving. Combined, these technologies had a dual use: to drive economic growth, and to plug into the government's surveillance and control apparatus over Chinese citizens.

This system manifests itself in a willingness to spend a lot of money on areas the government prioritizes, and to use private capital or entrepreneurs where necessary. K.O. Chia of the Hong Kong Venture Capital Association says the government studied the VC model carefully.

"They talked to us in 2003 when I was at Walden," he says. "The government understood VC as a strategic development tool. Only the governments of China and Israel get it. Beijing knew it was okay to lose $9 billion on failures if that other $1 billion succeeds and goes on to create the next great wave of entrepreneurs and companies."[4]

Wilcox relates a story of what this meant in practice. Shortly after he arrived in Shanghai, the municipal government sent a woman to work with SVB. She had identified 800 promising tech startups and asked SVB to help it identify the best ones; her finance department could then ask local banks to support those companies.

Over time, Wilcox found she had done a decent job of screening startups. "She didn't know the technology, but she identified 800 companies out of thousands. She could winnow it down. VCs are best for identifying good startups, but that's not the same thing as identifying which ones will succeed."

The government knew this too. It dangled the prospect of a banking license in front of SVB. Foreign banks could only operate via joint ventures, and SVB managed to tie up with Shanghai Pudong Development Bank. The government, eager to soak up the mysteries of venture debt, even gave SVB 50 percent of the JV, rather than the 10 to 20 percent that was typical. But once the government, or the Chinese banks it wanted SVB to mentor, felt they had learned enough, they set up competing institutions. SVB's own China business ended up being marginal (although it did prosper by banking Chinese VCs and startups in the US), and rivals such as Tencent's WeBank would become the biggest bankers to startups.

Nonetheless, SVB had felt it had no choice but to go along. Initially Wilcox thought they had cracked the China market, thanks to assiduous efforts to develop *guanxi* and be perceived as a good corporate actor. Indeed, Wilcox says big US venture capital firms in China have adapted by relying as much on *guanxi* as on their usual tire-kicking skills. "Many private VC funds in the US operate the same," Wilcox adds, noting most of them tend to follow the brand-name firms.

The difference in China was twofold: first, the country's size and venturesomeness meant it was throwing up unicorns at record pace; and second, the government was adept at channeling investments where it wanted them to go. VCs could add value by analyzing market fit, or finding a quality entrepreneur, or studying a great invention—or by becoming expert at judging government aims.

RENMINBI FUNDS

VCs didn't have the market to themselves, either. They learned to operate among a growing number of local funds. Initially these were privately owned. Jixun Foo at GGV says from 2000 to 2010, most capital in Chinese tech was from US dollar-denominated funds. Since then, renminbi-denominated funds cropped up, backed by various arms of government—ministries, SOEs, or municipal and provincial authorities—and by banks and wealthy individuals.

The government has encouraged private renminbi funds by opening STAR and other bourses that offer local investors an IPO exit. Renminbi funds tend to be shorter in duration, usually seven years to deploy capital and exit, with an option for another two years; US dollar funds follow the Silicon Valley norm of 10+2 years.

But, says Foo, "Tech capital is still driven by US dollar funds, especially for early-stage companies."

GOVERNMENT GUIDANCE FUNDS

Starting in the 2010s, state-operated VCs came on the scene. Beijing was concerned about the tech sector's dependence on foreign capital. It reminded Beijing of times when it was cut off from foreign sources of its defense technological needs, such as in 1960 when relations with the Soviet Union soured, and in 1989 when the West cut off military ties.

The golden age of China internet tech centered on the consumer internet, but from the Party's point of view, key technologies are always a facet of national security. Innovation was a way to help its military access the latest tech, and finance was the means.

This manifested itself in two ways. One was to help defense companies list on the local stock exchanges. Since the inauguration of the Shanghai and Shenzhen exchanges in 1990, regulators managed the IPO pipeline to favor SOEs, which is one reason why tech companies preferred the VIE route.

Starting in the early 2010s, China introduced Government Guidance Funds (GGFs). Initially they served as catalysts, with state entities accounting for only 5 to 15 percent of the fund, which promised some policy perks to private funds that put money in. But they operated on a parallel track, with private capital free to do as it pleased.

Under the leadership of Xi Jinping, these funds have become much larger and now more explicitly determine the direction for private money, including foreign funds. By early 2020, China had 1,741 GGFs managing Rmb4.76 trillion ($690 billion) of assets.

Of these, about one-fifth are aimed at technologies to be adapted by the military-security complex, to fulfill Xi's idea of an economy geared to serving both civilian and military needs. They tend to operate outside of any independent legal system or system of due process. They are meant to leverage private know-how and practices, but they are often badly run, rife with corruption, and usually end up investing in SOEs or big conglomerates instead of startups.[5]

"Government Guidance Funds don't know how to invest," says a managing partner at a US investment firm in Shanghai. "Look where the money comes from."

SMIC AND SEMICONDUCTORS

Nonetheless, GGFs are now a big source of funding for tech companies that the government wants to support, such as in semiconductors. China has a large semiconductor manufacturing industry but it steadily lags Taiwan, South Korea, and the US in producing the most advanced chips.

There have been VC-backed chip companies for a long time, led by SMIC, a pure-play foundry similar to TSMC.

It was founded in Shanghai (via a Caymans VIE) in 2000 by Richard Chang, a TI veteran who built and sold a Taiwanese foundry before returning to mainland China where he was born. He founded SMIC with investment from VCs Hambrecht & Quist Asia, Walden International, GIC, AsiaVest, NEA, and Goldman Sachs. Its biggest shareholders were Motorola and the Shanghai government.[6]

By 2004, SMIC was the world's fourth-largest foundry, and it listed that year on Nasdaq, despite never having come close to turning a profit. The IPO was a lucrative exit for the VCs. Larger-scale private equity would enter later, but SMIC's shareholding became more tied to municipal governments: the company just bled money, and only the Chinese government has the appetite to keep investing, in the hopes of creating a national champion that can create and own its own technology.

In 2019, amid rising tensions with the US, SMIC delisted from Nasdaq. Meanwhile, GGFs had become important shareholders in SMIC, led by one called the China National Integrated Circuit Industry Investment Fund—known as "the Big Fund"—which acquired a 23 percent stake in 2020 shortly before SMIC listed on Shanghai's STAR market.

THE BIG FUND

The head of the Big Fund, however, has since been arrested for corruption, amid allegations that GGFs of this kind were run by civil servants with no understanding of the industry. The Big Fund, established in 2014 by a mishmash of government agencies and SOEs, manages Rmb340 billion ($47 billion) with the task of achieving semiconductor independence. Where it invested, many other VCs followed—because if the Big Fund was allocating capital to a company, then it was a politically safe bet and maybe a smart investment since the company was enjoying so much state support.

Now under investigation, the Big Fund has ground to a halt. The reason for the investigation is murky. It may be that its managers were too focused on profits instead of national service, and made conservative bets into established companies rather than risky startups.[7]

Xi Jinping wants to repeat the success of "Two Bombs, One Satellite," with mass mobilization and patriotic gusto. However, if the Big Fund is found to be corrupt, then its taint could smear the private companies co-investing with it.[8]

Given there are nearly 1,800 such guidance funds, the fear of corruption hangs over the entire sector.

China is not unique in having an industrial policy. The US Congress passed its CHIPS and Science Act in 2022, which provides $39 billion in tax benefits and other incentives to manufacture chips in the US. It will channel funds to specific chipmakers such as Intel. But its primary focus is on funding basic research and offering tax breaks to encourage companies to enter the chips industry rather than trying to pick winners.

This harks to the American tradition of backing science and technology through government contracts to support an open system—well before the rise of VC.

THE US EXAMPLE: FEDERAL TELEGRAPH

The US engaged its first imperial war outside of its continental borders in 1898 against Spain. In the Caribbean it acquired Puerto Rico and made Cuba a protectorate, while in the Pacific it also seized Guam and the Philippines. Along the way the US also annexed Hawaii, the lynchpin of the Pacific Ocean (and which wouldn't become a state until 1959); and it would soon cement control of the Panama Canal.

Suddenly the US had a global empire that required military bases and a means of coordinating its Navy. It would soon turn to tech startups to meet that need—starting with the West Coast's first high-tech company, Federal Telegraph Company.

The Bay Area was mostly agricultural, although the 1849 gold rush made San Francisco the seat for mining and extraction companies, which required technological prowess. Stanford University was founded in 1885 to pursue researching into mining and civil engineering and soon gained national importance. It was here that Federal Telegraph, funded by a local banker, got its start with clever ways to use radio for secure, long-distance communications. The US Navy became Federal Telegraph's first big customer, providing it with a cushion to survive, just as it would support Fairchild Semiconductor and Intel in the 1960s and 1970s.[9]

Despite calls to nationalize the technology when the US entered the First World War in 1917, the government opted to keep Federal Telegraph private and independent, albeit as its de facto representative in the commercial sphere, chasing contracts in Latin America to block European rivals.

Too much government support usually turns out badly, though, as Federal Telegraph would go on to show. Following the breakout of the First World War, the company netted $1.6 million in Navy contracts—but only about $1 million reached the company's books. The rest involved shady side deals with the owners' private companies, and the scandal forced the Navy to cut its ties.

But Federal Telegraph's real problem was that its reliance on military largesse had caused it to miss out on technological developments: vacuum tubes. The Navy diversified its investments to RCA, an all-American radio company owned by General Electric, AT&T, Westinghouse, and United Fruit Company (whose role was to support RCA in those Latin American countries where United Fruit Company had plantations).

Federal Telegraph's other problem was that it was in California but the weight of America's military needs were Atlantic. This geographic weakness put the alarm into Stanford's provost, Frederick Terman, who doubled his efforts to nurture California's startup environment.[10]

Stanford would go on to support HP, Litton Industries, and Varian Associates—the tech giants of post-war San Francisco, all of which were sustained by military contracts, but which learned to commercialize so they could control their own fate.

THE COLD WAR

The Second World War, which began in Asia in 1936 and Europe in 1939, led to another round of military funding for research, particularly for the earliest computers. The US Army funded the first fully electronic digital computer, called ENIAC. This machine was all hardware, designed to do a single thing: in this case, calculate artillery fire. The Army funded research into hardware with a stored memory, so that instructions could be modified; this resulted in another machine, EDVAC, built in 1944.

Britain and the Soviet Union were also pouring government resources into developing computers. The US military, however, wanted its research to diffuse technology, not hog it for itself. It was very aware that its money was supporting companies that could never get a loan from a bank, and that a lively computer industry would provide the government with far more innovative results over time. It also didn't want to become dependent on a single vendor, as it had for a time with Federal Telegraph.

The US also had a very different philosophy about the purpose of government funding of research. In 1950, the government established the National Science Foundation (NSF). Its mission was to fund advanced science for its own sake, rather than to direct research into specific mandates. No other government had such an approach.

By the mid-1950s, especially following the invasion of South Korea by the North in 1950, military contracts supported the emergence of an industry on the East Coast. These big companies included RCA, IBM, and Sperry Rand, which sold computers to support specialized fields such as air defense, cryptography, and the design of nuclear weapons.[11]

Initially, there were hardly any startups for the military to look to. One reason startups had such a difficult time—and needed government funding—was because of tax. As part of Roosevelt's New Deal program, Congress in the 1930s had raised taxes on capital gains to 39 percent, and the top bracket for income tax to 79 percent.

Entrepreneurs found that once they began to expand their business, they faced punitive taxes.

One response was the founding of ARD, America's first VC, which scored with its investment in DEC, in 1957—the same year the Soviet Union ushered in the Space Age by launching Sputnik. Other responses involved the US doubling down on its involvement in high tech.

First, the DoD formed two critical agencies. One was DARPA, whose work would lay the foundations for the internet; the other was the National Aeronautics and Space Administration (NASA). These would become major procurers of electronics.

Second, Congress passed the National Defense Education Act in 1958, which poured money into scientific research. By now, more than half of national R&D was funded by the federal government, led by the DoD.[12]

Just as the NSF was founded in 1950 to fund science without political mandates, DARPA also had an unusually liberal framework. Designed to cut through bureaucratic red tape, it was also given a mission similar to a VC's: to make lots of big bets on many companies in the expectation that just a handful would bear fruit. The only difference is that DARPA wants solutions, whereas VCs want profits. DARPA was created to build technologies by farming out the work to contractors, not to oversee paperwork-intensive grants.[13] This kind of freedom made DARPA the ideal partner to Silicon Valley.

The government's requirement that learning from its contracts be diffused through the tech industry was a boon to Silicon Valley. Its open, egalitarian culture rewarded people who moved between companies or set up their own. This environment was more conducive to spreading the know-how. The Valley's budding ecosystem gained tremendously as a result, with innovations building quickly upon one another.

The third act by the US government to support its tech industry was to subsidize venture funds. Congress passed the Small Business Investment Act in 1958, creating the Small Business Investment Company (SBIC) program. These SBICs were venture funds supported by tax breaks and subsidized loans.

Georges Doriot of ARD was outraged by the government backing a raft of new competitors. In the end, no SBIC amounted to much; such is the problem of giving VCs easy money. But the government support did attract a lot of talent. Silicon Valley financiers such as William Draper III (of Sutter Hill Ventures) and banker George Quist (of Hambrecht & Quist) began their VC careers in SBICs.[14]

SBICs were kept small, but over time as a class they did deploy a lot of capital to startups—up to $1 billion by 1967.[15] Their presence broadened the VC industry, both in Silicon Valley and on the East Coast, and helped support the growth of other parts of the ecosystem, such as tech lawyers.

DOING BUSINESS WITH UNCLE SAM

Government support for VCs and tech companies should not be mistaken for an industrial policy promoting national champions. The US government needed certain technologies, and was willing to pay for them, which incentivized companies to develop them. The government wanted to ensure a wide, dynamic base of companies to choose from, rather than trying to determine which lived or died.

The first hot technology the government needed was the transistor, which it realized would be critical to winning the Cold War. Semiconductor companies such as Fairchild and its spinoffs got their start thanks to military contracts. By the end of the 1960s, though, commercial contracts began to outstrip government money.

IBM had a long history of selling computers to the military. But these projects weren't relevant to the commercial market, which demanded simplicity and low cost, whereas government contracts were not price sensitive and sought to meet very specific needs.

Eventually "Big Blue" stopped servicing the government and threw its resources behind developing mainframe computers for business customers. To cover a temporary loss of revenues, IBM granted its employees the first-ever corporate stock options, giving its people an incentive to buy into a rights offering.[16]

THE NAVY'S CHIP

As the interests of tech companies and the government began to diverge, the military funded its own research efforts for niche products. This could yield successes: the US Navy even invented the microprocessor independently of Intel or TI.

The Navy achieved this in 1970, via a chip company called Garrett AiResearch that, on contract from defense company Grumman, introduced a microprocessor designed to operate the electromechanics of the F-14 fighter jet. The chip, called the Central Air Data Computer, came out one year before Intel's 4004, the first microprocessor on the market.

But whereas Intel would go on to dominate chip design, making ever more miniature and powerful computers on a chip that propelled the adoption of PCs, the Air Force's chip didn't evolve or lead to anything else. It was built to do just one thing. While it was an engineering feat, helping make the F-14 the most sophisticated jet fighter in the world, the Central Air Data Computer was also a dead end.[17]

By the end of the 1970s, the tail was wagging the dog: the government changed its procurement policies to allow it to buy commercial technologies, lest it be shut out of the market.

Commercialization also opened the door to VC, which quickly replaced government as the source of funding and stability for early-stage companies. The DoD even lost the battle to have computer vendors program in a single, interoperable language: the new world of software would be powered instead by languages such as C++ (developed by AT&T in 1982) and Java (1991, Sun Microsystems), that existed for purely commercial reasons.[18]

LESS IS MORE: PRO-INNOVATION POLICIES

This didn't mean government was now irrelevant to the story of funding innovation in America. Now, however, its role was more about supporting the ecosystem. This usually meant getting out of the way.

Probably the most significant reform was by the US Labor

Department, which in 1979 reinterpreted the "prudent man" rule of the Employee Retirement Income Security Act (ERISA), which had been legislated in 1974.

ERISA established rules for corporate pension plans, including Rule 401(k) for the provision of employee pension funds. These rules included guidance on how funds could invest, to ensure companies safeguarded employees. Senator Lloyd Bentsen pushed the Labor Department to view "prudence" based on a total portfolio, not just individual investments.

This revision made it possible for pension funds to invest in an array of asset classes, including VC. This turbocharged the entire VC industry. In 1978, there were only 23 venture funds, managing about $500 million. By 1983, there were 230 VCs managing $11 billion, of which one-third came from pension funds. Such funding accelerated innovation and attracted yet more entrepreneurs and financiers to the tech industry.

Pension funds were hungry to get exposure to the next DEC, and they did: 1983 was also the year when tech IPOs exploded, with 900 deals in the US that raised $12.8 billion—more capital raised through IPOs than all the years previously back to 1971.[19] That was a staggering windfall for the entrepreneurs and early backers of these startups, and yet another reason for institutional money to seek exposure by investing in VC. This trend would reach its apotheosis with David Swensen's pursuit of alternative assets for Yale.

STATE-LED INNOVATION

In China, technology exists to serve the state—even if the founders and investors don't know it. Jack Ma thought the state could be reformed through the example Alibaba had set. His experience had been one commercial triumph after another, and in the process he helped tens of millions of small companies gain access to funding that state-owned banks could never provide. But when the state decided to assert itself, it did so swiftly and comprehensively.

The ascension of Xi Jinping marks a more aggressive assertion of state power in China. This began before the crackdown on internet companies. If Shenzhen became the city best representing the values of Deng Xiaoping, then Xi's city is Xiong'an, located about 100 kilometers south of Beijing.

Xiong'an is a new, planned city meant to relieve overpopulation in Beijing while showcasing Chinese values and technology. It is to be a "smart city," digitally connected by the internet-of-things and run by AI. The main form of transport, for example, will be electric vehicles, while payments will all be made using the digital yuan (not WeChat Pay or Alipay). Xiong'an's real estate is meant to be totally state-owned and planned, in contrast to the many corporate parks and prestige skyscrapers that define Shenzhen.[20]

This is just one expression of Xi's "common prosperity" drive. The Deng policies of growth and development led to a huge increase in inequality and corruption, and Xi is determined to reverse those trends—and avoid the social instability that plagues the US.

CRACKDOWN

The Chinese state has also bent private internet companies to its needs, notably suborning Tencent's WeChat to serve as a mass surveillance network. Once the Party became aware of the power of the company's data modeling and insights into user behavior, it could not allow a private company to do as it pleased with this power. Pony Ma was not given a choice: Tencent must hand over data to the government when ordered.[21]

Nationalization is also a possibility. The People's Bank of China, the central bank, forced Ant to sell 65 percent of its shares to SOEs led by Zhejiang Tourism Investment Group. The partners intend to establish a new joint venture running a credit-scoring service. Ant had always resisted government efforts for it to share its cache of consumer data on 1 billion people. Now that data belongs to the government.[22]

The crackdown on Big Tech companies didn't stop with Ant. The government set out tough rules to prevent monopolistic practices in the internet sector. It forced Tencent to stop producing shoot-em-up mobile games and start churning out games that serve propaganda purposes. Suddenly the founders of tech giants such as Meituan and Pinduoduo quit and donated billions of dollars' worth of stock to charity.

No one wanted to end up like Jack Ma, who disappeared from view and may have had his wealth stripped; he formally ceded control of Ant Group in January 2023, and in March the government broke Alibaba into six separate companies. Ma was not the only high-profile tech tycoon to lose his position.

In June 2021, ride-hailing platform Didi listed on the New York Stock Exchange, in an act of recklessness rivaling only Jack Ma's fiery speech. The company had been warned by regulators not to do the IPO, but it went ahead anyway. The deal was a success, raising $4.4 billion, which looked like payday for its VCs, including SoftBank, Tiger Global, and Tencent. But the day after the listing, China's cyber regulator announced it was investigating data breaches at Didi, citing national security concerns. The stock price collapsed and by December Didi had delisted—a stunning turn of events.

The final neutering of the internet tech sector followed in early 2022 when the government declared an entire industry illegal: online tutoring, a $100 billion sector heavily backed by all the major VC firms. Covid-19 fueled demand for learning from home, and in 2020 VCs poured $10.5 billion into the industry's unicorns.[23]

In March 2021, Xi declared after-school training was a social problem, and the government essentially regulated the industry out of existence. Private companies like Yuanfudao, an edutech valued at $17 billion, were wiped out. US-listed Tal Education had a $90 billion market cap in spring of 2021, but only $3 billion by 2023.

TOUGH LOVE?

There are many people in Asia's VC industry that defend China's crackdown, even if the handling has been rough. They point to America's failure to regulate Facebook, Google, and other Big Tech companies, regardless of whether the Presidency or Congress is controlled by Republicans or Democrats.

"Antitrust is a universal challenge," says one Beijing-based VC partner. "Facebook, Amazon and Alibaba control unprecedented amounts of data. We prefer regulators work with due process, but in the West there is legal and political entanglement. China has showed its own flexibility and capability to adjust without an election."

Gary Rieschel, founder of Qiming, puts it like this: "Facebook got away with it [data abuses and socially damaging algorithms] because the government hadn't put rules in place about data, how people should be compensated [for using their data]...[24]

"The China crackdown was a huge overreaction because the government is catching up. It didn't appreciate the extent of tech's data, insight, what was happening in the economy. They allowed things to run away from them, and maybe they should have paid more attention. It's hard when technology moves so quickly for a government to think ahead...I don't think companies are capped but the government will apply more regulations, earlier. The [monopolistic] behavior of Tencent and Alibaba, it was bad. We had investments in dozens of Alibaba and Tencent companies, and they would force a company to work with [just one of them]. Their reach and their monopolistic behavior around distribution of products and services had to be reckoned with."

Another VC says: "China believes the internet needs regulation. More governments will follow its example. Ant's going to come back, but regulated, like a bank. China's setting the pace, not the US." This particular VC, however, has recently relocated to Southeast Asia.

Investors say they are still focused on market plays. Some say they avoid investing alongside GGFs; others say their expertise involves understanding what sectors the government will nurture—hard tech like semiconductors, AI, smart cities, electric vehicles, robotics, healthcare.

VC DIMINISHED

But finding room for maneuver will get more difficult.

An investor who had stakes in Alibaba and Tencent says the spate of founders resigning their positions is troubling. "They know what's ahead. There's no desire for [a] founder to create a big-time tech company now. Bright entrepreneurs want to succeed and create a big market, but in China if you get too big for your britches, you get called in for a cup of coffee and told your success is because of the government's infrastructure. And if there's a personal agenda on top, it's a nightmare. So you can forget about innovation."

Deal flow has suffered in the wake of the crackdown, which has sent Chinese stocks tumbling, including in Hong Kong. In the first half of 2022, VC and PE firms raised $4.8 billion—94 percent less than the first half of 2021, according to data provider Preqin.[25]

Some of the biggest foreign investors in Chinese tech have been slashing their holdings: SoftBank has sold much of its Alibaba shares (see Chapter Fourteen), while in September 2022, Naspers began selling $7.6 billion of Tencent stock. These and other sales show some of the foreign investors that benefited from China the most are taking risk off the table.

The big funds that are dedicated to China still raised large rounds from global LPs in 2022. IDG Capital raised $900 million in June 2022. GGV and Qiming also raised new funds. Sequoia outdid them all, raising nearly $9 billion. Neil Shen has also tied his investment strategy closely to Xi's "common prosperity" goals, which promises a safer ride but one that will struggle to produce the returns that Sequoia's LPs previously enjoyed.

By 2023, the funding situation for China VCs had grown dire. Even leading brands are feeling stress in their portfolio valuations and in new fund raising. They are more prone to internal disputes as senior partners seek to leave.

Funding for RMB-denominated funding has become difficult. The biggest investors in these funds were local governments. But their budgets are being squeezed by woes in the real-estate sector and overspending on "Zero Covid" measures.

China-US tensions, on top of a rising interest rate environment, are causing global LPs to pull back from Chinese VC. New institutional investment from the Middle East is entering China, but it mainly backs state-owned enterprises, not startups.

Capital is drying up for large, later-stage or growth-equity investments. This also means VCs that just do early-stage investing are seeing LPs pull away, because they can't realize gains in later funding rounds. Only large, well-connected VCs with the ability to invest from seed to late stage are able win LPs' favor.

CAPITAL CRACKDOWN

The biggest worry for US-dollar VCs in China isn't the government's crackdown. It's the US response. Chinese innovation has been funded by foreign LPs and this might end.

The Trump administration forced long-simmering disputes about Chinese companies listed in the US to the fore. Any listco is meant to provide an independent audit to the Securities and Exchange Commission. But the Chinese government has blocked such moves on the grounds that the data is a national security issue. US regulators have threatened to kick out Chinese companies.

Diplomats have hammered out a tentative agreement to prevent Chinese companies from being delisted en masse. As of early 2023, the deal seems to be holding up, with the US Securities and Exchange Commission able to review audits conducted onshore in China. Beijing ultimately sought to compromise because it values foreign investment into its private sector.

Nonetheless there are political actors and bureaucrats in both countries who might wish the deal to fail. It is likely that some portion of Chinese companies will choose to delist from US exchanges.

Many Chinese companies are expected to relist in Hong Kong, with its US dollar-pegged currency and relatively liberal regulations. Hong Kong would provide global LPs with a viable exit.

HONG KONG'S ROLE?

Hong Kong will play an important role in China's ability to maintain access to international capital markets. Although the territory has not been involved in the tech sector since the last semiconductor assembly factories left in the 1980s, its financial services industry is the biggest in Asia, thanks to its rule of law, low tax, and English-language capabilities.

Finance is the most important link now in US-China relations. Wall Street firms remain the only pro-China industry in the US. Hong Kong is their most convenient gateway. The Xi Jinping administration has also floated the concept of a Greater Bay Area (GBA)—deliberately invoking the idea of San Francisco's high-tech Bay Area—in which Hong Kong would be more closely integrated with the hardware companies of Shenzhen, the assembly factories of Dongguan and other nearby cities, and the affluent consumer market of Guangzhou.

Hong Kong hosts global capital, and it also has high-quality universities that are gradually becoming sources of technological research and entrepreneurs.

GBA boosters such as George Lam, an ex-investment banker who is chairman of Cyberport, a Hong Kong government-backed tech incubator, argue this combination of stock markets, universities, consumers, hardware companies, and international norms can turn the GBA into the Silicon Valley of the twenty-first century. "We'll attract talent from everywhere," he said. "We'll be more open than Silicon Valley."[26]

"Companies in the GBA move five times faster than those in Silicon Valley, at prices that are five times cheaper," says Li Zexiang, a professor at Hong Kong University of Science and Technology, and a former research scientist at MIT's AI lab.

The city has never been a tech hub, and despite these advantages, it's unlikely to become one—the culture still favors banking, real-estate and legal jobs, and startup failures carry personal stigma—but in theory, it could become more involved in developing a broader tech ecosystem. The Hong Kong Stock Exchange now allows biotech companies to list without the traditional requirements of a profitable track record, and it hopes to attract more Chinese tech companies, such as Ant, now that the US markets are harder to access.

But turning the GBA into more than a political slogan will require big changes: there remains today a border between Hong Kong and the mainland, with different legal systems, different currencies, and different laws around the movement of data, people, and money.

The city has also tarnished its reputation internationally. In 2019, a misguided government proposal to effectively expose Hong Kong criminal law to mainland extraterritoriality sparked massive street protests that ended in a police crackdown and the imposition of authoritarian rule, which puts a question mark on the city's rule of law. This was followed by a response to Covid-19 that appeared to prioritize matching the mainland's "Zero Covid" lockdowns rather than support the city's economy or its international competitiveness.

Now that China has reopened after three years of pandemic-related isolation, business in Hong Kong is booming once again. It remains a hub for many VC and PE firms that want to be close to its international capital market.

SCHISM

But many wealthy Chinese, scarred by the tech crackdown and the bitter experience of arbitrary lockdowns, are flocking to Singapore and beyond, rather than investing in Hong Kong. The city's success comes from being an entrepot, a concept that is difficult to square with greater political and social integration with mainland China.

Even if Hong Kong retains its own character, it is now perceived by many in the West, particularly in the US, as "China." The US responded to the crackdown on protesters by abolishing longstanding rules that gave Hong Kong exports separate tax and administrative treatment. This sensibility leaks into the everyday. When OpenAI, a US startup, launched its generative AI applications, including DALL-E for images and ChatGPT for text, it barred residents of China from accessing its platform—including the people of Hong Kong.

Such divisions will make life harder for Hong Kong—and for VCs trying to straddle China and the West.

Even Sequoia, the king of VC in China, is struggling. Doug Leone, the firm's global managing partner, says collaboration between the US office and the standalone China team has "come to a screeching halt. The India-to-Southeast Asia corridor is wide open… by the vacuum left by China. This could go on for ten years, so we have to be ready for that."[27]

Sequoia Capital China can power on, albeit in splendid isolation. Or perhaps it too is seeing its influence slip under Xi Jinping's changing priorities. On January 20, 2023, *The Information* reported that Neil Shen, the lauded head of Sequoia China, lost his position on the Chinese People's Political Consultative Conference. So had Robin Li of Baidu and Ding Lei of NetEase.[28] Such roles are coveted for their implicit endorsement from the Communist Party's leadership.

Chin Chou of Morgan Stanley says that from the 1990s until 2015, the firm's private investments team had allocated the lion's share of capital to minority stakes in fast-growing Chinese companies run by dynamic entrepreneurs. Since then, the firm has done better investing in buying controlling stakes in established companies, while Chinese entrepreneurs have to focus more on cost-cutting. It's a time for finding exits rather than new investments in startups.[29]

China declared its anti-tech campaign over in early 2023. In January, Jack Ma announced he was stepping away from Ant Group. This in theory clears the way for Ant to revive its IPO, although at a lower valuation, because the company has been restricted to its payments business. Public-market investors will need time to determine what the company can achieve under tighter regulation before it lists.

Similarly, Beijing authorities said Didi can once again accept new users, which the market sees as a signal that it is out of the regulatory freezer. It is going to delist from New York and relist in Hong Kong. But the company has lost $40 billion in value since its ill-starred IPO on NYSE. It continues to burn through cash, and other Chinese government agencies, including the Ministry of State Security, continue to investigate the company for allegedly exposing user data, including sensitive information about government vehicles.

Private VC will continue to play a role in China, which has the scale and sophistication to produce world-class entrepreneurs and important innovation. But the scope for VC successes is narrowing. The government prefers to use its own financial resources to back important companies and technologies. China remains a world leader in AI, quantum computing, advanced manufacturing, electric vehicles, and mobile bandwidth. It will, over time, build a competitive chip industry, and double down on self-sustainability in all sensitive areas, from operating systems to space tech.

Along the way, though, China seems to have abandoned the openness that is the hallmark of innovative societies and dampened the animal spirits that motivate great entrepreneurs. Its rivalry with the US is problematic, but this does not explain the shift in mood among venture investors, even those with longstanding ties to China.

Beijing seems to recognize some of these problems, which may explain China's hasty exit from Zero Covid from late 2022 and its attempt to put the tech clampdown in the rearview mirror. The energy transition alone is a huge opportunity that will require vast amounts of investment into innovative companies.

For the period to the early 2030s, though, the exciting startup stories are more likely to be found in India and Southeast Asia—places where Leone says Sequoia will focus its investments for the next decade.

Morgan Stanley's Chou says, "The two big developments we see are, first, China is clearly transitioning from growth to buyout; and second, India is now a proper growth market."

India and Southeast Asia are populous emerging markets. Are they ready for VC—to the point they can become "the next China?"

13

INDIA AND SOUTHEAST ASIA: THE FRONTIER

THE 2020s look to be difficult for investing in China, but venture capitalists are excited by the opening of two vast frontiers: India and Southeast Asia.

These regions have long been connected in trade and culture by the rhythm of monsoons that have propelled Malay-crewed ships across the Bay of Bengal for millennia.

Both are large, with India's population today over 1.4 billion, and Southeast Asia's at 660 million, half living in Indonesia. Both have been relatively sleepy economies, but diverse, with pockets of enormous wealth and, in some places, a youthful emerging consumer class. English is widely spoken by the elites.

Most importantly to our story, both economies were traditionally dominated by family conglomerates or SOEs, but are now being transformed by a new wave of digitally savvy entrepreneurs.

The similarities diminish from there. We'll explore the India story, as it's the only potential peer competitor to China or the US, and wrap up our global tour in Southeast Asia.

INDIA: DISAPPOINTMENT OR HOPE?

When Ash Lilani, who headed SVB Global, organized the SVB icebreakers to Asia, his first stop wasn't China. It was Bangalore, India, which by 2003 had emerged as a global center for IT.

There was a tiny VC presence in this teeming country of (then) 1.1 billion people. Entrepreneurs were almost non-existent. Yet some people in Silicon Valley, most of them ethnic Indians like Lilani, were excited about the country's prospects—although initially as platforms to support US tech companies.

The US tech industry was still suffering from the dotcom hangover. "Hardware and software companies were burning cash because their costs were so high," Lilani says. "Why not outsource product development to Asia? And someday those markets will be big."[1]

Moreover, the loss of jobs in the US was giving the many Indian tech workers in America reason to return home, and take the culture of Silicon Valley with them.

Whereas the China market was primed for VC, India's was not. Its rise as an IT outsourcing center did not provide the supportive environment that India's VC pioneers had hoped for. India's moment would come but only a decade later. By the early 2020s, however, many VCs now regard India as the biggest opportunity.

How did India go from no-hoper to the greatest hope of all—and is the current optimism justified?

ANTI-BUSINESS LEGACY

India, the world's largest democracy, achieved independence from the British in 1947. It inherited a diverse population across a patchwork of states that are more like countries unto themselves.

China can also be said to be big and diverse but its ethnic Han majority, its tradition of a meritocratic bureaucracy, its single written language, and its unique relationship of a national Communist Party intertwined with the levers of government give it cohesion, akin to the

United States with its far-flung states. India is closer to the European Union, with many languages and distinct traditions—or perhaps it's more like a bigger Southeast Asia with a federal government on top. Moreover, its majority Hindu population is subdivided into castes, which constrains social mobility.

Finally, for much of its modern history, the prevailing attitude toward business and economics has been statist: for a long time the country's leaders defended India's entrenched poverty as "the Hindu rate of growth"—a poor excuse given the economy was about par with the likes of Taiwan and Korea in the 1950s, and wealthier than China, only to see these countries leave it far behind.

India's anti-business (especially anti-foreign business) stance was made clear in 1978 when IBM chose to exit the country rather than accept demands that its local business be partly nationalized.[2] The "license Raj" included high tariffs, import barriers, and plenty of red tape.

IT FLOURISHES

The government of Rajiv Gandhi began a modest liberalization campaign in 1984 and IT hubs began to emerge to provide basic programming for multinationals. In 1991, the administration of Narasimha Rao embarked on a broader liberalization drive, which his successor, Manmohan Singh, accelerated.

These efforts were not nearly as market-friendly as what Taiwan achieved in the 1970s and 1980s. Factories remain plagued by unreliable electricity or phone lines and threats of bribery. But given the steep cost differential, with Indian programmer labor priced at less than one-tenth of US workers, the opening was enough for a few big multinationals like General Electric, HP, and TI to open plants in Bangalore, the Tamil-speaking business capital of India's south.

The IT industry flourished, boosted by the demand among multinationals for cheap coders to solve their Y2K problem—most enterprise software had failed to take into account what would happen in the year 2000 because years were represented as two digits instead of four. Fears of crashing airplanes or broken factories led to a splurge on Indian IT.

In 1997, the IT sector achieved revenues of $5 billion and accounted for 1.3 percent of GDP, but by 2004, it had achieved revenues of $21 billion and was now 3.5 percent of the economy.[3] It was expanding from outsourcing to back-office processing and internet services. Wipro, one of three leading IT outsourcing companies, went IPO in the US and was the first company to offer stock options to employees in India.

But Wipro's US-style campuses were cut off from the rest of the country. Wipro, Infosys, and Tata Consultancy Services served exclusively foreign clients, not the domestic market. Shoddy infrastructure and unreliable electricity further isolated these companies. They became bubbles of an elite of well-trained engineers, mostly from the upper Hindu castes, amid a sea of a largely illiterate population.

There was none of the connectivity that marked Silicon Valley, and there were virtually no entrepreneurs—as the first VCs learned.

"Infosys, Wipro and Tata Consulting are still there; they're a steady part of the economy," says Tim Guleri, managing director at Sierra Ventures in San Francisco, who invests in Indian startups from afar. "But they haven't contributed to the venture life of the country. They're in the services business, not the innovation business."[4]

FIRST VC ATTEMPTS: DRAPER INTERNATIONAL

The first VC from overseas looking for tech entrepreneurs was started by William "Bill" Draper III. Bill was the son of William Henry of Draper, Gaither and Anderson, the first West Coast VC, and he went on to found his own shop, Sutter Hill Ventures, another leading Valley investor. Bill had interests in global and development affairs and was a senior ranking official with the United Nations.

In 1994, Bill co-founded Draper International, the first US VC to focus on finding startups in India, with local partners in Bangalore and Mumbai. The $55 million fund struggled to convince people to build a startup rather than sustain a family business, and was baffled by voluminous regulation.

Neither was there an obvious exit route: India had longstanding stock exchanges, but the securities regulator requires listed companies to be profitable, which blocks many new companies, and the investor base was hostile to the hefty valuations that VC-backed internet businesses commanded.

Draper International ended up focusing on US companies with an Indian presence, but it did begin to entrench the idea that Bangalore could develop a tech ecosystem.

EARLY INDO-US FUNDS: JUMPSTARTUP AND NEWPATH

The nascent VC scene was otherwise domestic, usually funded by local banks that didn't know what they were doing. In 1998, when Israel and Taiwan each boasted 100 or more local VCs, India had only 21 companies registered as such, managing a mere $700 million versus the $4 billion in Israel.[5]

There were a few professional ones. JumpStartUp was founded in Bangalore in 2000 by three partners with Silicon Valley backgrounds, including a Draper International veteran. SVB Global was among its backers. JumpStartUp was stymied by the same factors that Draper International encountered and moved its headquarters to Santa Clara to focus on US companies investing in India.

Perhaps the most quixotic of these global attempts was NewPath Ventures co-founded by Vinod Dham and Tushar Dave. As a youth, Dham went to study in the US in 1975 with a mere $8 to his name, and went on to become a legend at Intel, where he helped design its best-selling Pentium chip. Now he wanted to bring semiconductor manufacturing to India.

NewPath launched in 2002 as an incubator, backed by other VCs such as NEA. It was based in Bangalore and invested in a handful of Indo-US companies focused on chip design and related software. As with Israeli companies, these startups would place marketing and sales teams in the US while relying on Indian engineers.

"India in 2002 wasn't on the map," Dham told an interviewer. "People were afraid to set up in India, so all my investments at NewPath were in companies set up [in the US] that could utilize labor in India."[6] He made the bet that, in the wake of the dotcom crash, US companies would be desperate to reduce costs, and Indian talent could deliver.

The model had only mixed success, and Dham switched to becoming a traditional VC in the US but with a focus on leveraging the India network. As founder of NEA-IndoUS Ventures, Dham is still investing today, in chip design firms in the Valley—usually founded by Indians—using AI to manufacture ultra-fast processors.[7]

SCL AND SEMICONDUCTOR FAILURE

But India would remain difficult terrain for semiconductors. The government in the 1980s tried to follow Taiwan and Korea and become a semiconductor power. It set up the state-owned Semiconductor Complex Limited (SCL) in Punjab, near the elite Indian Institute of Engineering as well as aerospace and defense companies. SCL licensed older IP from Japanese and US companies and got to work.

Although India had plenty of talented engineers, the government sorely underestimated the capital required to import critical machinery and the challenges of running a chip fab with unreliable power and water. A disastrous fire accident set the factory back by years while TSMC and Samsung Electronics raced ahead—while investing billions to launch a single new fab.

SCL was never going to be sustainable; it found no commercial customers, not even domestically; its talented engineers began leaving for better opportunities. The government tried to sell it and found no takers. Today SCL exists as a lab doing R&D for India's space program, which is worthy—but India must import 100 percent of its chips.[8]

SVB GLOBAL

The SVB trip in 2003 played the same catalytic role in India as it would later do in China. Lilani hired out the Oberoi Hotel in Bangalore and gathered the small circle of local VCs, some promising startups, and Infosys and the telco Reliance "for gravitas," as he put it. Then the team flew in heavy-hitters from Sequoia, Accel, KP, Sierra, and other US funds. SVB opened an accelerator hub and offered desk space to US VCs interested in exploring opportunities in Bangalore.

"US VCs were ignoring India," says Sumir Chadha, a VC pioneer. "It was the back of beyond. Then came the SVB trip, and Sequoia and Accel saw the opportunity."[9] Lilani adds, "People in Silicon Valley mocked us. They couldn't believe we'd get on an airplane for 14 hours."

SUMIR CHADHA AND WESTBRIDGE

Chadha's own journey sums up the early India VC story. He is an American of Indian descent who worked at Goldman Sachs, first in New York and then in Singapore, as part of its Principal Investment Area. He wanted to write checks for stakes in Indian companies but had to apply to the government for permission—and didn't receive it.

"The government didn't know what foreign capital was, and they didn't want it," he says. Chadha returned to New York and in the aftermath of the dotcom crash decided to set up his own VC, Westbridge Capital, which specialized in backing Indian founders in the US.

He noticed changes in India, notably the growing penetration of cellphones. The government wasn't helping but it wasn't getting in the way of this new development—there was no "license Raj" for IT or telecoms. Chadha began looking to tap Indian entrepreneurs at the source, setting up an entity in Mauritius. (The island nation has emerged as the biggest channel for foreign direct investment into

India because of a double-taxation agreement and Mauritius's low 3 percent capital gains tax.)

He hoped finding entrepreneurs in IT services would attract more engineers and help perpetuate a tech industry. Software engineers in India were becoming well paid, forming the vanguard of a new, upper middle class. More Indian Institutes of Technology (IIT) graduates were returning from the US because they saw opportunities at home.

It worked, to a point, but he found entrepreneurs lacked sophistication or understanding of how to sell to US buyers, and there was little indigenous innovation. "The outsourcing companies could do the tech," says Ash Lilani, "but they couldn't create it."

WESTBRIDGE AND SEQUOIA

In 2005, Westbridge pivoted away from tech entrepreneurs and began investing more like a PE firm, looking for companies in traditional industries that needed growth capital.

The firm took another turn the following year when Chadha sold the business to Sequoia. Mike Mortiz at Sequoia had backed the firm's Beijing entry by finding Zhang Fan and Neil Shen and entrusting them to run a local entity, and he wanted to find a similar team to run a Sequoia India fund. Ash Lilani at SVB made the introduction to Chadha. Westbridge rebranded and looked to find entrepreneurs who could develop software for US buyers, while the US head office could find potential customers as well as LPs.

The relationship lasted for three years, enjoying a mini boom. Competition was light and Chadha could pick the best deals. "Those first years were great," Chadha says. "We had full independence." He also got the chance to work in the Silicon Valley office and learn from the veterans. "I got to listen in on the YouTube pitch, I saw the deals, I learned how VCs did the art of the venture."

But when Sequoia's top brass wanted to centralize the India operation, Chadha and his partners chafed, and in 2011 he left and restarted Westbridge, but as a growth-equity firm, not VC. He mostly avoided tech companies. Chadha says that at the time, VC in India could expect to return a mere 3×, versus the 20× or more that top funds could produce in the US and China.

The story has come full circle for Westbridge. Since around 2018, Chadha has begun investing in tech startups, which he says account for about 20 percent of the portfolio. "Over the next decade we will pivot fully to tech," he says. "The stars are aligning."

ACCEL INDIA

The first US firm to achieve real investment success backing Indian entrepreneurs was Accel. It drove arguably the two most important deals to date: Flipkart and Freshdesk.

Prashanth Prakash, a product manager working in the US, and Subrata Mitra, a computer scientist who did some of the earliest work on PCs in India, knew each other from studying in America. They both wanted to help create a tech industry in India, and Prakash wanted to be near his family in Bangalore.

They launched India's first internet company, Netkraft, to help Western companies build websites. "We were inspired by Netscape and what we saw in the US," Prakash says.[10] They raised money from JumpStartUp, and sold the company in 2004, after the dotcom bust. It made money for JumpStartUp but not enough to prevent the VC from closing its doors.

After Prakash and Mitra tried a few more businesses, they set up an incubator called Erasmic in 2004 to help entrepreneurs find talent, get started, and source capital. Mitra had friends at Google India, which ended up backing Erasmic's first fund.

Accel, meanwhile, was frequently returning to India on scouting missions after its first taste during the SVB trip. It acquired Erasmic in 2008 and rebranded it as Accel India. This relationship worked, in part because the US headquarters gave the local team full autonomy and helped them raise their first fund—$60 million, big for India at the time—and Prakash and Mitra are still partners at the business.

Finding entrepreneurs was hard because of the allure of traditional family offices, but also because there was no consumer market that a tech company could address. The rise of cellphones was changing that equation, however. Amazon had waded into India before e-commerce existed in the country, and it was spending a lot of money—more than any startup could match.

FLIPKART

One of Amazon's engineering talents was Sachin Bansal, a graduate of the elite IIT. He took the very unusual step of quitting in 2007 to launch his own company, which he and co-founder Binny Bansal (no relation) ran from a Bangalore apartment. The idea was to copy Amazon's origins and sell books online. They named the company Flipkart.

Their insight was that because few households were connected to the internet, most people did their searches from the office. And the biggest searchers of books were IT workers surfing on their lunch hour. So Flipkart sent people to Bangalore's physical bookshops and sold them the books they could see people searching for.

"They saw Amazon's obsession for the customer," Prakash says. "No one in Indian tech thought that way."

His peers thought the company was a loser but Accel put in $1 million. Initially not much happened because there was still no consumer internet. But shortly after the deal, Flipkart raised $10 million, seemingly out of the blue, from Tiger Global, a US hedge fund. They had no clue about Flipkart's team; they were just looking for the next China-sized opportunity and saw Flipkart had the most web traffic in India.

The Accel team stayed close to Flipkart and Mitra joined the board. They lobbied regulators to ensure the government wouldn't squash the rise of e-commerce. Flipkart raised more rounds, using proceeds to acquire businesses in digital distribution, social media, fashion, and electronics. By 2014 it struck deals with mobile operators and launched Big Billion Days, a copy of Alibaba's Singles Day, in which it heavily promoted the sale of cellphones—all the better to help the rising tide of consumers shop online.

Although Flipkart was by now the internet giant of India, the Silicon Valley model was still uncertain. Amazon proved a fierce competitor and Flipkart couldn't make a profit. It kept returning to VCs for more. This kind of behavior was normal in the US but unprecedented in India.

The speculation ended in 2018 when Walmart acquired a 77 percent stake in Flipkart for $16 billion, giving Accel an incredibly lucrative exit. This was a watershed for India's tech scene, motivating more waves of entrepreneurs and investors to the country.

China, it turned out, was not the only place that could produce Silicon Valley-sized startups.

JIO AND THE MOBILE REVOLUTION

The backbone of the Indian digital economy is mobile, but it's not just a copy of the China story. India is about mobile with the world's cheapest data, and that was made possible by Reliance Jio.

"We entered India thinking the internet would happen sooner, like in China," says Ben Mathias, partner at Vertex India, an arm of the Singaporean VC. "It didn't happen until Reliance Jio laid out its network, and the arrival of the Android phone."[11]

Reliance Industries is an old-school conglomerate run by the Ambani family. The two heirs, Mukesh and Anil, are rivals, which provides fodder for the Indian press. Their squabble forced Mukesh out of the group's telecoms business until 2010.

India had the world's largest mobile telecom industry after China, one that was increasingly competitive but unprofitable for the eight players vying to win market share. Mukesh Ambani jumped into the fray with a keen understanding that what would count was not talking, but data. Indians were overpaying for data, and couldn't afford enough to download Facebook or watch videos.[12]

He acquired a lesser player in 2010 because it also owned an internet service company that was seeking a license to operate 4G broadband. The other telcos ignored 4G because they made their money by selling voice calls.

Ambani rebranded the company Jio and laid a national network of optic fiber and telecom towers, while lobbying the government of Narendra Modi to let him combine voice and internet services over the same infrastructure. Then, when he launched Jio in 2016, he made domestic calls free and launched the cheapest data plans in the world. This was soon followed by a premium data plan—still very cheap—that offered perks and promotions. And he marketed the hell out of Jio, making it literally a Bollywood production.

The other networks scrambled to introduce 4G, but couldn't match the vast sums required to match Jio's expenditures on data infrastructure; Indian courts rejected lawsuits accusing Jio of predatory pricing. The eight telcos consolidated to four, with Jio enjoying the biggest market share. Meanwhile Flipkart's Big Billions Days was making a killing selling 4G handsets.

Facebook and other companies raced to buy stakes in Jio, but the bigger strategy for Ambani was to use Jio to knit together the rest of his share of the Reliance empire. Just as Alipay glued together Alibaba, super-cheap data would give Reliance a huge advantage.

In the meantime it has also transformed the digital economy and brought tens of millions of people online.

"The price of downloading 1 megabyte of data on Jio is just 10 percent of that in China, and only 5 percent of the cost in the US," Sumir Chadha says. "This makes services like TikTok way cheaper. Wireless data is growing faster in India than anywhere else, so our consumer internet boom will be even bigger."

THE INDIA STACK

The Indian government has also played a role in enhancing digital infrastructure. It created the "India Stack," layers of digital services to ensure 1 billion-plus people can access the internet.

This has been the work of the National Payments Corporation of India, launched in 2009 by the Manhohan Singh government. It took over the ATM networks to modernize retail payments. Second was the creation of the Unique Identification Authority of India, run by

Nandan Nilekani, the co-founder of Infosys. This body developed Aadhaar, the world's biggest biometric identity database.

The India Stack combines digital payments and digital identity. For example, the government can pay benefits like pensions directly into someone's bank account if they have a smartphone and an Aadhaar biometric identity. The next iteration of the India Stack was to allow people to transfer money via phones, a service called United Payments Interface (UPI).

UPI is a product that banks, e-commerce and financial technology companies use to serve as their own electronic wallets. UPI has brought money transmission fees to zero. This has taken away business from private digital-wallet operators, but it has allowed the rest of the digital economy to flourish. In 2020, UPI processed 12.5 trillion transactions valued at Rs21 trillion ($281 billion)—although in reality, UPI probably has fewer than 200 million active users, as banks and other players continue to compete on their own rails.[13]

The India Stack has even become an important tool of Indian diplomacy: the government touts it as a model for other emerging markets, making it an open platform rather than the restricted, closed-loop, highly surveilled superapps of China.

FRESHDESK: FIRST NASDAQ WIN

Flipkart was the first seminal moment in Indian VC. The second was Freshdesk, the first prominent startup to list on Nasdaq and prove that Indian founders could build a global company.

Flipkart took time to build into a huge company because it had to create a lot of the internet infrastructure as it went. The next generation of startups benefited from its legacy and grew faster.

One of these was Freshdesk, a business-focused software company that sold SaaS, centrally hosting the application and selling it to customers on a subscription basis. The idea has been around for decades but the growth of cloud computing in the 2000s made it popular.

Accel seeded Freshdesk with $1 million for 22.5 percent of the business. The company's users were global human resource and IT departments that wanted Indian-style support, but automated. Within five years the company was earning $100 million in revenues.

"There's another ten or more companies like this in the pipeline," says Shekhar Kirani, the partner at Accel India who wrote the first check. "These are companies that are global in scale from day one."[14]

The rise of global enterprise software companies has diversified India beyond the consumer internet, and given VCs a more reliable source of portfolio companies. "The death rate for SaaS companies is less than for consumer companies, which will fail if they can't get enough money or enough customers quickly," Kirani says.

Freshdesk rebranded to Freshworks for its IPO. The company raised $1.03 billion on Nasdaq in September 2021—a big payday for its backers, which also included Google India, Tiger Global, and Accel's US fund.

Now Freshworks has to learn how to execute at scale, because it's going toe-to-toe against incumbents like Salesforce. But its example is powerful.

"The IPO event was like a mini-India in New York, a showcase for the country," Kirani says. Noting the founder's humble background, he says, "If you have the intensity and enough VC money, you can build a great company and list it in the US. This deal helps our next set of companies imagine even bigger possibilities."

DOMESTIC EXITS TAKE OFF

The last trend is for Indian companies to IPO at home. This will be important to eventually developing a domestic LP base, because more than 90 percent of Indian VC funds represent foreign capital.

There have been some successes so far. One is Zomato, a restaurant guide (backers include Info Edge India, Sequoia, Temasek, and Ant Financial), which listed in July 2021 at a valuation of over $8 billion. PolicyBazaar, an insurance comparison site, was founded by Info Edge, Intel Capital, and Inventus Capital Partners, with SoftBank taking a large late-stage share. PolicyBazaar's parent company, FB Fintech, listed in November 2021, valued at $700 million.

Others have flopped—notably digital payments company Paytm, whose business model was undermined by the advent of UPI. But in the heady days of the VC boom and China's tech crackdown, the years 2016–2021 have transformed India. The Covid-19 pandemic has played a role too. Its economy is much more digital and efficient; small businesses and consumers are gaining access to services that were previously unaffordable; and India's huge population is a magnet for anyone looking to build the next big thing.

"We're seeing companies [in India] with growth rates over the last four to five years mimicking what we saw in China 15 years ago," says Morgan Stanley's Chin Chou. In early 2023, India's stock markets reached $3.2 trillion, making it now the world's fifth-largest equity market, surpassing the UK. That provides a more stable buttress for fast-growing companies.

THE NEXT SILICON VALLEY?

"They say software is eating the world," says Chadha. "But India is eating software."

Although only 5 percent of Indians speak English, its business elite is fluent, and many global CEOs are Indians, including the heads of Alphabet (Google), IBM, and Microsoft. While China is receding into itself, India's vast English-speaking diaspora is likely to play a greater role in global business and culture.

Chadha says, "What China did to manufacturing, India will do to software. Its products may not be creative, but they're cheaper and faster. India will compete with Silicon Valley in a way that China can't because of language."

Is this sustainable? Recent advances in AI are putting self-learning AI within reach. "Software is eating the world, but AI is eating software," is the motto of Jensen Huang, CEO of specialist chip designer Nvidia.[15]

The implication is that AI could replace coders and developers, which would threaten the Indian juggernaut. While it's just as likely that some programmers will learn to harness these tools for even greater breakthroughs, only elite tech companies may survive.

In the meantime, India has been on a winning streak. In 2021, more than 50 unicorns emerged—as many as it recorded in the previous five years combined, according to consultancy KPMG. The country has put "the Hindu rate of growth" behind it, thanks to a number of reforms, improved taxation, demographic trends, and the rise of its digital economy. For one quarter in 2021, the country notched a 20 percent rise in GDP.

COLD WINDS

There are limits to this bullishness, however. In 2022, a series of global macro problems—including rising inflation, rising interest rates, and supply-chain shocks—put an end to the VC party. Economic growth slowed precipitously. This affected VCs and startups everywhere, but this was India's first experience, as it was too unplugged to have noticed the dotcom crash of 2001.

India's tech scene is going through the same pain as brethren in the US. VC funds that deployed most of their capital in the boom years will see down valuations and difficult exits, and many will fail to launch a second fund. The startups and VCs that survive this freeze, on the other hand, will be well positioned for the inevitable thaw. India now boasts more unicorns ready to IPO than any other market outside of the US, including companies locally domiciled for a Mumbai listing and ones incorporated in Singapore or Mauritius that do global business and will list in the US.

The new mood of nationalism and self-reliance is also leading India to double down on industrial policy. The government is returning to semiconductors, never mind the SCL debacle. In 2019 India imported $21 billion in semiconductors, of which 37 percent came from China—a geopolitical problem.

In 2021 the government enticed Vendanta Resources, an Indian mining company, and Foxconn, the Taiwanese tech manufacturer, to build a semiconductor fab. The government is paying for half of the enterprise and providing subsidized land and utilities.

Vendanta is nowhere near the size of a Tata or a Reliance; Foxconn is not a chipmaker. But Foxconn is Apple's go-to contract assembler for making iPhones in China, and Apple (which now makes its own mobile chips) is starting to shift some of its production to southern India.

In a separate agreement, ISMC, a joint venture between Israel's Tower Semiconductor and Abu Dhabi-based Next Orbit Ventures, is committed to building a $3 billion fab.

At the same time, however, India has not learned how to integrate its government space, nuclear, and military programs with its commercial sector. Although India has a national security technical base, it imports virtually all of its armaments; it is not a techno-security state like the US, China, or Israel.

INDIA: BATTLEGROUND FOR THE FUTURE

India's budding technology sector has not produced globe-spanning platforms like Alibaba or Google; rather, India is considered a key battlefield, with US companies such as Amazon and Facebook vying with local players such as (Walmart-owned) Flipkart for local consumers.

The ambitions of Chinese companies such as Huawei, Xiaomi, and Tencent have been blunted over military tensions in the Himalayas in 2020. New Delhi banned many Chinese apps, citing concerns about abuses of Indian consumer data.

As of today, more than 300 China or China-related apps have been banned, including WeChat, TikTok, and even fintech apps produced by Singaporean companies partly owned by the likes of Alibaba and Tencent.

Chinese companies aren't the only ones that face challenges here. India has also pursued "data sovereignty," issuing rules that require global companies to store Indian consumer data in the country—an impediment to US tech companies that want to monetize such data by running analytics on it in cloud environments.

Jio's low-cost data and UPI's financial transactions make smartphones critical to India's economy, so manufacturing chips is the obvious next move. It will take a decade or more to tell if India succeeds. Its track record is poor, the technicalities are difficult, the country's physical infrastructure remains underdeveloped, and the economics are brutal. But this could lead to yet another wave of startups that will require VC funding—and success would give India the complete set of capabilities that today only China and Silicon Valley possess.

SOUTHEAST ASIA

This sprawling equatorial region, partly on the Asian mainland and partly a land of archipelagos, was off the map for VC until recently. The region has always depended on trade and foreign investment. It is not tied to a specific market, as Latin America is to the United States or Eastern Europe to Germany; rather it has enjoyed an array of trading partners, including Japan, Korea, China, India, and the West.

If one thing separates Southeast Asia from other emerging-market regions it is Singapore: no other grouping includes a triple-A rated, highly advanced hub of capital (although China has Hong Kong).

Singapore, as we saw in Chapter Six, emerged as an early hub of investment, thanks to government programs, the rise of its sovereign wealth funds, and some good universities. But the most talented Singaporean VCs migrated to China starting in the early 2000s, because that's where the action was.

BEFORE THE CRISIS: SEAVIC

Prior to this, there was an attempt by SEAVIC, the Singapore VC fund set up by Advent Capital, to launch country funds for other Southeast Asian markets. This fund was backed by the IFC, the private-sector arm of the World Bank, which had a mandate to invest in developing countries.

SEAVIC's managers were wary: an attempt to invest in Malaysia had failed due to unreliable political promises and a tendency by local businesses to mingle company and personal finances. Single-country funds are also risky because if they don't work, the VC can't allocate the capital elsewhere.

Nonetheless, the company launched funds for Thailand and Indonesia in the mid-1990s. They were disasters. "The Thais distrusted outside investors and assumed we were out to strip them," Peter Brooke wrote in his memoir. In Indonesia, "Groups of companies were controlled by the same families…Most privately held companies were linked to President Suharto."[16]

These countries suffered the worst of the 1997–1998 Asian Financial Crisis, which was the culmination of local crony capitalism, overborrowing in US dollars, greedy global banks that ignored their credit controls, and the heartless bets against local currencies by George Soros and other hedge funds. The economic wreckage swiftly led to political upheaval, including Suharto's humiliating concessions to get International Monetary Fund aid followed by his ouster, while Jakarta burned amid anti-ethnic Chinese riots.

SEAVIC wrote off its investments. "The Asian Financial Crisis crushed us," Brooke says.

FORMING A REGION

The AFC did, however, force governments and Southeast Asia's cliques of dominant business families to pursue sensible reforms and stable financial policies. This attracted foreign investment, revived the emerging middle class, and rebuilt the consumer markets.

In 2008, the ten member states of the Association of Southeast Asian Nations (ASEAN)—originally an anti-communist grouping from the Cold War—agreed to a new charter that aimed to move the region in the direction of the European Union.

ASEAN never met its loftier goals of integration, given the

difficulty of finding common ground in countries as diverse as Singapore, Vietnam, and the Philippines. But it did slash internal tariffs and become a useful talking shop.

ASEAN countries lack the military-science-tech complexes of the US, China, Japan, or Europe. Their economies remain dominated by a handful of family conglomerates, resource companies, and state-owned businesses. Nonetheless, the seeds of digitization were planted by the willingness of governments to allow competition to emerge against the entrenched interests.

LET IN THE CHALLENGERS

First among these was Malaysia, which allowed AirAsia to launch in 2001 as a low-cost airline; others then followed in neighboring countries. AirAsia was early to use digital technology, such as online ticket sales, to outcompete national champion carriers. By 2019, low-cost carriers carried more passengers within ASEAN than the national airlines.

This openness led to knock-on effects: the growth of tourism industries, easier business connectivity, and a spurt of infrastructure including new airports.

The most important impact has been on local logistics companies. E-commerce requires the last-mile delivery of goods, as well as warehouses and distribution. In the 2010s, VC-backed digital-first startups emerged to challenge the mainly government-owned delivery companies, including ride-hailing platforms such as Grab and Gojek.

The startups use technology, including AI, to provide faster, cheaper, and more transparent services that can reach even remote villages. Convenience and affordability encourage more e-commerce, and the easier connectivity is forging regional networks when before each ASEAN country was like an island unto itself.

This makes it easier for VCs based in Singapore to think about scale. Southeast Asia's markets have different regulatory, tax, and market practices. VC-backed digital companies, though, are able to centralize some of their operations, even if the sales and marketing remains fragmented.

RETURN OF THE INVESTORS

Meanwhile, some of the Singaporean investors who had gravitated to China returned. China's VC world had become intensely competitive and company valuations were skyrocketing. Startups in Southeast Asia were cheap, and there was little VC on the ground.

Peng Ong was working at Shanghai-based GSR (founded by Richard Lim, another of the Singapore crowd) when he decided to move to Jakarta in 2013, where he co-founded Monk's Hill Ventures.

"The longest tech bubble in history has helped," he says, noting that valuations in China, the US, India, and Europe have led many investors and entrepreneurs to look to new frontiers.[17]

"Most local tech companies are VC-backed," he says. What differentiates them from, say, China, is that many are founded by foreigners, which reflects the region's tradition of openness. "You can't move to Beijing without connections." But he has backed founders from the West—most but not all with a regional family background—who are new to the region or young returnees.

GROWTH STORY

Most regional startups are not reinventing the wheel. As in China in the 2000s, they are copying models from abroad and fitting them to local conditions. In both Southeast Asia and India, there are vast swaths of industries to be modernized, consumers to be plugged in. Simple tech-enabled business models can generate massive efficiencies, especially as more people use smartphones.

"With rising incomes, people can set aside some money for leisure and enjoyment," says Joo Hock Chia of Vertex, which is investing in tech companies that are digitizing small businesses catering to these new demands.[18]

Another returning investor was Jeffrey Chi, who moved to China in 2006 as one of the founding partners of Vickers Venture Partners, along with Finian Tan. He returned to Singapore in 2013.

VC'S NEXT GENERATION

"After China, the next story was Southeast Asia," Chi says, noting that Singapore's then President, Tony Tan, was still active in supporting commercialization of ideas out of local universities. This included funding and other incentives for VCs, and the government even supported firms established by foreigners.

These include Wavemaker Partners, established in 2003 with dual headquarters in Singapore and Los Angeles; Golden Gate Ventures, founded in 2011 by Vinnie Lauria of the US and Singaporean Jeffrey Paine; and Jungle Ventures, established in 2012 by India-born Amit Anand and Anurag Srivastava.

"Has this led to large startups?" Chi asks. "No, but the government is sponsoring research and attracting talent, and making it easier for startups to find people."[19]

The proof is in the rising amounts of VC money being deployed in Southeast Asia. Chi says the region's VCs invested $200 million in 2013, the year he returned from China. By 2017, VCs were investing $2 billion—and today the industry allocates $5 billion per annum: "Southeast Asia has really grown fast in the past ten years."

Although Singapore is the hub, every market in ASEAN has its own VC scene. Ong went to Jakarta; Tom Tsao of Gobi Partners moved from Shanghai to Kuala Lumpur in 2015.

SINGAPORE VC MATURES

Genping Liu was doing investment mainly in Taiwan, including with Vertex, which he joined as a partner in 2010. Southeast Asia's ecosystem was shallow compared to Taiwan, with its TSMC-related supply chains and mobile device makers. But he returned to Singapore in 2015, sensing that cross-border internet players were going to take off.

His first investment was a Series A round into Nium, a local fintech founded by an Indian, Prajit Nanu. The payments company was riding a boom in remittances—retail cross-border money transfers—and Liu liked the company's hustle. In 2020 the company achieved unicorn status.

"Today, VC in Southeast Asia is similar to VC in Silicon Valley," Liu says. "It's evolved. In 2010 there was no ecosystem. Then came Series A investors, then Series B. There's even late-stage companies entering that rely on global capital."[20]

The startup opportunities are also diverse. In Singapore there are deep tech companies. The region boasts enterprise SaaS players, consumer internet companies, fintech and blockchain companies, healthtech businesses, and agriculture digitization stories.

GRAB

Every market needs a champion to convince the world that the VC model works there too. In Southeast Asia, these would be Grab and Gojek. Neither originated in Singapore but both leveraged the Singaporean VC industry to reach dizzying heights.

Anthony Tan and Tan Hooi Ling, Harvard Business School graduates, wanted to adapt Uber's ride-hailing model for their native Malaysia. They launched the "My Teksi" app with a Harvard grant and backing from Cradle, a Malaysian government-backed fund for early-stage businesses.

Grab went on to expand into SME logistics, digital payments, and food delivery, with its mobile app considered the first major super-app outside of China. It has expanded to eight markets in Southeast Asia, moved its headquarters to Singapore, and become a colossus in serving small businesses.

It has also become a serial fundraiser, with one round after another propelling it to become Southeast Asia's first decacorn (valued at $10 billion). Its early seed and A rounds were backed by VCs such as Vertex and GGV, as well as Berlin-based Rheingau Partners and 500 Startups, an incubator.

By 2014, Grab was attracting growth-equity players such as Tiger Global and Hillhouse Capital, who valued it at $250 million.

The following year, Didi Chuxing—China's leading ride-hailing platform, backed by Tencent—joined the party, along with China Investment Corporation (a Beijing sovereign wealth fund) and SoftBank. SoftBank made several allocations, along with Japanese car manufacturers Honda Motor and Toyota Motor.

In 2018 Grab was the world's single largest recipient of VC, raising a mind-blowing $2.5 billion in a Series G round—a feat that also propelled Singapore into becoming a global leader in VC funding, and proved that Southeast Asia could support a tech business of this size.[21]

GRAB'S SPAC

The challenge for the founders was how to retain control of this unruly beast after seeing their stakes be constantly diluted. There was also the question of how long Grab could stay private: late-stage backers come in with the purpose of giving the startup a final valuation boost so they can cash out big time via an IPO.

But despite being infused with over $9 billion of VC money, the company wasn't anywhere close to being profitable. Public markets in the US were beginning to sour on these stories: Uber's IPO had been a disappointment, followed by the disaster of SoftBank-backed WeWork, a supposed disrupter of office space that wantonly burned cash; its IPO was pulled.

For these reasons, Grab opted to go public via a special purpose acquisition company (SPAC). SPACs are also known as blank-check companies: the company raises money and lists on a US exchange with a two-year mandate to find a company it can acquire—thus giving the acquiree a backdoor listing. Along the way, the owners of SPACs issue warrants to hedge funds that convert into stock once the acquisition is finalized, a valuable kicker.

For an acquired company, the SPAC route provides an easy way to get listed, as the regulation is light and there's no need for investment banks to take the founders on roadshows to woo institutional investors. Anthony Tan was also able to structure the deal to ensure he maintained de facto control of Grab, which he may not have been able to do with an IPO.

But that also means the company isn't subjected to the weight of market forces or investor scrutiny until after it goes public. SPACs only became popular during the late 2010s, bubble years for tech stocks and global stock markets; and they have fallen out of favor just as quickly now that the bubble has ended.

Grab's deal, sold to a blank-check firm called Altimeter Capital in 2021, was the largest-ever SPAC, which valued the company at $40 billion. However, the company had also just registered a net loss that year of $988 million. When it went public in December, public investors punished it and its share price cratered. The stock debuted at $12.40 a share; by October 2022, it had fallen to an all-time low of $2.86, giving the company a market cap of $11 billion, or about one-quarter of its hyped-up listing.

GOJEK

The environment for VC-backed startups has deteriorated across the board, but Grab's deal shows the perils of relying too much on the hype tactics of SoftBank, Tiger, and other late-stage players—especially once the macro environment changes. It also leaves Southeast Asia with an open question: can it grow a startup that's ready for center stage in New York?

Grab's regional rival, Indonesia's Gojek, may have an answer. Nadiem Makarim, an Indonesian who attended Harvard Business School and worked at McKinsey, had the idea of digitizing operations for the countless hordes of motorbike drivers.

He founded Gojek in Jakarta in 2008, and received his first VC money in 2014, from Openspace Ventures, the VC arm of Northstar Group, a local PE firm. Sequoia India joined in. The company released its app and had tens of millions of users practically from day one. This brought in a Who's Who of additional backers, including Tencent, Google, and Temasek, a Singaporean investment company.

Gojek became Indonesia's first unicorn and its first decacorn, later rebranding itself as GoTo after it acquired the country's biggest e-commerce platform, Tokopedia, in 2021. It has expanded into fintech, food delivery, entertainment, billing, video streaming, and more, with arms in four other regional markets. It is valued at $10 billion and its activities account for 2 percent of the country's GDP.

LOCAL HERO

It also has been cautious about its IPO plans. Unusually, Makarim wants to keep the company grounded in Indonesia. In April 2022 it listed on the Indonesia Stock Exchange. The deal was small, representing under 5 percent of its free float. It was meant to be a stepping stone for a later Nasdaq IPO, because the Jakarta market is too small to handle a company as large as GoTo. The company's caution is also because, like Grab, it is not yet profitable—and because it didn't want to see its stock price get hammered.

Its Jakarta IPO raised $1.1 billion, valuing the company at $32 billion. Since then the stock price has declined by one-third. As of April 2023, the company's value had declined to $6.5 billion. This may be in line with the general selloff of tech stocks in 2022, but the company will have to work hard to prepare for a successful debut in the US—and give its VC backers a handsome exit.

There are another 20 unicorns in Indonesia and many more in the rest of Southeast Asia. Their hopes, and those of their VCs, also rest on a regional champion proving itself in New York. The future of innovation lies with the risk takers being rewarded.

14

PLANET VC

INNOVATION occurred before the invention of VC. It relied on other, more traditional financing arrangements. But these were hard to scale—a wealthy benefactor could only invest within a personal network, and a corporate lab wanted to keep the technology in-house.

Nonetheless, the waves of innovation before the Age of Information yielded many bounties: the steam engine, the spinning jenny, Bessemer steel, penicillin, refrigerators, lightbulbs, automobiles, plastic, radio, airplanes, air conditioning, telephones, steamships, the pill.

VC emerged in sync with the commercialization of the transistor. It's hard to disentangle the two—or to separate them from virtually everything that followed, in business and in life.

"There's not a single device that doesn't use silicon," says Bill Tai, the angel investor. "Our computer and communication systems wouldn't exist without it."[1]

The evolution of digital technology is a familiar story: from giant mainframes the size of dining rooms to minicomputers and PCs; networks that led to the internet; miniaturization of products down to a cellphone and of processors measured in nanometers (a 2-nanometer chip puts 50 billion transistors on a space the size of a fingernail); the rise of apps and analytics to make sense of the explosion of data; cloud computing for storage and processing; robotics; AI; fintech and digital assets.

We are moving from the Age of Information and Telecommunications into a new wave of innovation. Today's venture capitalists are backing the ideas and technologies that will dominate headlines in the coming years: self-learning AI, quantum computing, brain-linked chips, virtual and augmented reality (which when synced 24/7 may create "the metaverse"); protein folding and genetic editing; and energy tech.

Less glamorously, most digital innovation winds up in iterative tools that improve a business's productivity. "The majority of increases in GDP have come from better asset utilization and other things related to the development of software," Tai says.

Traditional industries adopt digital processes, but a textile company, energy producer, or commercial bank is still making shirts, gas, or loans. The AI or other technology they are now using can lead to greater output per worker, better returns for shareholders, or lower prices for consumers, but the technology is invisible to the public.

Mark Andreessen, who co-founded Netscape in 1994 and then went into VC with his firm, Andreessen Horowitz, encapsulated this idea in a famous 2011 editorial he wrote for *The Wall Street Journal*, "Why Software is Eating the World."

"In some industries," he wrote, "particularly those with a heavy real-world component such as oil and gas, the software revolution is primarily an opportunity for incumbents. But in many industries, new software ideas will result in the rise of new Silicon Valley-style start-ups that invade existing industries with impunity," such as Amazon for books and Netflix for movies.

This wasn't just a case of one company outdoing the other with a better widget: the products themselves—books or movies, or phone calls or automobiles—had become software too.

In 2011, Andreessen also said this:

> It's not an accident that many of the biggest recent technology companies—including Google, Amazon, eBay and more—are American companies. Our combination of great research universities, a pro-risk business culture, deep pools of innovation-seeking equity capital and reliable business and contract law is unprecedented and unparalleled in the world.[2]

The story of *Planet VC* is the rise of new innovation clusters, enabled by the expansion of venture capital to previously hostile environments, which unlocked talent that is innate to humans everywhere.

"Innovation is a global phenomenon," says Greg Becker, who was CEO of SVB in the US before it collapsed in March 2023. "It's happening in critical centers around the world."

There are now huge, equally transformative companies in China, a fusion reactor of new tech in Israel, a growing embrace of risk-taking equity in Europe, and the rapid expansion of digitalization in India and Southeast Asia. Latin America, the Middle East, and Africa—everywhere—now boast their own nascent tech clusters.

PEAK VC

The year 2021 represented the peak of VC investments around the world. According to KPMG, VC investment reached $622 billion across nearly 39,000 deals, more than doubling the amount invested the year before. Of these, there were nine tech companies in Asia and the US that raised more than $1 billion each. The biggest recipients were software companies, along with consumer companies and enterprise tech. Sectors such as biotech, hardware, media, transportation, and energy received small allocations.

Global VC-backed exits achieved a record year of $1.38 trillion, more than double the previous year, thanks to a buoyant IPO market.

Figure 3 shows the value of VC investments around the world in 2020 and 2021.

Figure 3: Global VC investments

Country/region	VC investment ($bn)	
	2020	2021
US	145	315
Asia-Pacific	80	163
Europe	45	111
Americas ex-US	7	33
Global	277	622

Source: KPMG.[3]

These heady numbers represent the peak of a bubble that infused stock and bond markets as well. The world's central banks, led by the US Federal Reserve, kept interest rates at zero (or, in some European countries, negative), to resuscitate the economy after the Global Financial Crisis and to keep it afloat during the Covid-19 pandemic. This decades-long era of free money has caused many distortions, including the illusion that investments are also risk-free.

Ultra-loose money eventually led to inflation, a situation exacerbated by US-China tensions (which are leading to decoupling and an end to offshoring), and the Russian invasion of Ukraine in 2022. The Fed has been raising interest rates aggressively, which led to crashes in stock and bond markets, and in March 2023, runs on banks such as SVB. Many tech startups predicated their businesses on growth rather than profitability, but that growth was funded by VC money. Money is no longer free, so these models don't work. LPs are also pulling back from VC and other risk-taking asset classes, as they will now be able to generate returns on simple fixed-income instruments like treasury bonds.

VC investments in 2022 declined by 36 percent versus 2021, and it may be a long time before the 2021 results are matched, anywhere. If 2021 saw all regions rising together, will they fall together? Will the US reassert overall leadership, thanks to its deep and mature market? Will the closure of US markets to Chinese tech companies reduce the importance of Asia, or will Southeast Asia and India become new drivers?

The answer, for now, is that globalization of innovation is here to stay but VCs will find it in different sectors of industry. China's consumer opportunity came to an abrupt halt in 2020. Its private VCs are pivoting to enterprise software, advanced manufacturing, semiconductors, healthcare, and gene therapy; although the bulk of China's VC funds are ploughing into areas preferred by the government, such as electric vehicles and other environment-related companies. India may lack that hard tech, but it has huge opportunities for innovation in agriculture and food technology.

VCs that want to take advantage of this dispersion of technology will need to be onshore in multiple regions. Tech companies may be global, but VC is not. Once outside of the United States, it becomes a series of distinct venture industries in each market. The US firms that succeeded in China or India, like Sequoia and Accel, did so by creating autonomous local teams, and then helping them navigate US LPs and exits.

"Just as there is no such thing as 'Asia,' there are no companies that do India and China at the same time," says Jan Metzger, Citi's head banker in Asia.

VC investing outside the US tends to be country-focused. In the US, VC teams are more likely to be organized around sectors: healthcare, fintech, chip design. That's rare elsewhere, Metzger says.

Some markets are developing roles that connect to Silicon Valley, without becoming full-fledged replicas: Israel in hard tech; Taiwan in OEM and chips; London in fintech.

China is the closest place to a peer competitor, having evolved most of the kind of players found in Silicon Valley: hardtech, software, VC, law firms, banks, and other specialists in the startup universe. The biggest gap involves maturity—the US is now on its sixth decade—and the original source of funding, with dollar-based LPs still an important contributor to China's startups.

VC AND GEOPOLITICS

Sino-US competition is a problem for VCs, which are getting caught up in political disputes. Just as Covid-19 revived the idea in the West of manufacturing self-sufficiency, Sino-US tensions are now raising the specter of creating barriers to capital.

The US has the deepest pool of LP capital. In 2021, LPs allocated about $200 billion to VC, of which $128 billion came from the US.

"The biggest chunk of cash is in Menlo Park," says Larry Lopez, the former SVB Global executive, who's now partner at Australian Venture Consultants in Perth. "Silicon Valley is funding the most deals with the most dollars, even if the underlying companies are more global."[4]

Less of that money will go to China-focused VCs and startups. The Trump administration began with sanctioning doing business with specific companies such as Huawei that it believed were tied to the Chinese Communist Party or its military. The US not only forbade US companies from sharing technology or selling chips to Huawei; it also vowed to punish non-US companies that did so by threatening to cut them off from US technology and capital markets. Those moves cost Huawei its international leadership in telecom equipment and smartphones.

Then the administration of President Joe Biden expanded sanctions to Chinese tech companies that have developed AI and surveillance equipment used by the government to maintain control over the populace.

In October 2022, the US government passed sweeping export controls aimed at preventing Chinese semiconductor companies from accessing any US technology for use in AI and supercomputing. American-made algorithms remain vital to China's development of software in everything from autonomous vehicles to medical imaging.

Washington has also banned US nationals from working for Chinese chip companies—a direct strike at the returnees of mainland Chinese or Taiwanese origin who obtained a US passport during their time working in Silicon Valley.[5]

Of course, this is not a one-way street. China has long protected parts of its tech industry by banning foreign companies like Google and Facebook. It maintains strict controls on capital flows, and prohibits foreign investment in a huge part of its economy. Xi Jinping has made Chinese innovative self-sufficiency the centerpiece of his economic policy. His crackdown on the tech sector culminated in Beijing finally legalizing VIEs, but also putting them under heavy regulation.

The US, however, is now going all-out to prevent China from overtaking it in tech dominance. The venture capital industry is in its sights.

Since mid-2022, the US Congress has been considering legislation to create a "reverse CFIUS." CFIUS, or the Committee on Foreign Investment in the United States, is a Congressional body that screens the sale of US companies to foreigners and can block these if it sees a risk to national security. A reverse CFIUS would set up another committee that could prevent US companies or other sources of capital from investing in transactions that benefit either countries of "concern" (such as China or Russia), or their related entities.

This would present a huge challenge to China-dedicated VCs that rely on US dollar funding. They risk losing the ability to raise their next fund, and could be barred from exiting positions via IPOs in the US.

Weaponizing capital flows could also backfire on the US. Although its LP base is large, there are institutions in Asia, Europe, and the Middle East that would happily continue to invest in Chinese tech companies (and in dollars). The result might be that US shareholders, and US venture capitalists, miss out. VCs in other markets might benefit if US LPs are forced to diversify out of China. But here too there will be caution—the next generation of VCs in other countries may become wary of accepting money from American LPs if they think they risk a similar punishment.

Likewise, observers in other countries can be forgiven for being skeptical about America's campaign to contain China and punish Russia. What if one day the Washington and Big Tech elite decide that India (say) is hollowing out the US software sector, or otherwise challenging its supremacy?

BIG TECH TAMED

The US elite in Washington, Wall Street, and Silicon Valley wields power with confidence. Yet in the long run, this new relish for using financial or tech rules to thwart its enemies may end up damaging Silicon Valley more.

Big Tech has benefited from American openness, rule of law, a long period of financial stability, and little regulation. All four factors are now in question.

The US is widely viewed as the place to invest and build companies because of its rule of law. Despite racism or other problems, a businessperson of any color, sex, religion, and suasion can get a fair hearing in a US court. Entrepreneurs value this fairness, especially those who come from countries that wield justice more arbitrarily. The roster of high-powered foreigners running major US companies, from Microsoft to Google, is testament to this.

But the CHIPS Act and the Inflation Reduction Act of 2022 (with massive subsidies for companies deemed to be fighting climate change) raises the specter of an industrial policy that picks winners and targets foreign companies deemed hostile. Protectionism will always erode a nation's competitiveness, as companies lobby for favors rather than invest in their competitiveness, while consumers are denied the ability to buy the best products at the lowest price.

On top of these impersonal trends, America's gun violence, Donald Trump's racial baiting, and bureaucratic hassles around work visas (especially for university graduates) make foreigners feel unwelcome and unsafe.

Another strength of America's is its open financial markets. Foreigners, including the Chinese government, parked their excess savings in US assets because they believed in that same impartiality—buying Treasury bonds to ensure return *of* capital, rather than seeking a high return *on* capital. In response to Russia's invasion of Ukraine, however, the Joe Biden administration seized Russian central bank reserves and the assets of its oligarchs. Outsiders will now wonder if their assets might one day also be vulnerable to seizure.

Meanwhile, the safety of US financial markets rests on America's Treasury bonds being regarded as the ultimate safe haven, but the Republican Party in Congress continues to threaten a default if it doesn't get its way in other legislative matters.

Finally, regulation is coming to Big Tech. The Biden administration is suing Google and other companies for anti-competitive behavior, while both parties want to fight disinformation and abuse of user data in social media (although Democrats and Republicans don't agree on what it entails). The old Facebook motto, "Move fast and break things," is now perceived to be a recipe for releasing products without safeguards. Facial recognition and other aspects of AI are under regulatory scrutiny.

These factors all add up to headwinds for America's technology sector. The sector was crushed in 2022's financial market rout. Tesla lost 68 percent, Meta was down 66 percent, and Amazon's stock fell 51 percent that year. More broadly, the Nasdaq declined by 35 percent, far more than the 20 percent drop in the broad-market S&P 500 index.

It was the worst year for tech since the dotcom crash in 2001, and there is little prospect of them returning to bubble-era peaks. Big Tech companies are laying off workers at a time when the rest of the economy is adding jobs.

And yet 2023 has seen a new, unexpected resurgence in Silicon Valley, thanks to generative AI. Startups such as OpenAI (seed round backers included Y Combinator, Reid Hoffman Foundation and Khosla Ventures) have blown open the doors on powerful AIs that will transform cognitive roles across many industries. Similarly potent startups in China are attracting VC money, including from US-linked firms. The generative-AI story is quickly becoming the preserve of Big Tech (Microsoft acquired OpenAI in January 2023 for $10 billion) but VC firms will continue to invest in more waves of game-changing companies.

OPEN CULTURE, OPEN SOURCE

The US, despite its problems, will remain the primary center of innovation. It has the depth of experience, the biggest financial markets, the broadest ecosystem, and a vast and wealthy consumer base. It's unique. Silicon Valley's best long-term strategy is not to rely on taxpayer subsidies or hitting Chinese competitors with sanctions. It's to double down on US strengths such as openness. In a multipolar world, collaboration is going to become the new competitive advantage, and American startups are culturally attuned to this.

"The US has true leadership in not just creating companies but communities," says Young Sohn, a veteran CEO and investor.

Sohn's career is like *Planet VC* condensed—he set up Intel in Korea, ran other semiconductor companies such as Agilent and Oak Technology, founded startups like chip designer Inphi, sat on the board of UK AI chip specialist Arm (acquired by SoftBank in 2016 for $32 billion), invested as a VC at Silver Lake Partners, and ran Samsung Electronics in the US. Today he is back in the world of VC, as founding managing partner of Walden Catalyst Ventures, a new fund set up in partnership with Lip-Bu Tan—the godfather of Asian VC, still at it.

Sohn is backing companies using RISC-V open software, a trend that emerged from Berkeley, University of California during the 2010s. It's a non-profit project, supported by Berkeley and corporate developers from the likes of Arm, Google, Huawai, and Nvidia, to let people design chips without needed to get licensing or other IP controlled by semiconductor companies.

This offers a pathway to making chips more affordable to design, which could open doors to a new wave of VC-backed companies that can compete in niches against the behemoths such as TSMC and Samsung, whose fabs cost billions of dollars to build.

A taste of what may come is Snowflake Computing, a data management platform that uses cloud technology to help users store and analyze their data that's stored on the AWS, Google, or

Microsoft cloud platforms—what the company calls "data as a service."

Sutter Hill gave the startup $5 million in Series A funding in 2012; a Sutter Hill partner, Mike Speiser, ended up serving as Snowflake's first CEO. By the time of Snowflake's IPO in September 2020, Sutter Hill (its main fund and affiliates) owned 20.3 percent of the company. Sequoia and Altimeter Capital also owned large stakes.

The $4 billion IPO valued Snowflake at $70 billion, making it the largest software IPO in history. The public market loved this stock, which shot up by 258 percent over the next three months—for a moment making Snowflake more valuable than IBM.[6]

The stock has crashed in line with the market collapse in 2022, while IBM has proven more resilient; as of October 2022, Snowflake was valued at less than half IBM's $118 billion market cap. But its exciting ride showed the potential for new approaches to data—and netted Sutter Hill a $2.5 billion payout.

The irony is that Chinese tech companies like Alibaba and Tencent, coordinated by Beijing, are investing heavily in RISC-V-based chip design. Open-source code can be used and built upon by anyone, even if the US wants to cut them off from leading chip technology.

BLOCKCHAIN AND CRYPTO

Another twist on collaborative models is blockchain. In 2008, the pseudonymous Satoshi Nakamoto published a white paper describing how to transfer an electronic file as a form of value without requiring a central intermediary (like a bank) to facilitate it.

This triggered a craze for cryptocurrencies, which by 2020 and 2021 were attracting massive amounts of VC money into blockchain developers, gaming companies, and fintechs. Because crypto is a speculative asset, the hype reached epic proportions, with bitcoin being valued at $68,000 in 2021 (it had fallen to $19,000 by mid-2022). Andreessen Horowitz even rebranded itself as a16z and raised dedicated crypto funds.

The speculative bubble collapsed in 2022 in the wake of the US raising interest rates. Many smaller VCs are going to be wiped out, with even storied firms such as Sequoia writing off hundreds of millions of dollars from exposure to fraudulent crypto businesses.

Crypto provided an initial alternative to venture investing, however. Instead of raising equity to take stakes in a company, people could now buy tokens in a project. Those tokens might represent equity (although this soon raised the ire of securities regulators), or a voucher, or promise of a service.

Such models are sometimes referred to as "Web3," as opposed to monopolistic internet platforms such as Amazon or Facebook. It is also conflated with the metaverse, with blockchain serving as the infrastructure for money, identity, and property ownership. The 2022 crash may slow things down but many companies are still building on the back of decentralized protocols, including Asian governments, central banks, exchanges, and financial institutions. Even China, which banned Bitcoin and other private crypto assets, is rapidly building digital infrastructure using blockchain.

For VC, crypto opened new possibilities of how teams and companies can get funded. Combine this with other trends toward community building—such as RISC-V open source protocols—and the outlines of a more diverse investment landscape come into view.

The future of Web3 may well be decided in East Asia. Hong Kong is positioning itself to become a major center of liquidity and innovation in blockchain-based finance. Hong Kong's regulators, with the tacit backing of Beijing, have laid out licensing for "virtual asset service providers," providing a haven for many blockchain-related startups. The government is experimenting with a digital Hong Kong dollar, which could become an extension of China's own eRMB. Such digital expressions of money will turbocharge the tokenization of real assets, from real estate to bonds to niche investments such as collectibles.

Singapore too is eager to use blockchain-based platforms to reinvent cross-border payments that can settle in real time, instead of relying on slow and expensive correspondent banking relationships. DBS—about as official as it gets—operates a virtual-asset exchange.

In a great irony, the once libertarian, Wild West ethos of crypto may be reborn in East Asia as a blockchain infrastructure operated by companies backed by the Singaporean government, by Chinese banks, and by heavily regulated digital exchanges. This will, however, also provide many China-focused VCs with a viable sector for new investments, especially as pickings in the mainland become slim.

DO WE STILL NEED VC?

Do we still need VC, or has it outlived its usefulness? The free money is gone. The rise of scalable consumer platforms has run its course. The Covid-19 pandemic revealed our dependence on technology, but it also made a lot of Silicon Valley look trivial—people feared for their livelihoods and their lives, but VCs were backing multiple companies that could deliver a salad to your door in under 20 minutes. A backlash against social media has also cast tech in a bad light. The fruits of venture capital seem to pale against the big challenges in life, from the destruction of many middle-class jobs to environmental degradation. VC doesn't seem up to the job. It doesn't even appear interested.

Such perceptions are unfair to many of the best firms in VC, which have also continued to back startups in unfashionable sectors, from fertilizer tech to fusion, without fanfare. But even quality firms had to operate in an era of too much easy capital chasing too few original ideas.

Cracks in the VC model have been apparent since 2019. In May that year, Uber Technologies, the ride-hail darling, finally went to IPO. Its shares were priced at $45, at the low end of its proposed range, raising $81 billion. Its valuation of $82.4 billion was modestly higher than Uber's last private fund-raising valuation of $76 billion, but below the $100 billion figure that the company and its investment bankers had touted.

Uber's original founder, Travis Kalanick, who had been ousted over accusations of sexual harassment at the company, dumped 90 percent of his stock and walked away with $1.7 billion. But the stock was a dog: public-market investors were not impressed with Uber's lack of profitability.

Uber stock enjoyed a brief uptick in the giddy markets of 2021, but as of January 2023, it was a $59 billion company and its stock was trading at $29. Anyone who bought the IPO has lost one-third of their money.

Of course, this is not the case for Uber's early VCs, such as KP, which enjoyed high returns on their initial investment. The news was probably tougher for the late-stage backers that came in to pump up the valuation before listing: big financial institutions like Fidelity, Goldman Sachs, and BlackRock—and SoftBank.

This set the tone for other tech IPOs predicated on pumped-up valuations in private rounds. The outcome was similar for Uber's US rival, Lyft (backed by Andreesen Horowitz, Alibaba, Tencent, and SoftBank).

The most notorious flop was WeWork. The company was launched in 2019 by Adam Neumann, an Israeli entrepreneur in New York. It rapidly became the city's biggest real-estate owner by creating workspaces aimed at tech companies. Its growth and Neumann's chutzpah, framing WeWork as a tech company (a dubious claim), attracted plenty of backers.

But it was SoftBank that transformed WeWork into a juggernaut. Masayoshi Son met Neumann in 2017, shortly after Son launched SoftBank Vision Fund, a $100 billion fund dedicated to technology companies. Son was entranced by Neumann and invested $4.4 billion, valuing the company at $17 billion, far above its previous round.

EARLY STAGE TO LATE STAGE

We first met Son in 1999 in China, where he convinced Jack Ma to take $20 million that Alibaba wasn't asking for "to become bigger than Yahoo!" In China, there were dozens of startups fighting over the same ideas. Son realized the internet had turned technology into a winner-takes-all marketplace.

With software eating the world, the path to greatness was all about creating a monopoly—to be the one platform that captured all the eyeballs, all the attention. This model required huge influxes of capital, to squash or buy competitors, subsidize users, and spend on marketing.

The only Big Tech company that has achieved something like a monopoly through organic growth is Amazon; but for many years, as the company continually reinvested, it barely cut a profit. Son wanted a similar outcome but using capital as a shortcut. But Son also wanted to scale this model, which led to excesses.

In deals such as Alibaba, SoftBank was making early-stage investments where Son had a conviction about where the internet was headed. But then he moved into late-stage investing with the Vision Fund, a $100 billion behemoth. Now he had no special information about a company; he just had the most money to deploy.

US investors were more than happy to follow suit, with hedge funds such as Tiger Global and Coatue Management becoming prolific growth-equity funders. Early investors were happy because these rounds gave them opportunities to exit, but the whole operation only worked if there was an IPO with a huge valuation at the end.

This model isn't as reckless as it may seem. VCs need only one or two outsized hits in their portfolio to strike it rich. All the other duds are forgotten because they don't matter. Investors, looking back at their track record, define failures as juicy deals they turned down, not companies that lost money. The VC industry is designed to reward aggressiveness, and due diligence has never been its strong suit.

But there is a limit. The companies that do succeed and go public need to make money; they need to make business sense. The damn-the-torpedos approach, however, was distorted by the monetary glut. It took on a logic of its own, with the founder's original vision or idea swamped by the demands of VCs looking for a juicy up-round. The model made it easy to be a venture capitalist, which became all about financial engineering and a bit of networking.

"Uber didn't invent the GPS chip and the maps," Metzger says. "Amazon didn't invent the database. It's not like the 1980s, or the Fairchild days… that was about science, PhDs. Kleiner Perkins took a risk on whether these guys could get a transistor made out of sand. For the last 20 years, you weren't backing technology; you were backing bravery, systems integration, and a lot of cash."

That's what allowed Tiger Global to invest in 361 deals in 2021 (including many in India), an astounding pace of check-writing.[7]

THE MODEL CRACKS

The model was already falling apart, however. In 2019, WeWork registered to go IPO; its latest round had valued it at the ridiculous sum of $47 billion. By now, Neumann was more interested in partying than figuring out how to make WeWork profitable—and it was Son's money that gave him license. Son at one point declared WeWork would one day be worth $10 trillion, and more sober VCs such as Benchmark Capital were willing to go along. But WeWork reported a $1.8 billion loss as it headed to IPO. Much of its stated metrics were imaginary.

Following the disappointment of Uber's listing, WeWork was forced to shelve its IPO and SoftBank stepped in with a rescue package, which included a $1.5 billion purchase of stock from Neumann. Son's senior executives running the Vision Fund began to quit, but Son maneuvered WeWork to list via a SPAC.

The deal took place in March 2021, after WeWork announced it had now lost $3.2 billion the previous year—Covid-19 had put a halt to people going to work, and occupancy rates had plummeted. The SPAC acquisition now valued WeWork at $9 billion—high enough for earlier VCs like Benchmark to make a decent gain, but a disaster for SoftBank.

And the timing was bad. Many of Son's other outsized bets had also soured. The Vision Fund—and a successor, Vision Fund 2—were leaking money; SoftBank posted a $23.2 billion loss for April to June 2022.

Son's only recourse to keep the business alive was to sell his beloved Alibaba shares. But he faced crises in all directions: China's crackdown had hammered Alibaba's stock, which now traded barely above its 2014 IPO price. Moreover, selling Alibaba was a bitter move.

From March to September 2022, Son reduced SoftBank's stake in Alibaba from 23.7 percent to 14.6 percent. Although this did net $34 billion in proceeds, SoftBank had to surrender its board seat.

Son's forced sale of Alibaba stock is more than a closing chapter for the two companies. It's the end of an era. SoftBank isn't the only loser. The broader rout in 2022 of tech stocks has forced Tiger Global to write down its flagship fund by 50 percent, after fees, representing a loss of $17 billion in just four months.[8] Senior partners at Tiger and Coatue quit over the summer to launch their own funds—and perhaps avoid being tainted by the poor returns their portfolios are likely to record, after having invested in so many startups at the market's peak.

This isn't quite the end of VCs hyping valuations, however, regardless of the underlying company.

Mark Andreessen, whose "software eating the world" article chronicled the digital revolution in the making, announced in August 2022 that he was putting $350 million into a new startup—one vaguely meant to disrupt rental apartments, founded by Adam Neumann.

THE BUBBLE BURSTS

The worst excesses were committed in fintech. A rush of VCs raised fintech funds in 2020 and 2021, many focused on crypto projects and money-losing businesses such as BNPL (installment lending plans dressed up as digital businesses). Klarna, a Swedish fintech that led the BNPL trend, was valued at $45.6 billion in July 2021 during a funding round led by SoftBank's Vision Fund 2. One year later, as tech stocks crashed, the fintech was so desperate to raise additional capital it accepted a "down round," raising $800 million at a post-money valuation of $6.7 billion—an 85 percent drop.

But when it comes to burning VC money, nothing beats crypto. This hyped sector largely turned out to be unsustainable get-rich-quick schemes and scams. Crypto assets are the most speculative and volatile in the world, and were the first to be struck down when the Fed began to raise interest rates. As money exited the crypto ecosystem, coins based on faulty ideas of money and value (or just outright frauds) began to crash.

FTX, a prominent digital-asset exchange, collapsed in November 2022. One day it was valued at $26 billion; the next, it was worthless, and its founder, Sam Bankman-Fried, stood accused of fraud. Some of the world's most prominent investors—including Sequoia Capital ($150 million), SoftBank (about $100 million), Tiger Global ($38 million), and Temasek (a spectacular $275 million)—wrote off their entire investment in FTX.

They had plunged in without doing any due diligence, either not bothering to ask about FTX's obviously poor financial controls, or ignoring what they found. This is an extreme example of investment as FOMO, or fear of missing out, and Sequoia apologized to its LPs for its negligence. But bad investments in FTX were in line with what much of VC had become in the bubble years of 2019–21. Investors didn't need to ask about operations or understand the underlying technology; and anyway, most startups were innovating business models, not inventing new technologies. FTX hadn't invented anything—it was shoehorning a traditional financial institution into the Wild West of crypto.

The rapid hikes in interest rates have put an end to such cavalier investments. As with the dotcom bust of 2001, VCs and LPs are pulling in their horns. Many will be wiped out, even if it takes a few years for the damage on VC books to be realized.

The market collapse will be hardest on VCs on their first or second fund that deployed capital over the past several years. Their performance numbers will be bad and they will struggle to raise a third fund. Early-stage investors are least affected by the downturn because they focus on companies without a track record and which aren't expected to be generating profits (or even revenues). Late-stage investors can also survive through a strategic sale of their portfolio companies or by restructuring them to ensure they are profitable. Middle-stage funds are in the worst position, with their portfolio companies too immature for an exit, but now unlikely to receive additional VC money.

"There will be a flight to quality," SVB's Becker says. "VCs were about growth at all costs, but now they're all about unit economics, profitability, burn rates [of cash] and return on investment. Due diligence is back in vogue."

Sadly, it turned out SVB's own business model was not suited to the new era of rising interest rates. Although it banked up to 40,000 startups, most of these deposits were too large to be insured by the US Federal Deposit Insurance Corporation. SVB had succeeded by making itself the go-to bank for tech and VC, and few in Silicon Valley bothered to diversify their banking relationships. Unlike most banks, SVB's loan book was relatively small, because venture lending is still a niche service. Its assets were mostly in US Treasuries. However, as interest rates rose, the bank did not seem to consider its exposure to bonds, or to a highly concentrated group of companies whose business models were also upended.

Although the industry faces a rough patch, many VC funds are well capitalized. The have dry powder (cash) to spend on companies whose valuations are now more appealing. The danger is that on a risk-adjusted basis, LPs will prefer to invest in bonds that now provide a yield. Just as the dotcom bust cleared the way for companies like Amazon to build a durable e-commerce industry, this latest crash is setting the stage for something new. In this sense, the collapse of SVB is not so much the end of an era as a prelude to something new.

WANTED: NEW MODELS

We need innovation more than ever, including in VC itself. The mega-trend of the coming years is the energy transition to mitigate the worst effects of climate change. Will VCs play a role in this, or will they limit themselves to frivolous startups that make money but don't add much value to society? (Not because VC investors are necessarily frivolous people, but because their incentives make them back companies likely to rapidly scale.)

The rise in interest rates has burst the VC bubble, but even at its height, the industry was not that big. In 2021, VC's peak year with $622 billion deployed, the global economy reached $94 trillion of output. The industry may face some tough years, but its growth opportunity remains bigger than ever.

The investment requirements boggle the mind. The International Renewable Energy Agency calculates that to meet the targets in the Paris Agreement, cumulative investment in renewable energy needs to reach $27 trillion by 2050. That includes electrification and new infrastructure, renewable capacity, adapting fossil fuel companies, and improving energy efficiency.[9]

Technology will be critical to meeting these goals. The challenge for VC to remain relevant to the energy transition is scale. VC excels when the required capital is small and the potential upside is huge. Traditionally, energy companies are the opposite: capital-intensive businesses with utility-like returns. VCs sparked the early years of semiconductors, but today no VC can invest in companies as big as TSMC.

Even before the bubble, Silicon Valley—and by extension, the VC industry—was coming under fire for losing its social relevance and just becoming a short-term finance game. Even insiders recognized this, epitomized by Peter Thiel's quip about 140 characters instead of flying cars.

J. Storrs Hall is an engineer who pursued this question in his 2018 book, *Where Is My Flying Car?* He writes that the emphasis since the 1960s on information processing is perceived to benefit from Moore's Law, with a constant pace of miniaturization, speed, and falling costs. The common view is that heavy industry, construction, transportation, and energy do not enjoy such benefits. Entrepreneurs and financiers therefore favored "bits" over "atoms" and rapidly scaled electronic communications while other types of technology languished.

Hall believes this assumption is wrong: "We really, really should have had atomic batteries by now. And guess what? Your iPhone would never need charging, and your Tesla would have a range of 3.5 million miles."[10] The challenges are not technological, but problems of political will.

PERMANENT CAPITAL

The kind of developments Storrs describes could take decades to commercialize. Who's going to finance it? Government research labs are still important for making breakthroughs. In January 2023, scientists at the Lawrence Livermore government lab in California announced a milestone in nuclear fusion, which could one day power the world without any carbon emissions or radioactivity. But just as Bell Labs invented the transistor, it took private money and entrepreneurial founders to launch the Age of Information, and that will be the case for new technologies as well.

Corporate research labs are going to be back in vogue too: it's companies like Microsoft and Google that are making the biggest investments into AI.

When things go bad in VC, people like to say there's too much capital chasing too few opportunities. But this is not true. We need far more equity capital to back risky ventures and meet the challenge of climate change.

"VC will come up with disruptive ideas in energy transition," says Becker. "It isn't suited to invest in mass-scale businesses like wind farms, but VC-backed companies will develop the chips that make renewable energy businesses more efficient."

The industry is experimenting with new models that involve ways to sustain investments over a longer period of time.

VCs are keen to blur into PE and public asset management. If hedge funds like Tiger Global can dive into a VC's world, why can't a VC grow into something bigger?

Kathy Xu at Capital Today in Shanghai has created dedicated "evergreen" funds to hold stock in her favorite companies after her

VC funds matured. She argues that VCs rely on luck when it comes to finding the right founder, but the size of their investment and the time they hold it is in their control. Compounding returns can make a portfolio company far more lucrative over time.

Sequoia is experimenting with a model of "permanent capital" so it can support companies it likes even after they have gone public. It is the biggest traditional VC in terms of assets under management, with $85 billion in 2022. But compare that to the biggest PE shop: Blackstone, with $941 billion, is more than ten times bigger. And BlackRock, the asset management company, manages around $8.5 trillion, 100 times the size of Sequoia.

VC has always been a niche industry. This is because of its mission, finding the best new companies. But it may also reflect the fact that VCs are still run as partnerships: a small team of (mostly) white men making gut calls about entrepreneurs.

In the 1990s, the big Wall Street investment banks were still run as partnerships. They all went public—Goldman Sachs was the last, in 1998—in order to raise permanent capital, share ownership among their employees, and to use publicly traded securities to finance any strategic acquisitions.

Most VCs are too small to go public, but the needs for innovation are bigger: the energy transition to mitigate climate change will demand lots of technology, and someone has to find a way to take a risk on funding it. We are going to need larger financial institutions that have VC DNA in their blood.

Larger institutions would also have the resources to turn VC into a global business. It's already a global phenomenon, but largely confined to individual markets. Banking used to be the same, but scale changed that. Might similar cross-border scale help VC support global-sized solutions, applying AI, robotics, and data analytics to carbon sequestration, new infrastructure to support electric vehicles, new grids to store and transfer energy, new ways to manufacture and move goods? The answer, somehow, must be yes.

THE NEW AGE

A new breed of VC is experimenting with ways to invest in bigger, lab-backed private companies for longer, in order to support their ability to build meaningful but difficult businesses.

One example is Tokyo-based Nemesis Technologies, a VC that launched in early 2023, led by managing partner Pierre Mauriès. Japan—like Germany, Hong Kong, and many other places—has lots of university labs that do not commercialize their research, in part because their projects require far more capital than, say, a SaaS startup, and they lack the hyper-scalability that consumer internet companies gun for.

"We're not looking for unicorns to list, but to build gorillas that can stay private for as long as possible," Mauriès says, with an eye on climate tech.[11]

To do this he is relying on blockchain technology to underpin the fund and create a new set of incentives. Initially, Nemesis's fund will be structured like a typical, 10-year VC vehicle. It is issuing digital tokens on two blockchain fintechs that will eventually sponsor them on the Osaka Digital Exchange (ODX), a digital-asset exchange being built by two of Japan's biggest financial groups, SMBC and SBI Holdings.

The idea is that, as regulations and market demand allow, Nemesis will IPO its fund on ODX, selling units in the fund to both retail and institutional investors—in effect turning individual investors into LPs. Once listed, the fund will convert to an open-ended structure, obliging tokenholders to a relatively short (three or four year) lockup, but otherwise creating ample liquidity.

By transforming a VC fund into a blockchain-based asset, Nemesis hopes to create something akin to Sequoia's permanent capital, letting LPs trade the token, whose price would presumably reflect some valuation of the fund's portfolio. Nemesis, meanwhile, would likely sell down its holdings through a secondary market rather than push startups to list prematurely.

This echoes crowdfunding models such as Israel's OurCrowd, which also enables individuals to become LPs and fund a variety of projects sourced worldwide. OurCrowd has committed $2.1 billion in funds, spread across 42 funds—a lot of small bets for angel investors. Nemesis hopes to launch a $500 million fund that makes concerted, large-sized bets on behalf of institutional and, one day, retail investors. It's changing the incentives to make bets on technology, rather than on markets, using digital technology to recreate the conditions that favored operationally savvy VCs such as KP in the 1970s.

One aspect of a blockchain-based approach is that digital assets trade around the clock and across borders. A digital-asset exchange such as Coinbase or ODX, while complying with local regulations, is still a global market. Regardless of whether Nemesis succeeds, its experiment shows one way that VC firms—not just tech clusters—are globalizing.

The old model of VC was very local, with local teams investing in local companies. The foundations are being laid for both innovation and its financing to be distributed.

Crypto, for all its faults, showed a different way to invest in projects and technologies. The Web3 movement highlights incentive mechanisms that will shake up how startups get funded. Covid-19 forced the world's white-collar workers to work from home and severed the need for people to be tied to a single office or location. Open-source technology such as RISC-V enables teams to collaborate on sophisticated software with few restrictions. Ongoing improvements in AI, bandwidth, computing power and augmented or virtual reality will make collaboration even more powerful.

In previous waves of innovation, anchor technologies reinforced one another. Railroads led to huge advances in steelmaking and mining; the radio gave rise to broadcasting networks. The manifold technologies unleashed by the humble transistor have a powerful network effect. The convergence of, say, AI with supercomputing or mobile bandwidth enables even greater innovation in downstream applications, from mobile games to gene editing.

The virtual nature of software has allowed this convergence to occur across borders. As companies unbundle various functions from a physical location, the funding opportunity will also become detached.

Geopolitics seems to be pulling countries apart, and along with them, supply chains and access to technology. But globalization isn't over. It's merely shifting, from manufacturing to services, and now to distributed tech projects. The new vogue for industrial policy in the West, to match Chinese mercantilism, may result in beggar-thy-neighbor competition, but it could also support variation and resiliency. Capital flows remain one of the strongest bonds between countries. The VC industry connects entrepreneurs and investors. If the world's governments aren't able to coordinate to meet global challenges, it will be up to private networks to fill the void.

The challenge for the emerging age—for now, looking like the Age of AI, but who can be sure?—is to scale it, so that new forms of venture investing can find 100 or 1,000 times more startups to back. That will call upon the ingenuity and the risk-taking capital of people, projects, and companies from around the world, with the added value coming from how these pieces are assembled, and how AI itself is deployed in capital decisions.

Silicon Valley taught the world how to align interests for unlocking innovation. It's now up to Planet VC to transform the financing of change into a sustainable future.

ACKNOWLEDGMENTS

THE authors relied on many industry experts to tell this story. We are grateful for their input. Any errors are ours. Some of our sources prefer to remain anonymous but have our thanks, as do:

Greg Becker, Sumir Chadha, Jeffrey Chi, Joo Hock Chia, K.O. Chia, Chin Chou, David Cohen, Michael Eisenberg, Jixun Foo, J.P. Gan, Tim Guleri, Robby Hilkowitz, Darren Ho, Simon Ho, Jing Hong, Mark Hsu, Harry Kellogg, Shekhar Kirani, David Lam, George Lam, Rocky Lee, Ash Lilani, Genping Liu, Peter Liu, Larry Lopez, Jon Medved, Jan Metzger, Peter Mok, Edmond Ng, Peng Ong, Prashanth Prakash, Gary Rieschel, Stuart Schonburger, Yossi Sela, Young Sohn, Chang Sun, Finian Tan, Bill Tai, Tom Tsao, Ken Wilcox, and Avi Zeevi.

Terrance Philips would like to express appreciation to his family, colleagues, and clients. Finally, he would like to thank the men and women of SVB Financial Group that gave their all to support the innovation space. Your achievements and the good times will never be forgotten. Together they made this an amazing journey.

Jame DiBiasio thanks Mabel Leung for her love and support.

ABOUT THE AUTHORS

TERRANCE PHILIPS

Terrance Philips was a senior banker at SVB for nearly 12 years, where he helped build its international businesses. SVB was a unique institution, specializing in venture debt (debt for startups and the VCs backing them). This is an incredibly niche part of the world of private capital, but it gave SVB an unparalleled view on the VC industry worldwide. Terrance is using his incredible network to win interviews for the authors with the VC industry, from pioneers to executives at today's hottest firms. Terrance is currently a managing director at Citibank based in Hong Kong, where he now leads Citi Private Bank's private equity client coverage, serving Asia's biggest private equity firms investing locally and covering the world's largest global PE firms investing into the region.

JAME DIBIASIO

Jame DiBiasio is a writer and journalist. Based in Hong Kong since 1997, he founded various financial trade publications for the region. In 2017, he launched his own media business, DigFin, to focus on fintech, and sold it to banking group AMTD in 2021. He is author of *Cowries To Crypto*, a history of money; as well as two books on Asian history covering medieval temple societies in Cambodia and Burma. He is also co-author of *Block Kong*, profiling blockchain entrepreneurs in Hong Kong. In his spare time Jame writes international thrillers.

REFERENCES

CHAPTER 1

1 Foo, Jixun, interview with Philips and DiBiasio, January 5, 2022.

2 Tan, Finian, interview with Jame DiBiasio, December 22, 2021.

3 "China PE/VC Successful Case Studies," internal PDF of China Venture Capital Association, August 2020, pp. 39–47.

4 "The Untold Story of the Baidu IPO," Static Chaos, SeekingAlpha.com, August 23, 2009.

CHAPTER 2

1 Crafts, Nicholas and Mills, Terence C., "Six Centuries of British Growth: A Time-Series Perspective," *European Review of Economic History*, Volume 21, Issue 2, May 2017, pp. 141–158.

2 Adams, Stephen, "Before the Garage: Beginnings of Silicon Valley, 1909–1960," YouTube video, October 24, 2015.

3 Moritz, Michael, "Michael Moritz, Partner, Sequoia Capital," YouTube video, February 8, 2019.

4 Nicholas, Tom, *VC: An American History* (Harvard University Press, Cambridge, MA, and London, 2019), pp. 53–106.

5 Nicholas, p. 96.

6 Ante, Spencer, *Creative Capital: Georges Doriot and the Birth of Venture Capital* (Harvard Business Press, Boston, MA, 2008), pp. xiii–xix.

7 "Texas Instruments Incorporated," www.encyclopedia.com.

8 Ante, pp. 175–198.

9 "Ken Olsen," www.wikipedia.com.

CHAPTER 3

1 Brooke, Peter with Penrice, Daniel, *A Vision for Venture Capital: Realizing the Promise of Global Venture Capital and Private Equity* (New Venture Press, Boston, MA, 2009), pp. 40–57.

2 Ante, pp. 241–256.

3 Ante, pp. 221–240.

4 Nicholas, p. 159.

5 Hoefler, Don, "Silicon Valley USA," *Electronic News*, January 11, 1971, archived at www.netvalley.com.

6 Rock, Arthur, "Silicon Genesis: Oral Histories of Semiconductor Technology," Stanford University Libraries video interview, November 12, 2002.

7 Saxenian, AnnaLee, *The New Argonauts: Regional Advantage in a Global Economy* (Harvard University Press, Cambridge, MA, 2006), p. 50.

8 Tsao, Tom, interview with Philips and DiBiasio, July 23, 2022.

9 Saxenian, p. 51.

10 Ante, pp. 183–230.

11 Rock, ibid.

12 Brooke, pp. 3–20.

13 Brooke, p. 56.

14 Dubocage, Emmanuelle and Rivaud-Danset, Dorothee, "The Development of Venture Capital in Europe: The Role of Public Policy," hosted at www.nomurafoundation.or.jp.

15 Jackson, Michael, "Meet the Investor: Michael Jackson, Mangrove Capital Partners," LPEA.lu website, November 2, 2016.

16 Chi, Jeffrey, interview with Jame DiBiasio, October 4, 2021.

17 Shin, Gabriel, "Past, Present, Future: A Brief History of VC in Europe, part 1," Vauban website, October 12, 2021.

18 "Top 10 Most Active VC Firms In Europe 2022," Ventroduce.com.

19 Lewin, Amy and Shead, Sam, "The US VCs are Coming to Europe," Sifted.eu, February 10, 2020.

20 Zennström, Niklas, "European Tech Must Learn to Embrace Failure," *Financial Times*, October 4, 2022.

CHAPTER 4

1 Broitman, Doron, "High-tech Continues to Blossom, But the Rest of Israel's Economy Can't Keep Up," Ctech, Calcalistech.com, March 21, 2022.

2 Ben-David, Ricky, "Israeli Tech Companies Raised $25.6 Billion in 'Extraordinary' 2021—Report," *Times of Israel*, January 3, 2022.

3 Shulman, Sophie, "Israeli Companies on Wall Street Reach Historic $300 Billion Market Cap Landmark," Ctech, calcalistech.com, June 17, 2021.

4 www.managementstudyguide.com/israel-economic-crisis-of-1983.htm.

5 Saxenian, pp. 104–108.

6 Crittenden, Ann, "Venture Capitalist: A Rise to Riches," *New York Times*, January 6, 1981.

7 Senor, Dan and Singer, Saul, *Start-Up Nation: The Story of Israel's Economic Miracle* (Twelve, New York, 2009), p. 167

8 Sela, Yossi, interview with Philips and DiBiasio, January, 25, 2021.

9 Avnimelech, Gil, "VC Policy: Yozma Program 15-Years Perspective," April 4, 2016, SSRN, papers.ssrn.com/sol3/papers.cfm?abstract_id=2758195.

10 Eisenberg, Michael, interview with Jame DiBiasio, April 28, 2022.

11 Avnimelech, ibid.

12 Sela, ibid.

13 Eisenberg, ibid.

14 Simchayoff, Elad, "The Company That Created a Generation of Tech Dreamers," medium.com, October 2, 2020.

15 Hilkowitz, Robby, interview with Jame DiBiasio, August 2, 2021.

16 Zeevi, Avi, interview with Philips and DiBiasio, January 26, 2021.

17 Medved, Jonathan, interview with Philips and DiBiasio, March 16, 2022.

18 Saxenian, pp. 108–109.

19 Sela, ibid.

20 Schleifer, Theodore, "Why Silicon Valley's Accomplishments on Gender Aren't as Good as They Seem," Vox.com, February 10, 2020.

21 Vanderschoot, Kelsey, "Closing the Funding Gap for Women Entrepreneurs," DMagazine.com, July 19, 2022.

22 Hodgson, Leah, "Singapore Tops List in VC Funding Per Capita," Pitchbook.com, June 1, 2022.

CHAPTER 5

1 Saxenian, pp. 124–125.

2 Saxenian, pp. 96–102.

3 Miller, Chris, *Chip War: The Fight For the World's Most Critical Technology* (Scribner, New York, 2022), pp. 53–54.

4 Saxenian, pp. 132–134.

5 Hsu, Mark, interview with Philips and DiBiasio, January 30, 2021.

6 "Ta-Lin Hsu, Founder and Chairman of H&Q Asia Pacific," *The Mercury News*, John Boudreau, April 10, 2010.

7 Liu, Peter, interview with Philips and DiBiasio, February 4, 2021.

8 Chang, Morris, "Silicon Genesis: Oral Histories of Semiconductor Technology," Stanford University Libraries, interviewed August 24, 2007.

9 Wessner, Charles, editor, 21st Century Manufacturing, appendix A3, Taiwan's Industrial Technology Research Institute: *A Cradle of Future Industries* (The National Academies Press, Washington, DC, 2013).

10 Landler, Mark, "The Silicon Godfather: The Man Behind Taiwan's Rise in the Chip Industry," *New York Times*, February 1, 2000.

11 Robert Tsao, interviewed by Ling-Fei Lin, "Taiwanese IT Pioneers: Robert H.C. Tsao," Computer History Museum, February 17, 2011.

12 Tsao, ibid.

13 Chang, ibid.

14 Marinissen, Eric Jan, "Pioneering in Asia with the US Venture Capital Model," *IEEE Design & Test of Computers*, Volume 29, Issue 6, December, 2012, pp. 52–55.

15 Saxenian, p. 144.

16 Sharma, Ruchir, "Pound for Pound, Taiwan is the Most Important Place in the World," *New York Times*, December 14, 2020.

17 Saxenian, pp. 31–32.

18 Saxenian, pp. 148–153.

CHAPTER 6

1 Mok, Peter, email to Philips and DiBiasio, December 13, 2020.

2 Chua, Joo Hok, interview with Jame DiBiasio, May 6, 2022.

3 Brooke, pp. 58–77.

4 Brooke, pp. 78–99.

5 Nicholas, p. 229.

6 Brooke, p. 92.

7 Brooke, ibid.

8 Joo, ibid.

9 Tai, Bill, interview with Philips and DiBiasio, February 4, 2021.

10 Liu, Peter, interview with Philips and DiBiasio, February 4, 2021.

11 Tan, Finian, interview with Jame DiBiasio, December 22, 2021.

12 Lim, Sharon, "Singapore's TIF Ventures Senior Team Leaves En Masse," *Private Equity International*, October 1, 2007.

13 Chi, Jeffrey, interview with Jame DiBiasio, October 4, 2021.

14 Lopez, Larry, interview with Philips and DiBiasio, February 4, 2021.

15 Ng, Edmond, interview with Philips and DiBiasio, December 13, 2020.

CHAPTER 7

1 Valentine, Don, "Silicon Genesis: Oral Histories of Semiconductor Technology," Stanford University Libraries, interview recorded April 21, 2004.

2 Cowen, Tyler, "Jeremy Grantham on Investing in Green Tech (Ep. 165)," Conversations with Tyler podcast, November 30, 2022.

3 Nicholas, p. 212.

4 National Venture Capital Association, 2021 Yearbook, p. 13.

5 "Brush Electric Co.," Case Western Reserve University, Encyclopedia of Cleveland History online entry.

6 Lamoreaux, Naomi and Sokoloff, Kenneth, "The Organization and Finance of

Innovation in American History," *Financing Innovation in the United States, 1870 to the Present* (MIT Press, Cambridge, MA, 2007), pp. 3–12.

7 Chandler, Alfred D., Jr, *Shaping the Industrial Century: The Remarkable Story of the Revolution of the Modern Chemical and Pharmaceutical Industries*, Harvard Studies in Business History, Issue 46 (Harvard University Press, Cambridge, MA, and London, 2005), pp. 6–11.

8 Neal, Larry and Davis, Lance, "Why Did Finance Capitalism and the Second Industrial Revolution Arise in the 1890s?," *Financing Innovation in the United States, 1870 to the Present* (MIT Press, Cambridge, MA, 2007), pp. 131–133.

9 O'Sullivan, Mary, "Funding New Industries: A Historical Perspective on the Financing Role of the U.S. Stock Market in the Twentieth Century," *Financing Innovation in the United States, 1870 to the Present* (MIT Press, Cambridge, MA, 2007), p. 193.

10 Chandler, pp. 295–300.

11 Rock, ibid.

12 Nicholas, p. 216.

13 Ante, ibid.

14 Valentine, ibid.

15 Valentine, ibid.

CHAPTER 8

1 Khanna, Dan, *The Rise, Decline, and Renewal of Silicon Valley's High Technology Industry*, Routledge Library Editions: The Economics and Business of Technology, Volume 25 (Garland Publishing, London and New York, 1997), pp. 15–25.

2 Khanna, ibid.

3 Khanna, p. 22.

4 Chandler, pp. 301–308.

5 Miller, pp. 88–90.

6 Chandler, ibid.

7 Khanna, pp. 119–136.

8 Marquardt, David, "Oral History with David F. Marquardt," Carole Kolker, Computer History Museum, October 11, 2011 and February 28, 2012.

9 Chandler, pp. 301–308.

10 Nicholas, pp. 233–262.

11 Chandler, p. 307.

12 Ibid, pp. 35–37.

13 Krugman, Paul, "The Myth of Asia's Miracle," *Foreign Affairs*; Nov/Dec 1994, Vol. 73, Issue 6, pp. 62–79.

14 Chia, K.O., interview with Philips and DiBiasio, April 12, 2021.

15 Hamada, Yasuyuki, "Venture Capital in Japan," *Economic Journal of Hokkaido University*, Issue 38, October 2009, pp. 1–12.

16 Kenney, Martin, Han, Kyonghee and Tanaka, Shoko, "Venture Capital: Taiwan and Japan," *The Globalization of Venture Capital*, https://citeseerx.ist.psu.edu/viewdoc/download?doi=10.1.1.727.4222&rep=rep1&type=pdf.

17 Brooke, pp. 97–99.

18 Byford, Sam, "How the iPhone Won Over Japan and Gave the World Emoji," *The Verge*, June 29, 2017, p. 50.

19 Sutherland, Ed, "Japan's SoftBank Uses iPhone to Beat Rival," *Cult of Mac*, July 8, 2010.

20 Kelts, Roland, "Japan Once Led Global Tech Innovation. How Did It Fall So Behind?" *Rest of World*, May 12, 2022.

21 Oda, Shoko and Maki, Ayaka, "IPOs in Japan Haven't Been This Hot Since the Dotcom Bubble," *Bloomberg News*, December 20, 2020.

CHAPTER 9

1 McCullough, Brian, "A Revealing Look at the Dotcom Bubble of 2000: And How It Shapes Our Lives Today," December 4, 2018, Ideas.TED.com.

2 Berlin, Leslie, "Lessons of Survival, From the Dotcom Attic," *New York Times*, November 21, 2008.

3 Cheung, Tai Ming, *Innovate to Dominate: The Rise of the Chinese Techno-Security State* (Cornell University Press, Ithaca, NY and London, 2022), pp. 1–13.

4 Miller, p. 172.

5 Blank, Steve, "China Startup Report: Introduction to Chinese Venture Capital," StartupGrind.com.

6 Blank, ibid.

7 Saxenian, pp. 235–237.

8 Daxue Consulting, "A Brief History of Startup Investments in China," May 1, 2020, www.daxueconsulting.com.

9 Ho, Simon, interview with Philips and DiBiasio, November 11, 2021.

10 Yang, Yingzhi, "Sequoia, Tencent and IDG Are the Top Investors in Chinese Unicorns, Says Report," *South China Morning Post*, May 14, 2019.

11 *Bloomberg News*, "China Tech Investor Defies Skeptics with $900 Million Fundraise," June 30, 2022.

12 Liu, Peter, interview with Philips and DiBiasio, December 19, 2020.

13 Vanderklippe, Nathan, "How Goldman Sachs Won and Lost With China's Alibaba," *The Globe and Mail*, July 4, 2014.

14 Rieschel, Gary, interview with Jame DiBiasio, December 16, 2022.

15 Inoue, Atsuo, *Aiming High: Masayoshi Son, SoftBank, and Disrupting Silicon Valley* (Hodder & Stoughton, London, 2021), p. 147.

16 Liu, Shiying and Avery, Martha, *Alibaba: The Inside Story Behind Jack Ma and the Creation of the World's Largest Online Marketplace* (Collins Business, New York, 2009), pp. 67–72.

17 Schonberger, Stuart, interview with Philips and DiBiasio, March 23, 2021.

18 VerWey, John, "Chinese Semiconductor Industrial Policy: Past and Present," *Journal of International Commerce and Economics*, United States International Trade Commission, July 2019, p. 10.

19 VerWey, p. 11.

20 Chia, K.O., interview with Philips and DiBiasio, April 12, 2021.

21 Allison, Graham and Schmidt, Eric, "China's 5G Soars Over America's," *Wall Street Journal*, February 16, 2022.

22 Lau, Fiona, "1997: A New Shade of Red," *IFR Asia*, July 17, 2017.

23 Saxenian, pp. 248–249.

24 Gargan, Edward, "Hong Kong's Peregrine Soared Like a Falcon, Sank Like a Reckless Bank," *New York Times*, January 13, 1998.

25 Lee, Rocky, interview with Philips and DiBiasio, December 23, 2020.

26 Einhorn, Bruce, "Sina.com: Is This Any Way to Dress Up for an IPO?," Bloomberg online, October 11, 1999.

27 Saxenian, p. 185.

28 Chevalerias, Philippe, "The Taiwanese Economy After the Miracle," China Perspectives online, March 2010, p. 37.

29 Ezell, Stephen, "The Evolution of Taiwan's Trade Linkages with the U.S. and Global Economies," Information Technology and Innovation Foundation website, October 25, 2001.

CHAPTER 10

1 Kellogg, Harry, interview with Philips and DiBiasio, December 5, 2020.

2 Lopez, Larry, interview with Philips and DiBiasio, February 4, 2021.

3 Wilcox, Ken, interview with authors, March 13, 2021.

4 Lilani, Ash, interview with authors, February 11, 2021.

5 Mok, Peter, email to authors, December 13, 2020.

6 Tsao, Thomas, interview with Philips and DiBiasio, July 23, 2022.

CHAPTER 11

1 Valentine, Don, "Silicon Genesis: Oral Histories of Semiconductor Technology," Stanford University Libraries, interview recorded April 21, 2004.

2 Chou, Chin, interview with Philips and DiBiasio, February 24, 2021.

3 Moritz, ibid.

4 Phelps, Edmund, *Mass Flourishing* (Princeton University Press, Princeton, NJ and Oxford, 2013), p. 205.

5 Shen, Neil, "Sequoia's Neil Shen to Entrepreneurs: 'Follow Your Heart'," Stanford Graduate School of Business online, November 12, 2015.

6 Chen, George, "Sequoia Capital China Founding Partner Zhang resigns," *Reuters*, February 2, 2009.

7 China First Capital blog, "Kleiner Perkins Adrift in China," May 3, 2010.

8 Xu, Kathy, "Venture in China Today, Venture is Eating the Investment World," Capital Allocators with Ted Seides YouTube channel, March 28, 2022.

9 Metzger, Jan, interview with Philips and DiBiasio, July 4, 2022.

10 Li, Lillian, Twitter post, March 27, 2022.

11 Chen, Lulu Yilun, *Influence Empire: The Story of Tencent and China's Tech Ambition* (Hodder & Stoughton, London, 2020), pp. 32–33.

12 Chen, pp. 36–37.

13 Liu and Avery, pp. 67–72.

14 Ng, Edmond, interview with Philips and DiBiasio, December 13, 2020.

15 Rieschel, Gary, interview with Philips and DiBiasio, December 16, 2022.

16 Liu Zhengzheng and Qiu Zhili, "Kathy Xu, The Queen of Venture Capital," *Forbes China*, December 2014, pp. 76–79.

17 Chen, pp. 64–66.

18 Chen, "Business QuickTake: Alibaba," Bloomberg, November 20, 2017.

19 Rieschel, interview with Jame DiBiasio, December 16, 2022.

20 Lam, David, interview with Philips and DiBiasio, February 25, 2021.

21 Hong, Jing, interview with Philips and DiBiasio, February 8, 2022.

22 Bhidé, Amar, *The Venturesome Economy: How Innovation Sustains Prosperity in a More Connected World* (Princeton University Press, Princeton, NJ, and Oxford, 2008, e-book version).

23 Dychtwald, Zak, "China's New Innovation Advantage," *Harvard Business Review* online, May/June 2021.

CHAPTER 12

1 Ruehl, Mercedes, Riordan, Primrose and Kinder, Tabby, "Global Investors in Limbo After Ant IPO Torpedoed By Beijing," *Financial Times*, January 15, 2021.

2 Wilcox, Ken, interview with Philips and DiBiasio, March 13, 2021.

3 Daxue Consulting, ibid.

4 Chia, K.O., interview with Philips and DiBiasio, April 12, 2021.

5 Cheung, pp. 119–224.

6 Meikle, Brad, "VC's Windfall from SMIC IPO," BuyoutsInsider.com, March 22, 2004.

7 Li Yuan, "Xi Jinping's Vision for Tech Self-Reliance in China Runs into Reality," *New York Times*, August 29, 2022.

8 White, Edward and Liu, Qianer, "China's Big Fund Corruption Probe Casts Shadow Over Chip Sector," *Financial Times*, September 29, 2022.

9 Adams, Stephen, "Arc of Empire: The Federal Telegraph Company, the US Navy, and the Beginnings of Silicon Valley," *The Business History Review*, June 2017, p. 10.

10 Adams, pp. 29–31.

11 Fabrizio, Kira and Mowery, David, "The Federal Role in Financing Major Innovations: Information Technology During the Postwar Period," *Financing Innovation in the United States: 1870 to the Present* (MIT Press, Cambridge, MA, 2007), pp. 295–299.

12 Lamoreaux and Sokoloff, pp. 21–23.

13 "Cloning DARPA," *The Economist*, June 5, 2021, pp. 67–78.

14 Nicholas, pp. 107–141.

15 Ante, pp. 147–174.

16 Usselman, Steven, "Learning the Hard Way: IBM and the Sources of Innovation in Early Computing," *Financing Innovation in the United States: 1870 to the Present* (MIT Press, Cambridge, MA, 2007), pp. 343–347.

17 Fallon, Sarah, "The Secret History of the First Microprocessor, the F-14, and Me," *Wired*, December 23, 2020, p. 77.

18 Fabrizio and Mowery, pp. 300–304.

19 Ante, pp. 241–256.

20 Stokols, Andrew, "Xiong'an: Designing a 'Modern Socialist City'," *The Space Between* Substack newsletter, May 25, 2021.

21 Chen, pp. 245–246.

22 Zhu, Julie, "Chinese State Firms to Take Big Stake in Ant's Credit-Scoring JV," *Reuters*, September 1, 2021.

23 Week in China, "Taught a Tough Lesson," November 26, 2021.

24 Rieschel, Gary, China Money Network podcast.

25 McMorrow, Ryan, and Lockett, Hudson, "Sequoia Targets $9bn China Fundraising Despite Tech Crackdown," *Financial Times*, July 5, 2022.

26 Lam, George, interview with Philips and DiBiasio, May 31, 2021.

27 Leone, Doug, "Fireside Chat: Douglas Leone and Mohit Bhatnagar," YouTube video, August 16, 2020.

28 Oster, Shai and Osawa, Juro, "Sequoia China Chief Leaves Beijing's Top Political Advisory Body," *The Information*, January 20, 2023.

29 Chou, Chin, remarks at the Hong Kong Venture Capital Association conference, January 13, 2023.

CHAPTER 13

1 Lilani, Ash, interview with Philips and DiBiasio, December 2, 2020.

2 Saxenian, p. 274.

3 Saxenian, p. 299.

4 Guleri, Tim, interview with Philips and DiBiasio, March 7, 2021.

5 Saxenian, p. 302.

6 Takahashi, Dean, "Interview with Vinod Dham, Father of the Pentium, on Life in Technology and Venture Investing," VentureBeat.com, July 3, 2008.

7 Takahashi, Dean, "Vinod Dham, Father of the Pentium, Takes on AI Chips with Agent-Based AlphaICs," VentureBeat.com, August 8, 2018.

8 Asianometry YouTube channel, "India's Semiconductor Failure," undated.

9 Chadha, Sumir, interview with Philips and DiBiasio, November 10, 2021.

10 Prakash, Prashanth, interview with Jame DiBiasio, July 13, 2022.

11 Mathias, Ben, interview with Jame DiBiasio, May 23, 2022.

12 Asianometry YouTube video, "Reliance: The Rise of India's Biggest Telecom," no date.

13 DiBiasio, Jame, "What is the India Stack? Nandan Nilekani explains," DigFinGroup.com, July 28, 2020.

14 Kirani, Shekhar, interview with Jame DiBiasio, August 3, 2022.

15 Simonite, Tom, "Nvidia CEO: Software is Eating the World, but AI is Going to Eat Software," *MIT Technology Review*, May 12, 2017.

16 Brooke, pp. 100–127.

17 Ong, Peng T., interview with Jame DiBiasio, February 9, 2022.

18 Joo, Hock Chia, interview with Jame DiBiasio, May 6, 2022.

19 Chi, Jeffrey, interview with Jame DiBiasio, October 4, 2021.

20 Liu, Genping, interview with Jame DiBiasio, May 8, 2022.

21 *Straits Times* online, "Grab Emerges as Largest Venture Capital Recipient in the World for First-Quarter 2018," April 11, 2018.

CHAPTER 13

1 Tai, Bill, interview with Philips and DiBiasio, August 16, 2022.

2 Andreessen, Mark, "Why Software is Eating the World," *Wall Street Journal* online, August 20, 2011.

3 KPMG Private Enterprise, "Venture Pulse" reports, Q1 2020 through Q3 2022, www.assets.kpmg.

4 Lopez, Larry, interview with Philips and DiBiasio, February 4, 2021.

5 Hille, Kathrin, Liu, Quaner, Olcott, Eleanor, Waters, Richard, Sevastopulo, Demetri, Inagaki, Kana, and Song, Jung-a, "China's Chip Industry Set for Deep Pain from US Export Controls," *Financial Times*, October 9, 2022.

6 Fox, Matthew, "Cloud-Storage Firm Snowflake is Now More Valuable Than IBM After 258% Post-IPO Rally," *Markets Insider*, December 9, 2020.

7 Singh, Manish, "Tiger Global to Slow Startup Investments for Two Quarters, Eyes New Fund Later This Year," Techcrunch.com, July 11, 2022.

8 Fletcher, Laurence, "Tiger Global Hit by $17bn Losses in Tech Rout," *Financial Times*, May 10, 2022.

9 Irena.org/financeinvestment/investment-needs.

10 Storrs Hall, J., *Where is My Flying Car?* (Stripe Press, London, 2018), pp. 157–158.

11 DiBiasio, Jame, "VC, Seeking Tech Gorillas, Prepares for Digital IPO," DigFin, January 17, 2023.

INDEX

Page numbers in italics indicate figures.

CPSIA information can be obtained
at www.ICGtesting.com
Printed in the USA
JSHW010924080623
42782JS00002B/5